D0931468

Volume V, SAGE SERIES ON POLITICS AND THE LEGAL ORDER,
Joel B. Grossman, *Series Editor*

JUDICIAL POLITICS IN WEST GERMANY

A Study of the Federal Constitutional Court

DONALD P. KOMMERS

University of Notre Dame

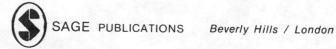

SAGE PUBLICATIONS   *Beverly Hills / London*

For information address:

SAGE PUBLICATIONS, INC.
275 South Beverly Drive
Beverly Hills, California 90212

SAGE PUBLICATIONS LTD.
St George's House / 44 Hatton Garden
London EC1N 8ER

Printed in the United States of America

International Standard Book Number 0-8039-0125-9
Library of Congress Catalog Card No. 72-98037

FIRST PRINTING

JUDICIAL POLITICS IN WEST GERMANY:
A STUDY OF THE FEDERAL CONSTITUTIONAL COURT

The SAGE Series on
POLITICS AND THE LEGAL ORDER

Editor: **Joel B. Grossman,** University of Wisconsin

CONTENTS

To the memory of my father

EDITOR'S FOREWORD

Professor Kommers has written an important book with appeal to a diverse audience of scholars and professionals. It is must reading for specialists in German politics and law. For those with an interest in comparative politics, it provides a significant building block of vital information and intelligent analysis about the contitutional process in a major industrial nation. And for those whose specialty is judicial politics, even with an American emphasis, the book offers a confirmation of the need to understand the political roots of a constitutional court. Reading about the establishment and development of "another" constitutional court offers rich insights into the development of our own constitutional system, and particularly into our own experience with the power of judicial review.

The study of comparative judicial politics is still in its infancy. As Professor Kommers recognizes, the gap between highly abstract theorizing and single country studies is still quite large. Yet that gap is not unbridgeable. What is needed is a greater accumulation of knowledge about national judicial systems which is also sensitive to the needs of theory-building and verification. This book certainly meets that need. It delves deeply into the lore and traditions of the German legal system, and the influence of this culture on the postwar Court, noting at the same time how the very idea of a constitutional court was a sharp break from the German tradition of political, not judicial, control. Yet it does so from the perspective, and with the language, of a social scientist.

The Federal Constitutional Court has prospered because, like its American counterpart, it met an important political need—the need for an institution to authoritatively settle major disputes not settled elsewhere in the system. Professor Kommers shows convincingly how favorable political conditions contributed to the acceptance of judicial review in West Germany. A competitive and pluralist politics, a commitment to a system of checks and balances, a thriving economy and middle-class population, a commitment to compromise differences in the interests of political stability, and a formal commitment to protecting individual rights and liberties all support balanced but effective judicial power. These are not the only conditions under which strong judicial power can, or will, thrive; witness the contrary experience in Great Britain, and, for other reasons, in Japan. But they do contribute to our understanding of how and why juridical democracy has become established in West Germany in so short a period of time.

Joel B. Grossman
Madison, Wisconsin
20 September 1975

PREFACE

This is a study of the Federal Constitutional Court (*Bundesverfassungs-gericht*) of West Germany. My principal goal is to examine the Constitutional Court as a judicial structure and to describe its relationship to German politics. That courts of law, constitutional courts especially, are parts of political systems is a proposition no longer to be denied. Judicial structures cannot be properly understood apart from the wider legal and political context within which they originate and operate. Accordingly, following a short introductory chapter, the study opens with an examination of the historical and intellectual foundations of judicial review in Germany and then proceeds to a description of the constitutional, legal, and political setting in which the Constitutional Court functions (Chapter 2). It continues with an analysis of the Court as a governmental structure, including an investigation of its origin, jurisdiction (authority), and internal organization (Chapter 3).

The main emphasis of this study, however, is upon the Constitutional Court as a *law-making* institution or, more accurately stated, as an instrument for the making of constitutional policy. By policy, I refer to those authoritative prescriptions, values, norms, or rules derived from interpretations (by the Court) of the Basic Law of the German Federal Republic. In looking at the Court as policy-maker, I start with the justices themselves, inquiring into their backgrounds, their values, their conceptions of the judicial role, and the circumstances of their recruitment (Chapter 4). This is followed by an examination of decision-making procedures inside the Court and an analysis of the techniques and strategies calculated to realize judicial policy goals (Chapter 5). The study then moves on to a rather detailed report of judicial policies in selected areas of German constitutional law and a consideration of the Court's main political roles (Chapter 6). Finally, I have tried to measure, with the limited tools at my disposal, the Court's influence on West Germany's political system as well as its impact on public policy (Chapter 7). The study concludes with a brief summary of the meaning that the Court has had for political life in the Federal Republic (Chapter 8).

In writing this book, I have relied most heavily upon various historical documents, standard library resources, records and decisions of the Federal Constitutional Court, personal interviews with judges and other public officials, attitude surveys and public opinion data, newspaper reports and government bulletins, and personal letters received from German judicial scholars, judges, and other persons professionally interested in the Constitutional Court. I have also drawn on some of my own previously published work which has appeared in *Jahrbuch des Oeffentlichen Rechts* (Volume 20, 1971), *American Journal of Jurisprudence* (Volume 16, 1971), and *Frontiers of Judicial Research* (New York: John Wiley, 1969). Most of the sources used in this book appear in the German language; unless otherwise indicated, all direct quotations which appear in the text are my own translations from the original.

While the concepts around which the chapters are organized constitute rather specific criteria of relevance in the selection and organization of data, this book contains a large amount of descriptive material, much more, actually, than I wanted originally to incorporate. But a beginning study of a major political institution of the Western world needs to be buttressed by a foundation of detailed information. I will be satisfied if this book provides my colleagues with a basis on which to frame better research designs for the comparative study of constitutional courts.

The intellectual origins of this book are in part traceable to a combination of graduate training in American constitutional law and an abiding interest in Germany, as well as to early articles on German judicial review and the Federal Constitutional Court by R. Taylor Cole, Edward McWhinney, Gerhard Leibholz, and Carl Friedrich. Under the stimulus of these articles and with the support of Notre Dame's Program of West European Studies, I spent several weeks in the library and archives of the Federal Constitutional Court in Karlsruhe, West Germany, during the summer of 1966, after which plans for this book began to take shape. Several more years were required to gather the materials and prepare this manuscript for publication.

During these years of research and writing, I acquired many debts and wish now to acknowledge some of them. I am indebted first to several institutions and agencies without whose generous financial support this book would not have been possible. I am most grateful to the Program of West European Studies, University of Notre Dame, which enabled me to spend the academic year 1967-1968 as a special research guest of the Federal Constitutional Court. A supplementary grant from the American Philosophical Society, which I also gratefully acknowledge, made it possible for me to extend my residence in Germany to a full calendar year. A second gesture of generosity from the

Program of Western European Studies allowed me to spend the summer of 1969 at Harvard's International Legal Studies Center to begin writing the manuscript. I am thankful, too, for a Faculty Research Grant from the Social Science Research Council for the purpose of carrying out the field research stage of my work in Germany during 1967-1968. The assistance of *Inter-Nationes* (West Germany), permitting me to return briefly to the Federal Constitutional Court in September 1969, is also gratefully acknowledged. Finally, while a resident scholar in political science and constitutional law at the University of Cologne under an Alexander von Humboldt Fellowship from September 1971 through August 1972, I managed to find time to finish a first draft of the manuscript and to update the study. I am extremely indebted to both the Alexander von Humboldt Foundation (West Germany) and the National Endowment for the Humanities for making that year possible.

This study owes much to many people. Let me begin with a word of thanks to the President of the Federal Constitutional Court, Dr. Gebhard Müller, who provided me with comfortable working quarters, permitted me access to court records and facilities, and tolerated my presence inside Prinz Max Palais, almost on a daily basis, for an entire year. I want also to acknowledge the cooperation of Dr. Josef Mackert, director of the library of the Federal Constitutional Court, but I am indebted most of all to his chief assistant, Franz Schneider, whose untiring patience and vast bibliographical knowledge helped to make my year at the Court productive. For long hours of consultation and friendly advice on various aspects of this study, I am indebted to several law clerks and civil servants employed by the Court during my research stay in Karlsruhe. I particularly wish to thank Dr. Peter Wittig (legal assistant to President Müller), Dr. Christian Starck (legal assistant to Justice Scholtissek), Dr. Gerd Roellecke (legal assistant to Justice Leibholz), Dr. Walter Rudi Wand (administrative assistant to President Müller), and Dr. Reinhard Rupprecht (high civil servant). Their mastery of detail about the work and operations of the Constitutional Court saved me from a host of errors. More recently, I have also benefitted from the advice and assistance of Dr. Wolfgang Zierlein (administrative assistant of President Benda). Finally, my most heartfelt thanks are reserved for the Justices of the Federal Constitutional Court. Large portions of this manuscript would have been impossible to write without the generous giving of their time and views. Twenty-six Justices, on and off the bench, cheerfully submitted to interviews running at least an hour in length and frequently much longer. Some sitting Justices were always at my disposal, ready to answer questions at almost a moment's notice. Among those who gave so freely of their time, I want to mention especially Justices Willi Geiger, Gerhard Leibholz, Hans Rupp, Hans Kutscher, and Gregor Geller.

Outside the Court, I received, at various points in time, valuable assistance from other persons. Professor Rudolf Wildenmann and Dr. Max Kaase of Mannheim University were extremely gracious in helping me prepare and translate a questionnaire mailed to selected political elites in Germany. I also thank them for allowing me to use relevant portions of public opinion surveys carried out in Germany by the Mannheim University Social Science Research Institute. Acknowledged, too, is the help of Professor Ferdinand Hermens, University of Cologne, who made the resources of the Research Institute of Political Science available to me during the winter semester of 1971. I owe much also to Professor Martin Kriele, University of Cologne, with whom I was associated as a Humboldt Fellow during the summer semester of 1972, for sharpening my understanding of German constitutional law. Finally, I am personally indebted to several American colleagues who commented extensively on the manuscript. Professor Lewis D. Edinger, Columbia University, Professor Walter F. Murphy, Princeton University, and Professor Joseph Tanenhaus, State University of New York at Stony Brook read all of the manuscript except the last two chapters. Professor Joel B. Grossman, University of Wisconsin, read the manuscript in full. I relied heavily upon their comments and suggestions in the final revision of the manuscript, wholly reorganizing and rewriting certain sections in the process. For typing the manuscript, I wish to thank Carmela Rulli, Shirley Schneck, and Marie Meilner.

These last words are reserved for three persons who have contributed more than they know to the totality of my work in recent years. Each has had an abiding interest in my scholarly activity. Each has proffered me his good counsel—solicited and unsolicited—for which I shall always be grateful. Each remains a valued colleague in the academy. Thus, I offer my heartfelt thanks, long overdue, to Professor Stephen D. Kertesz, University of Notre Dame, who offered me the first real opportunity to exploit my interest in the Federal Constitutional Court; to Dr. George N. Shuster, University of Notre Dame, who has helped to sustain my interest in German affairs; and to Professor David Fellman, University of Wisconsin, who first introduced me to the world of scholarship.

D.P.K.

ABBREVIATIONS

BGBl   *Bundesgesetz* (Federal Statutes).

BGH   *Bundesgerichtshof* (Federal Supreme Court).

BGHSt   *Entscheidungen des Bundesgerichtshofes in Strafsachen* (Decisions of the Federal Supreme Court in Criminal Matters). Official Reports.

BGHZ   *Entscheidungen des Bundesgerichtshofes in Zivilsachen* (Decisions of the Federal Supreme Court in Civil Matters). Official Reports.

BVerfGE   *Entscheidungen des Bundesverfassungsgerichts* (Decisions of the Federal Constitutional Court). Official Reports.

BVerfGG   *Bundesverfassungsgerichtsgesetz* (Federal Constitutional Court Act).

CDU   *Christlich-Demokratische Union* (Christian Democratic Union).

CSU   *Christlich-Soziale Union* (Christian Social Union).

DP   *Deutsche Partei* (German Party).

FDP   *Freie Demokratische Partei* (Free Democratic Party).

KPD   *Kommunistische Partei Deutschlands* (Communist Party of Germany).

SED   *Sozialistische Einheitspartei Deutschland* (Socialist Unity Party of [East] Germany).

SPD   *Sozialdemokratische Partei Deutschlands* (Social Democratic Party of [West] Germany).

WMA   *Wahlmannerauschuss* (Judicial Selection Committee).

1

INTRODUCTION:

COMPARATIVE JUDICIAL POLITICS

Judicial scholars are just now beginning to fix their attention on the study of foreign courts. They are confining their work mainly to specialized constitutional courts or to high appellate courts endowed with authority to rule on constitutional questions. The attraction of these courts as favorable targets of comparative judicial research stems in part from their resemblance, both in structure and function, to the U.S. Supreme Court. Most studies have hitherto been either very general or exploratory in nature, barely scratching the surface of the tribunals under examination, or very limited in scope, confined largely to judicial background studies and studies which probe the relationship between judges' values and judicial policy. Moreover, nearly all these studies have been carried out in single nations; few are the subject of systematic multinational comparison. Still, it is fair to say that this literature constitutes the broad outlines of a new and emerging subfield or branch of political science elusively described as public law. [1]

We can place these remarks in perspective by specifying a few of those influences pushing judicial research in a comparative direction. These influences include changing intellectual perspectives in political science as well as developments in the real world of judicial politics. Among the former is the increasingly comparative focus of political science itself. Although political scientists are far from unified in their conceptions of how comparative research should proceed, they seem persuaded that the advancement of knowledge about politics depends on the orderly study of political institutions and processes across national boundaries. The stress on the phenomenon of political development in comparative research today, and the role—however marginal—that courts and judges play in that development, are directing greater attention than before to judicial institutions in a variety of political systems and cultures.[2]

A second and related influence is the increasing use of systems theory (or analysis) as an analytical framework for the study of politics. The concept of systems analysis is relatively simple. In the plain words of Webster, a system is "a complex unity formed of many diverse parts subject to a plan or serving a common purpose" or, alternatively, "a set of units combined by nature or art to form an integral, organic, or organized whole."[3] As an analytical device, the notion of system might be applied to a judicial institution. The Federal Constitutional Court, for example, could be regarded as an organized whole whose intermingling parts (judicial roles, decisional procedures, personal values of judges, etc.) mesh in such a way as to sustain it as a living organism. But there must be something to generate movement among the Court's working parts; a dormant institution no less than dormant muscles is apt to atrophy from disuse. In a word, the Court depends for its survival upon factors external to it—its legal, political, social, and ideological environment. It operates by responding to demands and claims pressed upon it by individuals, groups, and institutions along with the support it receives for its activities from the general public. When the Court responds to a claim or demand—say in the form of a judicial decision—it presumably affects the political order in such a way as to result in still further pressures on the Court. These demands and responses, according to the theory, help to sustain the Court as an institution (or political structure) and define its relationship to the political system as a whole.[4] In the technical language of Gabriel Almond, the main advantage of the system concept "is that it analytically differentiates the object of study from its environment, directs attention to the interaction with other systems in its environment, to its own conversion characteristics, and to its maintenance and adaptive properties."[5]

Another advantage of the systems concept is that it gives us a convenient albeit rough paradigm for research on foreign judicial structures. For one thing, it allows us to focus on judicial policy and policy-making; for another, it directs our attention to the relationship between political culture and judicial policy. This approach is also coincident, happily, with recent efforts on the part of judicial scholars in the United States to reassert the primacy of judicial policy and the importance of policy consciousness among judges;[6] it is also coincident with recent pleas of political scientists for policy analysis studies across national boundaries.[7] It might be noted that this study of the Federal Constitutional Court employs some of the concepts on which systems theory is based but it does so on an extremely selective basis and seeks consciously to avoid, while perhaps not altogether successfully, the inelegant terminology or jargon which is part of its baggage.

Interest in comparative judicial politics has soared, too, because of the postwar emergence of foreign judicial tribunals patterned after or comparable to the U.S. Supreme Court. What makes these tribunals interesting objects of study is their establishment in legal and political cultures where the practice of judicial review historically has been very weak or altogether unknown. The spread of judicial review since 1945 to non-English-speaking nations particularly is a truly remarkable phenomenon of our time. Today the constitutions of over 50 nations with varying political systems, civic cultures, and legal traditions include provisions sanctioning some form of judicial control over constitutionality.[8] In some of these countries, it is too early to tell whether judicial review will take hold; in others, judicial review has not worked at all; in still others, judicial review has since been abolished, usually under the impact of military takeovers. Outside the Anglo-American legal tradition, judicial review seems to have had its most favorable reception in advanced constitutional democracies; since 1950, the constitutional courts of some of these countries have created impressive bodies of constitutional or political jurisprudence. The West German Federal Constitutional Court is one such tribunal; others are the Supreme Court of Japan, the Constitutional Court of Italy, the Constitutional Court of Austria, and the Supreme Court of India. This development offers both conventional constitutional law scholars and students oriented toward judicial process studies excellent opportunities to think comparatively about their subject.[9]

Comparative judicial research must be discriminating. American scholars interested in the political jurisprudence of foreign constitutional tribunals should probably, for purposes of comparability, limit their studies to judicial structures whose functions are similar to those of the U.S. Supreme Court; they might also judiciously limit their studies to advanced political democracies. That West Germany, for example, has a constitutional court staffed with full-time professional judges vested with wide powers of judicial review and operating in an advanced, pluralistic, federal, democratic state powered by a modern party system within a parliamentary framework literally excites wonder about the roles and capacities of that tribunal in its wider environment. At the same time, we have the opportunity to observe the operation of judicial review in an institutional setting and politico-legal context that differs markedly from those of the United States. It is an opportunity to see how judicial policies interlace with aspects of German politics and how the pattern compares to that of the United States.

One of the functions of modern political systems is "rule adjudication," where courts play an important if not dominant role.[10] Thus, we may reasonably regard judicial tribunals as parts of political systems. One of the advantages of the comparative approach, especially if combined with a broad systems perspective, is that it allows us clearly to expose the judiciary's complex interconnections with the political system. Yet what courts do is not always political in nature; to specify the political uses of courts and the conditions of judicial influence on politics and public policies would seem to be one of the chief tasks of judicial research. And if the object of study is a major appellate tribunal with authority to decide constitutional questions, like the Federal Constitutional Court, its policies may also have important consequences for the political system as a whole.

All this, of course, raises questions about how to proceed with the comparative study of judicial institutions. Certainly comparative judicial research has as one of its objectives the systematic transnational study of constitutional courts and their roles in political systems. But our need now is to start at the beginning by compiling information about existing constitutional courts throughout the world and weaving it into an intelligible unity. A modest beginning is on a nation-by-nation basis, particularly since few scholars have the competence, let alone the resources, to engage in multinational research of meaningful scope and depth. This study of the Federal Constitutional Court represents that modest beginning.

My research paradigm is equally modest. It includes a rather simple set of questions about the Federal Constitutional Court: Why did the Germans decide to establish a constitutional court? What were their expectations regarding the role of the Court—and of judicial review—in the German political system? Has the Court measured up to these expectations? Who are the judges and why were they selected? Who goes to the Constitutional Court for redress and why? How have judicial personalities influenced the Court's policies? What political influences have impinged upon the Court? How have the Court's policies influenced the political process? What functions does the Court perform in the German system? In what measure has the Court contributed to the stability of West Germany's democracy? What are its capacities for continuing to do so? In what measure has the Court managed to marshall the support of the German public?

With regard to general research strategy, I have been very selective in the choice of topics or concepts around which to structure this book. I refer to the notions of setting, structure, actors, process, policy, and impact. There is nothing particularly original about them; some of these "organizing ideas" have been drawn from decision-making theory and some from systems theory.[11] Indeed, they overlap to a large extent. The wisdom of such eclecticism is that it is parsimonious, allowing the cumulation of *politically relevant* data about the Federal Constitutional Court.[12] Better organization or arrangement of material is possible, I have no doubt. But this is a matter which I would prefer to submit to the judgment of fellow colleagues in judicial research.

It may be useful briefly, to define the organizing concepts of this book. *Setting* refers to selected elements of the political and legal environment which influence the operations of the Federal Constitutional Court; it includes also the historical background out of which the Court may be said to have emerged. *Structure* refers to the Court's organization together with its authority, jurisdiction, and internal workways. *Actors* refer to the principal decision-makers—namely, the Justices—including their recruitment, socialization, backgrounds, and values. *Process* refers to the procedures, techniques, and methods of arriving at policy decisions, together with judicial strategies calculated to realize judicial policy goals. *Policy* is what the judges decide and involves the further consideration of judicial roles and the limits of judicial power. *Impact*, finally, deals with the effects of judicial decisions upon other political institutions, the public mind, and the Court itself.

At the risk of repetition, this approach is favored for the following reasons: First, it is an orderly way to collect data on the political role of a judicial institution; second, it directs attention to the relationship among all the above elements of judicial politics; third, it recognizes the primacy of judicial policy-making; finally, it provides us with a basis for assessing the institutional performance of a judicial tribunal over time and, in this book, how the institution has served West Germany's fledgling constitutional democracy.

NOTES

1. Recent works falling into the growing genre of comparative judicial studies are Glendon Schubert and David J. Danelski (eds.), *Comparative Judicial Behavior* (New York: Oxford University Press, 1969); David J. Danelski, "The People and the Court in Japan," Chap. 3, Donald P. Kommers, "The Federal Constitutional Court in the West German Political System," Chap. 4, Fred L. Morrison, "The Swiss Federal Court: Judicial Decision Making and Recruitment," Chap. 5, and Glendon A. Schubert,

"The Dimensions of Decisional Response: Opinion and Voting Behavior of the Australian High Court," Chap. 6, in Grossman and Tanenhaus (eds.), *Frontiers of Judicial Research* (New York: John Wiley, 1969); Ulf Torgersen, "The Role of the Supreme Court in the Norwegian Political System," in Schubert (ed.), *Judicial Decision-Making* (New York: Free Press, 1963); Henry J. Abraham, *The Judicial Process: An Introductory Analysis of the Courts of the United States, England, and France*, 2nd ed. (New York: Oxford University Press, 1968); S.R. Peck "The Supreme Court of Canada, 1958-1966: A Search for Policy Through Scalogram Analysis," *Canadian Bar Review*, 45 (1967): 666-725; Glendon Schubert, "Judges and Political Leadership," in Edinger (ed.), *Political Leadership in Industrialized Societies: Studies in Comparative Analysis* (New York: John Wiley, 1967), Chap. 8; and Walter F. Murphy and Joseph Tanenhaus, "Constitutional Courts, Public Opinion, and Political Representation," in Danielson and Murphy (eds.), *Modern American Democracy* (New York: Holt, Rinehart & Winston, 1968). Several studies of judicial review in countries other than the United States, some of which are cited in note 9 below, have also appeared in recent years. For a criticism of many of these studies, see Theodore L. Becker, *Comparative Judicial Politics* (Chicago: Rand McNally, 1970). The emergence of comparative judicial politics as an important concern within modern political science was the recent decision, in August 1973, by the Executive Council of the International Political Science Association to establish a permanent Research Committee on Comparative Judicial Studies. A selection of the papers formally presented at the 1973 IPSA meeting are included in the symposium, "The Political Impact of Constitutional Courts," *Notre Dame Lawyer* 49 (June 1974): 953-1050.

2. See Gabriel A. Almond and G. Bingham Powell, Jr., *Comparative Politics: A Developmental Approach* (Boston: Little, Brown, 1966), pp. 158-163. For other studies which use the concept of political development as a research focus, see the bibliography in James A. Bill and Robert L. Hardgrave, Jr., *Comparative Politics: The Quest for Theory* (Columbus, Ohio: Charles E. Merrill, 1973), pp. 243-245.

3. *Webster's Third New International Dictionary* (1969), s.v. "system."

4. A major influence on the development of systems theory as a framework of political analysis is David Easton, "An Approach to the Analysis of Political Systems," *World Politics*, 9 (1957): 383-400. Easton's approach is elaborated further in his *A Framework for Political Analysis* (Englewood Cliffs, N.J.: Prentice-Hall, 1965) and *A Systems Analysis of Political Life* (New York: John Wiley, 1965). Several judicial scholars have adopted systems theory to their studies of American courts. Examples are Walter F. Murphy,

Elements of Judicial Strategy (Chicago: University of Chicago Press, 1964); Glendon Schubert, *Judicial Policy-Making* (Chicago: Scott, Foresman, 1965); Joel B. Grossman, "A Model for Judicial Policy Analysis: The Supreme Court and the Sit-In Cases," in Grossman and Tanenhaus, *Frontiers,* op. cit., pp. 405-460; and Sheldon Goldman and Thomas P. Jahnige, *The Federal Courts as a Political System* (New York: Harper & Row, 1971).

5. Gabriel A. Almond, "Political Theory and Political Science," *American Political Science Review,* 60 (1966): 876.

6. Since C.H. Pritchett's classic study, *The Roosevelt Court: A Study in Judicial Politics and Values, 1937-1947* (New York: Macmillan, 1948), the accent of our research has been on judicial *behavior* rather than on judicial *policy.* The apotheosis of the behavioral movement, which underscored the importance of psychological variables and personal values in the determination of judicial behavior, may well have been represented by Glendon Schubert, *The Judicial Mind* (Evanston: Northwestern University Press, 1965). In recent years, however, there has been a reemphasis on the study of judicial policy, especially as it evolves within the context of social and institutional forces and intergovernmental relationships. See, for example, Richard Wells and Joel Grossman, "The Concept of Judicial Policy-Making; A critique," *Journal of Public Law,* 15 (1966): 286-310; Samuel Krislov, *The Supreme Court in the Political Process* (New York: Macmillan, 1965) and Martin M. Shapiro, *Law and Politics in the Supreme Court* (New York: Free Press, 1964). See also Shapiro's *The Supreme Court and Public Policy* (Chicago: Scott, Foresman, 1969). Extremely important also is an early article by Robert A. Dahl, "Decision-Making in a Democracy: The Supreme Court as a National Policy-Maker," *Journal of Public Law,* 4 (1957): 279-295.

7. See Richard Rose, "Comparing Public Policy: An Overview," *European Journal of Political Research,* 1 (April 1973): 67-93. See also Arnold J. Heidenheimer, "The Politics of Public Education, Health and Welfare in the U.S. and Western Europe" (delivered at the Sixty-Sixth Annual Meeting of American Political Science Association, Los Angeles, 1970).

9. For recent studies of constitutional courts and judicial review in political systems other than the Anglo-American, see Richard D. Baker, *Judicial Review in Mexico: A Study of the Amparo Suit* (Austin: University of Texas Press, 1971); Mauro Cappelletti, *Judicial Review in the Contemporary World* (Indianapolis: Bobbs-Merrill, 1971); John M. Maki, *Court and Constitution in Japan: Selected Supreme Court Decisions, 1948-60* (Seattle: University of Washington Press, 1964); Donald P. Kommers, "Judicial Review in Italy and West Germany," *Jahrbuch des Oeffentlichen Rechts,* 20 (1971): 111-134; Mauro Cappelletti and John C. Adams, "Judicial Review of Legislation:

European Antecedents and Adaptations," *Harvard Law Review,* 79 (1966): 1207-1224; and Dimitrije Kulic, "The Constitutional Court of Yugoslavia," *Jahrbuch des Oeffentlichen Rechts*, 18 (1969): 79-94. The most comprehensive survey of judicial review around the world is Hermann Mosler (ed.), *Constitutional Review in the World Today: National Reports and Comparative Studies* (Cologne and Berlin: Carl Heymanns Verlag KG, 1961).

10. See Almond and Powell, *Comparative Politics,* op. cit., p. 158.

11. James A. Robinson and R. Roger Majak have listed the components of decision-making as (1) the decision situation, (2) the decision participants, (3) the decision organization, (4) the decision process, and (5) the decision outcome. See their article "The Theory of Decision-Making," in Charlesworth (ed.), *Contemporary Political Analysis* (New York: Free Press, 1967), pp. 178-179.

12. See Roy C. Macridis, "Comparative Politics and the Study of Government," *Comparative Politics*, 1 (1968): 82.

2

SETTING

This chapter seeks to provide background for an understanding of the Federal Constitutional Court and its relationship to West Germany's political system. It seeks to chart the historical development of constitutional jurisdiction in Germany, to describe the legal order of which the Constitutional Court is a part, and to identify elements of the political system that are relevant to the Court's operations.

CONSTITUTIONAL JURISDICTION IN GERMAN HISTORY

Since much of this book deals with judicial review in today's Germany, it will be helpful at the start to indicate precisely what we mean by judicial review and to mention some of the propositions on which it is based. At the same time, it will be necessary to differentiate between *judicial* review and *constitutional* review, activities with wholly different origins in the German experience.

Together, these activities exhaust the notion of *constitutional jurisdiction*.

Judicial review itself can mean two things: It may indicate the broad authority of courts to examine executive and administrative measures to ascertain if they conform to ordinary law; or it may refer to the authority of courts to invalidate legislation and other official state acts on constitutional grounds. We use the term here in the latter sense of measuring an act of government against some provision of a constitution; by a constitution, of course, we mean a written document specifying the relationships of power within government, limits of power on government, and rights of citizens against government.

Both the scope of judicial review and the institutional form it embodies vary among nations. In some countries, it is limited to specified courts; in others, to specified disputes; in still others, to specified litigants.[1] Whatever its structural variation, judicial review involves several assumptions concerning the role of the constitution and the judiciary. First, it implies a recognition of the constitution as a fundamental law taking precedence over all other forms of law. Second, it implies that all other laws and legal regulations—criminal and civil, statutory and administrative, public and private—must ultimately be sanctioned by the fundamental law. Third, it implies the authority of courts to invalidate the unconstitutional actions of other government agencies or public officials.

It is tempting to suggest that the form in which judicial review appears in a constitutional polity is an expression of the extent to which these propositions are accepted. In the United States, for example, judicial review is not limited in the ways noted above. Most American courts, state or federal, may invalidate any law in a case properly brought and appropriately raised by any person under the U.S. Constitution, at least until such time as the legislature withdraws that authority. What is also interesting about the American experience is that judicial review was not conferred upon courts by the express language of the Constitution; it was a judge-made convention, originating in the post-colonial period with *Marbury v. Madison*; in the course of time it gained enough popular and elite acceptance to become one of the linchpins of American government.[2]

There is no comparable German tradition of judicial review; if anything, the mainstream of German jurisprudence is averse to this process. Yet countervailing currents supportive of judicial review do course through German constitutional history. Admittedly, these currents are weak and almost never continuous, and they are to be found more frequently in the writings of legal scholars than in the behavior of courts. Still, this history is important, and we shall have to consider it if we are to appreciate the contemporary shape of judicial review in the German Federal Republic.

Before doing so, however, it is imperative to underscore the German distinction between judicial review and constitutional review. Judicial review (*richterliche Prüfungsrecht*) is a procedure by which courts determine the constitutionality of laws in the ordinary course of litigation; it is mainly a twentieth-century development in Germany. Constitutional review (*Staatsgerichtsbarkeit*) antedates judicial review, going back at least to early nineteenth-century German state constitutions; it is a judicial procedure for the resolution of controversies between units or levels of government about their respective rights and duties under the constitution. Disputes concerning the legitimacy of elections and referenda, ministerial impeachments, and the validity of amendments to the constitution were, in general, other examples of constitutional review. Constitutional review in Germany, unlike judicial review in the United States, never included the authority of a court to nullify legislative acts on constitutional grounds.[3] Both judicial review and constitutional review are species of what now is generally known as constitutional jurisdiction (*Verfassungsgerichtsbarkeit*).

Even if judicial review had not been incorporated expressly into the Basic Law of 1949, the Federal Constitutional Court would have been established to exercise constitutional review. Judicialization of the procedure for outlawing political parties is merely one of its several provisions that would seem to call for a judicial structure like the Federal Constitutional Court. In founding the Court, the Germans relied almost exclusively upon their own history and institutional precedents. Yet it is difficult to treat the history of constitutional review and its various historical manifestations without at the same time referring to the parallel development of the idea of judicial review. Both are interwoven in German legal history.

Constitutional Review

Constitutional review in Germany can be observed in embryo form during the days of the Holy Roman Empire. There was a need for unity among the commonwealths of the Empire and peace among their warring princes. Late in the fifteenth century, Maximilian I created a Court of the Imperial Chamber known as the *Reichskammergericht*, before which the princes were to lay their political controversies with one another. By the seventeenth century, the Imperial Court and some local courts were increasingly used to enforce the "constitutional" rights of estates against crown princes.[4] Their relations were fixed by compacts or treaties—in effect, constitutions—governing their mutual rights and obligations. Constitutional review might be said to have begun at the point where judicial decrees enforced the corporate rights of estates.

Constitutional review in modern form emerged from nineteenth-century efforts to preserve the confederation of German states established by the Congress of Vienna in 1815. Articles later formulated by the Congress demanded that the states submit their constitutional disputes to the Reich Assembly.[5] The Reich was even obligated to intervene in a constitutional dispute within a state if necessary to protect the latter's constitution. When deciding such cases, however, the Assembly had to resolve itself into something resembling a judicial forum; the Assembly was required to afford the conflicting parties a complete hearing and to support its decision with a doctrinal rationalization.[6]

Article 61 of the May 15, 1820, Vienna Accords (*Schlussakte*) also permitted the states to submit their internal constitutional disputes to the Assembly.[7] This provision is the direct antecedent of the 1871 Imperial Constitution's Article 76, empowering the

Bundesrat to settle state constitutional conflicts. The legislature, incidentally, was the principal forum for the resolution of constitutional conflicts under most of Germany's monarchical constitutions, as with the 1864 Constitution of the North German Federation.[8] Not until the emergence of Germany's democratic constitutions do we find these disputes once again being heard by independent law courts: By the Federal Supreme Court (*Reichsgericht*) under the Frankfurt Constitution of 1849, by the High State Court (*Staatsgerichtshof*) under the Constitution of 1919, and by the Federal Constitutional Court (*Bundesverfassungsgericht*) under the Basic Law of 1949.

Many of the jurisdictional and structural antecedents of the Federal Constitutional Court can be traced to the Frankfurt Constitution and even to some of the earlier state constitutions, particularly those of several South German states known for their liberal political traditions.[9] These constitutions were very specific regarding (1) the nature of constitutional disputes, (2) the parties who could bring such conflicts, (3) the procedures to be employed in such cases, and (4) the type of tribunal to decide them. Altogether, the four elements equalled a good working definition of constitutional review. First, a constitutional dispute was one that could arise only under fundamental law. Second, it involved only official agencies of government or, more precisely, those vital state organs whose constitutional duty it was to form the political will of the state. Third, it was brought on original jurisdiction and usually in the form of a simple complaint (*Beschwerde*), unfettered by the procedural rules of an ordinary lawsuit. Fourth, a constitutional dispute usually was put into the hands of a tribunal created outside the regular judicial establishment.

Even the recruitment of Federal Constitutional Court Justices has its roots in these early state constitutions. According to the Württemberg Constitution of 1819, the *Staatsgerichtshof* was to have a president, named by the King, and twelve judges, a portion of whom had to have legal qualifications. The King was to select half the judges and the Estates Parliament the other half.[10] Parliament's role in selecting judges reflected awareness of the court's political character, which explains the effort to make it a representative institution. Württemberg's tribunal seemed actually to be a forum for negotiation; *Kompromissgericht* (Court of Compromise) was the label attached to the constitutional tribunal established by the Kurhesse Constitution of 1831.[11]

These states never wholly abandoned their traditions of constitutional review. Bavaria, for example, had an active constitutional court during the Weimar period. The Bavarian *Staatsgerichtshof* could decide constitutional complaints brought by agencies of government and other constitutional disputes that could not be resolved by any other court.[12] Even Prussia had a *Staatsgerichtshof* to decide controversies between government and legislature and to hear cases initiated against a minister by at least 100 members of the state parliament.[13] With the coming of the Nazi regime, constitutional review was abolished, but was reestablished after World War II in most of the states located in the zones of Western occupation.

At the national level, the *Reichsgericht*, created under the Constitution of 1849, was the first tribunal to be vested with full power of constitutional review. The Frankfurt National Assembly, influenced in part by the pro-American constitutionalist views of intellectual liberals such as Friedrich Ludwig von Rönne and Robert von Mohl, set up a genuine federal state, provided for the separation of powers, and, most importantly, created a high court modeled after the U.S. Supreme Court.[14] The court's constitutional jurisdiction included (1) complaints by a state against national laws allegedly in violation of the Constitution, (2) complaints by the national government against the states for the same reason, (3) conflicts of opinion between the two houses of parliament over the meaning of the Constitution, (4) constitutional disputes between a state government and its popular assembly, and (5) complaints of German citizens claiming some violation of personal rights guaranteed by the Constitution.[15]

The *Reichsgericht* never functioned, however; it fell, along with Frankfurt's democracy, when the Constitution and the popular assembly it created were crushed under the heel of Prussia's boot at the fortress of Rastatt on July 23, 1849. Still, its failure to operate does not diminish the importance of constitutional review as a concept vital to the German theory of constitutional government. The *Reichsgericht*, like many state constitutional courts, was an institutional expression of a strong German insistence that relations among official centers of power be subject to law as interpreted by an independent tribunal.

Many of the *Reichsgericht's* powers were eventually inherited by the Weimar Republic's *Staatsgerichtshof*. Unlike the Frankfurt tribunal, however, the *Staatsgerichtshof* had no authority to hear the constitutional complaints or ordinary citizens. The gradual establishment, beginning in 1867, of a separate system of administrative courts in the German states was deemed sufficient to ensure official behavior consistent with the Constitution.[16]

The *Staatsgerichtshof's* jurisdiction included the authority—when not assigned to another national court—

(1) to settle constitutional disputes within the separate states as well as public law disputes among the states and between the states and the Reich (Article 19);

(2) to resolve differences of opinion concerning state administration of national laws (Article 15);

(3) to decide controversies, on the motion of a state or the national government, involving the distribution of property following a change in state boundaries (Article 18);

(4) to hear Reichstag complaints against the national President, Chancellor, and ministers for violations of the constitution (Article 59); and

(5) to decide controversies between states and Reich regarding the transfer of state railroads (Article 90), state waterways (Article 171), and state post and telegraph (Article 170) facilities to the national government.

The court also received limited jurisdiction over treaties by the law of June 9, 1921, which organized the *Staatsgerichtshof*.[17]

It is important to add, however, that the *Staatsgerichtshof* was not an independent tribunal with full-time judges. It functioned largely as a branch of the Supreme Court (*Reichsgericht*). Different sets of judges were required to decide the separate matters coming before the court. Article 15, 18, and 19 cases—dealing mainly with questions of law—were decided by a seven-judge panel composed of the President of the *Reichsgericht* presiding, three additional judges from the *Reichsgericht* (chosen by their colleagues), and one judge each from the Prussian, Bavarian, and Saxon Administrative Court of Appeals. Article 90, 170, and 171 cases—dealing mainly with questions of fact—were also decided by a seven-man panel under the chairmanship of the *Reichsgericht's* President, but four of its members were chosen by Parliament. Article 59 cases were decided by a much larger panel of fifteen members with even wider public representation.[18]

Although this is not the place to describe the work of the *Staatsgerichtshof*, it is necessary to mention generally its decisions in the electoral field where the court expanded the concept of constitutional review by regarding political parties as organs of the state capable of invoking the court's jurisdiction. Several cases involved suits by political parties against state governments which the court accepted under Article 19, vesting the court with jurisdiction over constitutional conflicts within states. In deciding these cases, the court developed the notion, rejected by most of the Weimar Constitution's leading commentators, that political parties are constitutionally necessary instruments of democracy.[19] In short, the court went beyond the juridical assumptions of Weimar's founders to emphasize that the Republic was, in a constitutional sense, a *Parteienstaat* (party state), a notion that has also been incorporated, but not without controversy, into the jurisprudence of the Federal Constitutional Court.[20] The *Staatsgerichtshof* maintained that the right of political parties to invoke the court's constitutional review powers derived from their status as constitutional organs of the state; they had the quality of such organs by virtue of their role in helping to form the "will of the state" through elections and other activities.[21]

` Whether in protecting the rights of political parties the *Staatsgerichtshof* struck a blow for Weimar democracy is hard to say. Several German states had banned radical left and right parties. In four of six cases coming before the *Staatsgerichtshof*, the ban was lifted.[22] (Under the Basic Law of 1949, the authority to ban political parties is the exclusive preserve of the Federal Constitutional Court.) But in one of its last decisions upholding a national ban on Prussia's Social Democratic Party, the *Staatsgerichtshof* helped to seal the fate of the Weimar Republic. This was the decision of October 25, 1932, when the court sustained the constitutionality of von Papen's seizure of the Prussian government under the emergency provisions of Article 48.[23]

We have strayed slightly from our path. Let us reenter it and conclude by underscoring once again the special character of constitutional review. Constitutional review is to be confused neither with the ordinary jurisdiction of German courts generally nor with the jurisdiction of specialized public law courts such as administrative tribunals. Constitutional review does not involve a dispute arising in the course of an ordinary lawsuit. Nor does it deal with the protection of individual rights; that is the function of specialized tribunals such as administrative courts. Historically, administrative law and constitutional law have been sharply distinguished in the German legal order. The juridical basis of the distinction, according to Franz W. Jerusalem, is that the former concerns the execution of the state's will once it is made, whereas the latter concerns those organs of government which actually form the state's will.[24] Constitutional review is therefore limited to disputes between primary organs of government or to those constitutionally prescribed units or the political system.

Judicial Review

The predominant German teaching during the nineteenth century was that courts did not have the authority to nullify legislative acts. The legislature was the supreme law-maker. The supremacy of parliament was supported by the doctrine of sovereignty and the doctrine of separation of powers. The German idea of law, to be discussed in greater detail later, constituted a third support. Traditional German teaching holds that statutes are the sole source of law. It follows that judicial decisions may not be regarded as sources of

law as in the Anglo-American legal system. The German judge's
first and only duty is to enforce the law as it is written.

In the second half of the nineteenth century, however, German legal
scholars did come to accept a limited form of judicial review. Then,
as now, they distinguished sharply between a law's formal and
material constitutionality; the latter implied the enactment and
promulgation of a statute in strict accordance with the procedures
laid down in the constitution, while the former implied the
compatibility of the statute's content with substantive constitutional
norms. The near unanimous view in Germany was that courts
generally did have the authority to review the formal, but not the
material, constitutionality of statutes.[25]

Even so, judicial review received measurable support during this
time. Robert von Mohl, familiar with both the *Federalist Papers*
and the work of the U.S. Supreme Court, defended judicial review
in a major legal treatise published in 1860.[26] In 1862, over a
thousand lawyers, judges, and legal scholars attending the third
annual meeting of German jurists went on record in favor of
judicial review, with Rudolph von Jhering emerging as their leading
spokesman.[27] Their views had little effect on the judiciary as
such. Still, in 1875, the Hanseatic Appeals Court struck down a
local tax law as violative of the right to property protected by
Article 19 of the Bremen Constitution.[28] (It is of some interest
that this first recorded instance of judicial review occurred in the
liberal political atmosphere of one of Germany's historic free
cities.) Several years later, however, the Imperial Court overruled
the decision. There, the conventional German view was reasserted:

"[It is said that] the ordinance should be denied the force of
binding law, because it is only an act of ordinary legislation,
while the constitution is a law of a higher order. . . .This view
cannot be acceded to. . . .[The] correct view is as follows: the
constitutional provision that well-acquired rights must not be
injured, is to be understood only as a rule for the legislative
power itself to interpret, and does not signify that a command
given by the legislative power should be left disregarded by the
judge because it injures well-acquired rights."[29]

It is not difficult to see why this view prevailed under the Monarchy (1871-1918). The German Empire was an expression of Prussian hegemony; it was marked by a powerful executive and a feeble parliament; the Constitution said very little about individual freedoms; the Reich's power proceeded from the sovereigns of each state, not from the people; the Constitution could be amended by ordinary legislation; and the Bundesrat reserved to itself authority to decide constitutional disputes within and among states. Remarked Otto von Gierke in 1910: "It is a fundamental deficiency of our public law that there exists no protection of constitutional principles by an independent court of justice."[30]

The Weimar Republic provided a climate somewhat more favorable to judicial review's reception. First, the 1919 Constitution, drawing inspiration from the Frankfurt Constitution of 1849, established a liberal democratic state and articulated a bill of rights that restricted the government. In a radical departure from the main juridical premise of the Imperial Constitution, it proclaimed that the state's power proceeded from the people. Judicial review was not, of course, the logical consequence of these provisions. Yet their net effect was a significant reduction, doctrinally, of the state's power over citizen and society, raising the possibility that courts might be used for the purpose of entertaining constitutional objections against laws.

Second, the Weimar period was coincident with the rise of the "free law" school (*Freirechtsschule*) of judicial interpretation led by Ernst Fuchs and Herman Kantorowicz. This school held that the judge was not bound to the letter of the law; rather, he was free to follow its true spirit and even to create new law if warranted by the circumstances of a case.[31] A related development was the tendency of a large part of the judiciary increasingly to assert its independence from the legislature, which may have stemmed partially from the judiciary's abiding antipathy toward the Weimar Republic.[32] The free law advocates in any event were unable to break down Germany's solid wall of legal positivism. But the wall did crack under their battering, leaving an opening, however slight, into which judicial review might be wedged.

Third, judicial review had strong support in the Weimar National

Assembly, for it was valued by many at the time as an important principle of limited government. The American experience with judicial review was well known, and judicial review was about to be incorporated into the constitutions of several other European nations. It is true that opponents of judicial review prevailed in the National Assembly, but they chose not expressly to deny to the courts authority to review legislation.[33] Hugo Preuss, the principal author of the Weimar Constitution, warned the National Assembly, accurately as it turned out, that judicial review would prevail if the Constitution did not expressly forbid it.[34]

Finally, constitutional provisions on court organization and jurisdiction were in themselves ambiguous enough to ensure that judicial review would remain an open question. Under Article 13, the *Reichsgericht*, the court of last resort in civil and criminal matters, had jurisdiction to resolve doubts or differences of opinion on whether state law is compatible with national law on the petition of a state or the national government, although in finance matters this authority was shared with the High Finance Court (*Reichsfin-anzhof*). It is somewhat surprising that Article 13 jurisdiction was not vested in the *Staatsgerichtshof* since, under Article 19, as noted earlier, it had jurisdiction generally to decide public law disputes between the states and the Reich, along with constitutional disputes arising within the states. At any rate, the question never wholly put to rest was whether these high courts, in settling *bona fide* public law disputes or doubts about the compatibility of state and national laws, could use the Constitution as a standard for measuring the validity of national laws.

The conjunction of all these features then—the liberalism of Weimar's Constitution, the "free law" school of judicial interpretation, the acceptance of judicial review by an influential minority in the National Assembly, and the ambiguity of constitutional provisions relating to the power of the judiciary—served to accelerate the pace of debate on judicial review during the 1920s; it was a debate which took up considerable space in the legal literature of the time.[35]

Great legal scholars were to be found on both sides of the question. Gerhard Anschütz, Weimar's leading constitutional authority, maintained, as Preuss had earlier, that courts had no power to examine the constitutionality of laws.[36] He was joined in this view by other authoritative commentators like Walter Jellinek, Richard Thoma, Julius Hatschek, Friedrich Giese, Gustav Radbruch, Leo Wittmayer, and Franz W. Jersualem.[37] Equally strong voices in support of judicial review were Hans Fritz Abraham, Hans Nawiasky, Fritz Poetzsch, Edward Hubrich, Rudolf Stammler, and Heinrich Triepel.[38] Those against judicial review generally argued that since the Constitution could be amended by legislation it could not, as in the United States, be regarded as law superior to ordinary law. Those in favor of judicial review mainly argued that the fundamental rights accorded to citizens under the constitution would be worthless if they were to be put at the mercy of the legislature.

The swelling debate in the legal literature was marked by several decisions of the *Reichsgericht* and other high national courts between 1921 and 1929, in which the doctrine of judicial review was accepted. On April 26, 1921, the *Reichsfinanzhof* suggested in a dictum that a tax law could be examined in light of the constitution.[39] In the same week, coincidentally, the *Reichsgericht* affirmed its own authority to review national legislation on constitutional grounds, a dictum it repeated a few months later in still another case involving a local police regulation impinging on free assembly.[40] Having laid its groundwork, the *Reichsgericht* could confidently claim: "It is indeed a recognized principle that the courts are fundamentally empowered to examine the formal and material constitutionality of [national] laws and regulations."[41] This was, of course, a fundamental misreading of German legal history; nevertheless, on October 21, 1924, the *Reichsversorgungsgericht* (High Pension Court) joined the chorus of high courts favoring judicial review.[42] Finally, in the Decision of November 4, 1925, the *Reichsgericht* for the first time went beyond the dicta of its previous decisions to consider directly the constitutionality of the Revaluation Act of 1925. Although the Act was sustained over the objection that it impaired a constitutional right to property, the Court's decision is important for its lengthy justification of judicial review.[43] Finally, on April 19, 1929, the *Reichsgericht* invalidated a national law that made pension and other welfare claims of police officials the subject of an administrative proceeding. This was a violation of the constitution, said the court, since under Article 129 police officials are entitled to have their claims heard in regular courts of law.[44]

These decisions caused considerable uneasiness among German legal scholars and law-makers. How conflicting interpretations of the constitution among the high courts were to be resolved was not the least of the problems that bothered them. In this connection, it is interesting to note that soon after the original 1921 decisions of the *Finanzgericht* and the *Reichsgericht* a bill was introduced into the Reichstag to confer judicial review exclusively on the *Staatsgerichtshof*. The bill contained provisions for concrete and abstract judicial review proceedings that are almost identical to those over which the Federal Constitutional Court presides today.[45] The bill failed to pass, leaving the matter of judicial review where it was before—namely, in the courts.

The attempt to establish the doctrine of judicial review in German law owes much to the efforts of Walter C. Simon, president of the *Reichsgericht* from 1922 to 1929. (By virtue of his position, by the way, he was also president of the *Staatsgerichtshof*.) Unhappy with the results of his labors, he wrote:

"During the seven years of my office I have tried to heighten the position of the *Reichsgericht* unceasingly but unsuccessfully. I wanted it to be like the Supreme Court of the United States, a high organ of the Commonwealth equal in rank to the Cabinet, having immediate intercourse with the President of the Republic; for in my opinion a republican commonwealth will never find a check on the overbearing power of parliamentarianism and the secret influence of ministerial bureaucracy if the Supreme Court is not perfectly independent and on the same footing with both the other powers of the state. Until now, the *Reichsgerichtshof* has not found a Chief Justice Marshall."[46]

Simon's comment betrayed his own mistrust of Weimar's democracy, and here he spoke for the large majority of German judges. As the Weimar Republic's leading historian has pointed out, judicial review was invoked most often to support largely conservative and propertied interests.[47] At any rate, Simon's influence came to an end when he resigned as president of the *Reichsgericht* in 1929, following a clash between the government and the court.

What was the experience of state courts with judicial review during the Weimar Republic? This final consideration need not detain us long. Courts generally held firm to the German tradition that judges are subject to law and have the duty to apply it, even over conflicting constitutional norms. Yet differing policies toward judicial review were beginning to emerge. Most state constitutions said nothing about judicial review.[48] Following the lead of the *Reichsgericht*, most courts accepted judicial review in principle, although they seldom used it to void legislation.[49] Bavaria had the most liberal policy on judicial review, for its Constitution conferred on all courts explicit authority to review laws in light of both state and national constitutions.[50] Even the Prussian Constitution was thought to imply judicial review, a major departure from the 1850 Constitution which expressly forbade judicial review.[51] Only the Oldenburg and Schaumburg-Lippe Constitutions denied the courts judicial review; in Oldenburg, the authority to review the constitutionality of laws was vested in the legislature instead.[52] The significance of these general developments was that constitutions in Germany were slowly coming to be recognized as laws of higher obligation, controlling all other law, and not simply as political documents broadly defining the governmental system.

Needless to say, judicial review was not exercised during Hitler's regime, for judicial review makes sense only in political systems where power is limited by written constitutions. National Socialism rejected both the principle of the written constitution and that of limited power. The *Volksgeist* replaced the constitution, while the *Führer* principle denied the finite character of power. In the end, *Volk* fully merged with *Führer*, leaving no room for checks and balances, individual rights, judicial review, or an independent judiciary.[53] Thus, the Nazi regime broke radically with the dominant tradition of German constitutionalism.

When the German states were reconstructed after World War II judicial review emerged once more, this time as an articulate principle of the written constitution, although in most of the states its exercise was confined to a specialized constitutional court. Contrary to the impressions of some people, there is no clear evidence to show that the United States or the Allies insisted upon putting judicial review into these state constitutions. The Allies insisted upon the judiciary's independence, but that was all. The Germans had their own history upon which to draw, while the Weimar experience might have taught them to organize judicial review more efficiently.

THE GERMAN
LEGAL SYSTEM

Any understanding of the Federal Constitutional Court requires some awareness also of the legal system in which it functions. German ideas on law and the judicial role, legal training, socialization of judges, practices and procedures of courts, and judicial structure impinge upon the Constitutional Court in vital ways. We shall treat these and other relevant aspects of the legal system in the following sections on (1) the meaning of law, (2) the system of legal education, and (3) the organization of the judiciary.

The Meaning of Law

Germany is part of the civil law system that is predominant in Western Europe. Civil law, which is based on the Roman codes, was received into Germany in the middle ages through the mediation of Italian glossators.[54] At first, Roman law mingled with local customary law to produce codes whose variations tended actually to impede Germany's commercial and political development. These variations and the influence of the Napoleonic Code, imposed during the French occupation of the Rhineland, generated the nineteenth-century movement for the codification of German private law. By the end of the century, German law had been systematically arranged and unified in several codes which still exist. Criminal law was codified in 1871; criminal and civil procedure in 1877; general private law in 1896; commercial law in 1897. The codifications followed Germany's political unification in 1871, facilitating, in turn, the unification of the court system in 1877. As Fritz Baur pointed out, codification reflected "the optimistic belief that all legally relevant human relations could be thus rationally comprehended and constructed."[55]

The drive for legal unity, powered in part by fierce nationalistic feeling, had meaning for the organization of the state in Germany. Under the influence of thinkers like Hobbes, Rousseau, and Montesquieu, German intellectuals, much as their contemporaries elsewhere in Europe, were very much attracted by the notions of sovereignty and separation of powers. To observe that the convergence of these ideas with the legal philosophy of Kant, Fichte, Hegel, and other thinkers culminated in the view that law is solely the product of legislation and the state is the exclusive source of law blurs, of course, important distinctions between schools of German jurisprudence. Yet, the one notion that emerges clearly out of all these ideas is the reality and ubiquity of the state. Indeed, it can be said fairly that the state is the dominant idea of nineteenth-century German jurisprudence.[56] It was commonly assumed that law and justice could be nurtured only within the bosom of that perfect society known as the state.

The primacy of the state in German jurisprudence influenced attitudes toward the role of the courts. This role is suggested by the following propositions which fairly well summarize the German, and largely continental, theory of law and judicial authority: That the state is the source of all law; that the locus of all law-making authority within the state is the sovereign legislature; that law is a closed system of logically arranged and internally coherent rules; that law, to be just, must be specific in content yet general in the sense of applying to all persons; that all legal disputes must be resolved by reference to such laws; that courts of law, independent of the legislature, are the proper agencies for interpreting law; that laws be interpreted literally and in strict accordance with the legislator's will; the function of courts, therefore, is to administer the law as written, requiring on the part of the judge a posture of absolute neutrality; in a word, the judge is a cog in the wheel of judicial administration, unmoved by feeling or even conscience.

This model of judicial administration is obviously exaggerated. It obscures many points of similarity between civil and common law systems and it accentuates the difference between judicial roles in the two systems. Nevertheless, the model broadly identifies a mind-set that helps to explain traditional German attitudes toward law and the judicial role. The German judge does not, like the common law judge, view his decisions as sources of law. He is even reluctant to base his decisions on general principles of law—to be distinguished from general laws—fearing that he may stray from the straight and narrow path of the law's letter. For example, one reason Germans have never accepted equity as a source of law is that equity bestows on judges independent "legislative" power. Moreover, equity contains the seeds of possible injustice since, by definition, it constitutes a departure from the equal application of general law.

The dominant school of German legal philosophy, as many of the above postulates about law suggest, remains that of legal positivism (analytical jurisprudence). By 1900, legal positivism had completely overshadowed the natural law and historical schools of jurisprudence. It holds that the rights and obligations of citizens are exhausted by general law; as such it leaves little room for judicial review. In legal positivism, law and politics, like law and morals, are separate domains. Similarly, politics and adjudication are mutually exclusive concerns. Legal positivism has been blamed for much that went wrong with Germany after 1933. This view may well have some merit. At the same time it is important to underscore the close connection between positivistic jurisprudence and the traditional German notion of *Rechtsstaat*. Legal positivists in Germany have long insisted, despite their separation of the spheres of law and ethics, that a state based on law (*Recht*) is the only means of securing individual persons against the arbitrary exercise of power (*Macht*). In Germany, limited government has been identified traditionally with the idea of *Rechtsstaat*.

The *Rechtsstaat* is doubtless an important element of constitutional government. Still, one might note the large gap separating the German idea of *Rechtsstaat* from the Anglo-American notion of constitutionalism. The German *Rechtsstaat* is largely neutral toward the political goals of the state or the specific institutional form that the state embodies. It does not, for example, presuppose parliamentary democracy, as in English theory, or judicial review, as in American theory. Nor does it exhaust the many classical ideas on justice to be found in Western political thought. In the *Rechtsstaat*, individual rights are secured by *general* laws elaborated in comprehensive codes that govern the conduct and mutual relations of citizens. We might parenthetically observe that in the Nazi regime citizens did not enjoy the protection of law in this positivistic sense, for there law was both politicized and personalized, and equal protection of law wholly denied. Seen from this perspective, legal positivism was rejected by the Nazi system.

Legal Education

Professional training and education is probably more important than any other background factor in the determination of judicial attitudes toward the Basic Law of 1949 and judicial review. Law school is the place where traditional thought-forms regarding the judicial process are taught. It is the place where the future judge learns and absorbs the values, spirit, and lore of his legal system. Legal education is important for us because of its potential impact upon the Federal Constitutional Court; it constitutes a force capable of generating or diminishing support for a regime of judicial review.

German legal education, which treats the codes as the embodiment of law and justice, views the judicial process largely in mechanistic terms. The staple of legal education in Germany is still code law: the Civil Code, Criminal Code, Commercial Code, Code of Civil Procedure, Code of Criminal Procedure, and, in the area of public law, the Code of Administrative Procedure. The student's main responsibility is to devour these codes and to listen, if he wishes, to the turgid lectures of professors who authoritatively delineate their meaning. Henry Adams may not have been far off when he noted, recalling his student days at the University of Berlin—when analytical jurisprudence was at its zenith—that "in the Civil Law he found the lecture system in its deadliest form as it flourished in the thirteenth century."[57]

Yet, German legal education and attitudes toward law are changing. Any full assessment of this change would have to consider the impact of the assault upon analytical jurisprudence mounted by the "free law" school of judicial interpretation during and before the Weimar period, the jurisprudence of interests popularized by Professor Philipp Heck about the same time, and the natural law school after 1945, when judicial review was incorporated into the constitutions of several German states.[58]

Rigidities which once characterized legal education in Germany are beginning to loosen. Even an American law student would feel at home with some aspects of contemporary German legal education. While code commentaries are the principal learning tools in law schools, judicial decisions are growing in importance. The decisions of the Federal Supreme Court (*Bundesgerichtshof*), particularly in criminal law, are vitally important, as the battered volumes of reports in any German law school library will show. In their examinations, students are expected to refer to these decisions, to deal with them critically, and then to decide the problem at hand, on whatever authority they regard as superior; this might be a judicial decision, a standard commentary or, more likely, the opinion of their professor.

A second development that would meet the eye of our American student is the increasing liberality of the law school curriculum. The German tradition has been one of rather sharp cleavage between law and social science. Student demands for curriculum reform (much stronger than among American law students), the rising prominence—and respectability—of social science faculties in German universities, and the problems associated with a modern industrial society are forging new links between law and social science. The University of Cologne is representative. Students are now offered courses in the history of Weimar's political parties, the foreign relations of the Common Market, and several other courses, such as law and pollution, which involve cross-disciplinary considerations. A proposal before the North Rhine-Westphalia legislature would widen student options even further, possibly to include courses in sociology and psychology.

It is of particular interest here to note that there are no courses in constitutional law based on the decisions of the Federal Constitutional Court, although these decisions, unlike the decisions of other courts, are regarded as primary sources of law. Still, if a German law student is asked where the constitutional law of his country is to be found, he is likely to reply, "In the Basic Law of 1949," or, put otherwise, in the constitutional code. Like other areas of German law, authoritative commentaries are the chief tools in the study of constitutional law; they are bulky volumes which explain the meaning of the Basic Law, clause by clause, with the same detailed attention to historical and logical analyses which characterize commentaries on the civil code. Citations to Constitutional Court decisions in such commentaries are of course frequent, but authors do not always regard them as the most authoritative interpretations of the Basic Law. Authors of commentaries, ordinarily professors of law, often rank their own views as equal to those of the Court. Unbound by any doctrine of *stare decisis*, they are free to base their interpretations on the "constitutional code"; judicial decisions are of secondary importance.

German students now learn constitutional law mainly through courses in constitutional history (*Verfassungsgeschichte*) and the general theory of the state (*Allgemeine Staatslehre*). But here, too, changes are to be observed, especially as younger professors educated in the Federal Republic move into German law faculties. For one thing, as German law students have noticed, there are increasing references to Federal Constitutional Court decisions in public law courses. For another, one of the most widely used commentaries on the Basic Law, published in 1966, is based almost exclusively upon the Court's decisions.[59] Written in fact by two Justices of the Constitutional Court, it is now in its fourth edition.

A former law clerk at the Constitutional Court, now a distinguished teacher of public law, is the first to edit and publish the Court's leading cases.[60] Since then at least one other collection of cases has been published.[61] Important also is the fact that several Constitutional Court Justices and former law clerks hold professorships in German law schools; their influence in heightening awareness of the Constitutional Court among German law students should not be underestimated.

The Judicial System

Court Organization: Germany has a uniform judicial system. Court organization, the basic structure of which is fixed by federal law, is the same throughout the country. Federal codes of civil and criminal procedure govern the practice and proceedings of all regular German courts. National law also provides for the jurisdiction and procedures of public law tribunals. But there is no separate system of federal courts. All courts, except the highest appellate courts in the nation, are state courts. While federal law specifies the basic organization of the judiciary, state law provides for the establishment and administration of the courts. The states, through their ministries of justice, are also in charge of the training, recruitment, and supervision of judges. The division of federal and state authority over the judiciary is a structural characteristic of some consequence, as we note later, for the exercise of judicial review.

Specialization is another important feature of the German judiciary. Private law and public law are divided into specialized jurisdictions. For each of these jurisdictional areas, separate courts, with their own independent hierarchy, have been created. Thus, ordinary civil and criminal jurisdiction is vested in what are called regular courts (*ordentliche Gerichte*). Within these courts, there is further specialization since many of them are divided into civil, criminal, commercial, and juvenile chambers, not to mention special panels that deal mainly with noncontentious matters. In addition, each state has a separate system of administrative, revenue, labor, and social ·courts. (Each state also has one constitutional court.) The supreme courts of appeal for each of these areas of basic jurisdiction are federal tribunals. They include the Federal Supreme Court (*Bundesgerichtshof*), Federal Administrative Court (*Bundesverwaltungsgericht*), Federal Labor Court (*Bundesarbeitsgericht*), Federal Social Court (*Bundessozialgericht*), and the Federal Finance Court (*Bundesfinanzhof*).

The regular courts operate at four levels. At the lowest level are the *Amtsgerichte* (local courts). They operate in towns or other limited geographical areas and exercise jurisdiction over minor civil suits and petty criminal offenses. They also perform many nonjudicial functions such as administering estates, drafting wills and conveyances, keeping registers, appointing guardians, and supervising executors and trustees in bankruptcy. Next come the *Landgerichte* (district courts). They are the trial courts of general jurisdiction; within their territorial limits, they also serve as final courts of appeal for the local courts. The court of last resort in each state is the *Oberlandesgericht* (court of appeals), although it has original jurisdiction in cases involving high treason and betrayal of the Basic Law. The final court of appeals is the Federal Supreme Court in Karlsruhe.[62]

Specialized public law courts operate at three levels. In the case of administrative jurisdiction, for example, administrative courts (*Verwaltungsgerichte*) are at the lowest level. The intermediate court is called an *Oberverwaltungsgericht* (High Administrative Court); each state has at least one such intermediate court except that Lower Saxony and Schleswig-Holstein have established a common High Administrative Court with jurisdiction over both states. The court of last resort is the Federal Administrative Court in Berlin. (The Federal Labor Court and the Federal Social Court are located in Kassel.) Fiscal courts, however, are organized at only two levels, composed simply of state fiscal courts, of which there are a total of fifteen, and the Federal Finance Court in Munich.[63]

German judicial structure is also marked by the collegial character of its courts. Only the local courts are one-judge tribunals, although in criminal cases the judge is assisted by lay judges. All other courts function in panels of three to five judges.

The high federal courts are very large. The Federal Supreme Court has 104 judges who are assigned to one of ten civil senates, five criminal senates, and seven senates for other fields. The remaining federal courts are also divided into senates, each of which is composed of five judges and headed by a senate president. Originally the Basic Law provided for the creation of another federal tribunal to resolve jurisdictional conflicts among these high federal courts. It was never established. Instead, the Bundestag established a *Gemeinsamer Senat* (Common Senate) composed of the presidents of the five high federal courts to resolve such conflicts.[64]

The scope of the judicial system, presented in Table 1, can perhaps be better appreciated by noting that Germany, with one-fourth the population of the United States, has over twice as many judges. The 12,934 professional judges holding office in 1972 is in sharp contrast to the approximately 5,687 (5,265 state and 422 federal) judges holding office in the United States.[65] Perhaps this difference is more sharply illustrated by contrasting the German state of Baden-Württemberg with Michigan; both are relatively equal in population—around eight and one-half million—although Baden-Württemberg is territorially much smaller. Baden-Württemberg has 1,248 ordinary court judges in addition to 279 judges who preside over labor, fiscal, social, and administrative courts, dwarfing Michigan's mere 138 full-time professional judges.[66]

These figures say something about the scope of German law and the litigious behavior of Germans. There is hardly an area of human relations in Germany untouched by some rule, order, or regulation. These rules may range from the private rental agreement specifying that a certain detergent be used when scrubbing the front steps of the house every Saturday afternoon to the Bavarian ordinance that requires parents to keep their children quiet each day between 1 and 3 p.m. And contrary to popular belief, Germans, like other people, break laws, occasioning lawsuits. What is more, Germans seem very much disposed to seek judicial redress of grievances, more so than Americans, a trait which Herbert J. Spiro attributes to the particularity of German code law as well as to a

TABLE 1

THE GERMAN JUDICIARY: 1972

Court	No. of Courts	No. of Judges
State		
Regular Courts	891	10,094
(Local Courts)	(776)	
(District Courts)	(93)	
(Courts of Appeal)	(20)	
Administrative Courts	41	844
Social Courts	60	931
Labor Courts	116	354
Fiscal Courts	13	270
Federal		
Federal Supreme Court	1	104
Federal Administrative Court	1	66
Federal Labor Court	1	17
Federal Social Court	1	40
Federal Finance Court	1	40
Federal Patent Court	1	158
Federal Constitutional Court	1	16

SOURCE: *BRD-DDR Systemvergleich: Bericht und Materialien zur Lage der Nation* (Bonn: Westdeutscher Verlag, 1972), II: p. 297 and *Statistisches Jahrbuch für die Bundesrepublik Deutschland 1972* (Stuttgart and Mainz: Verlag W. Kohlhammer GMBH, 1972), p. 98.

general German disinclination to settle controversies by negotiation or political means.[67] An equally plausible explanation is that German justice is speedy and relatively inexpensive to secure.

Decision-making in the courts follows a traditional pattern. At the trial level, German judges play a much more active role in the judicial process than do American or British judges. In administrative, social, and revenue, but most of all in criminal courts, judges themselves seek to establish facts independent of what attorneys in the case may have put forward by way of evidence. After the facts are established, the judges consult with one another, under the chairmanship of the court's president if a collegial court is involved, and then vote. Differences of opinion on both facts and law are thrashed out until a majority is found. There is no record of these consultations. They are secret, and judges are honor-bound to reveal nothing about the nature of their internal deliberations.[68]

On appellate review, it is customary to assign a case to one of the judges, known as the *Berichterstatter* who is in charge of preparing for his colleagues a report and recommendation on what should be done with it. The report is discussed in conference and a vote taken. Once again, a majority decides. Although the judges may have been deeply divided among themselves, the court speaks to the parties and to the public with one voice in an anonymous institutional opinion, a practice followed by the Federal Constitutional Court until 1971.

Judges: When more than seventy years ago Hugo Münsterberg compared the political system of the United States with Imperial Germany, he wrote disparagingly of the "chronic dilettantism" of American public life. By contrast, he noted that "the career of experts in all functions of public activity is the pride of Germany—where the school committeeman or the major or the diplomat climbs up step by step, and reaches the greatest effectiveness by his life-long specialization."[69] So it is with legal professionals in Germany; the legal profession is so stratified that there is little crossover from one legal career to another.

A word about the training of judges (and lawyers) is in order. After three and a half years (seven semesters) of formal study, in which the student must successfully complete certain prescribed courses, he may take his first state examination. If successful he becomes a *Referendar*—a junior barrister—and enters upon two and a half more years of practical training. During this time, he is required to spend limited periods (from three to six months) as an assistant in the office of a public prosecutor, an ordinary court (civil and criminal), an administrative court, an administrative agency, and an attorney. When he completes his practical training, he may then take his second or major state examination, the successful completion of which renders him qualified for judicial office. It is at this point that the student chooses his career. He may become a judge, state prosecutor, civil servant, or notary public, may enter private law practice, or may join the legal staff of some corporation, labor union, or other association. If he decides to become a judge, he goes through still another three-year period of in-service training, during which time he holds the rank and title of *Assessor*. If his stewardship meets with the approval of his superiors in the Ministry of Justice, he is awarded a judgeship with lifetime tenure and security.[70] And there he will undoubtedly remain, seldom interacting with other members of the legal profession, with the exception perhaps of public prosecutors. E.J. Cohn writes, "Sociologically it appears doubtful whether it is possible to speak of a German legal profession at all. Judges and state attorneys [prosecutors] usually entertain closer social contact with civil service circles than with attorneys. There is little fellowship between Bench and Bar in Germany."[71]

The psychological link between bench and civil service is deeply rooted. During Imperial Germany and the Weimar period judges were regarded as part of the civil service. Indeed both civil servants and judges were subject to the same system of regulation. Though judges now enjoy independent status in Germany, being subject to a set of laws (*Richtergesetz*) different from those that govern the behavior of civil servants (*Beamtengesetz*), the two professions are still similarly structured with comparable tenure, salaries, ranks, promotion procedures, and retirement conditions. Below the federal level, nearly all judicial appointments are made by state ministers of justice. The typical appointee begins his career in the lowest court. His ascent within the judiciary is uncommonly slow. Promotion depends usually on the recommendation of higher-ranking judges. Many judges are never promoted. Little wonder that German judges are not known for their independence; according to one authority, the judiciary does not "attract or encourage the most forceful and energetic personality types."[72]

Germans themselves have often commented on the conservative and bureaucratic character of their judicial establishment. For example, one judge who spent a lifetime on a criminal court described the typical judge as "sober, suspicious, reserved, and not open to new ideas."[73] Ralf Dahrendorf, a noted sociologist, has remarked that "the majority of judges are . . . driven by an ethos of duty and service to the state, concerned above all with the values of order and security."[74] Judicial background studies have tended to reinforce the conservative image of the German judiciary. Recent studies have shown that most judges have upper-middle-class backgrounds, that upwards of fifty percent have fathers in the civil service, and that only a tiny percentage—around two percent—have lower-class backgrounds.[75]

Occasionally the above criticisms and findings are used (misused?) to suggest that German judges are antagonistic to political democracy. The hostility of the judiciary to the Weimar Republic was, of course, well known; so was the judiciary's subservience to the Third Reich. In the Federal Republic, however, there is no manifest judicial antagonism toward democracy, even though a substantial number of judges now in office served in the judiciary prior to 1945. Criticism of German judges for their lack of sympathy for democracy must be viewed with skepticism today, as younger judges trained since the 1945-1950 period and within the framework of a more liberal system of legal education replace an older generation of judges. Actually, a survey of 1,032 regular court judges by the Mannheim University Social Science Research Institute in 1973 showed that they were overwhelmingly in support of the democratic order established by the Basic Law.[76]

Nevertheless, the Mannheim study found a high incidence of conservative political attitudes among German judges, notwithstanding the interesting finding that forty-two percent of the judges in the sample expressed a preference for the continuation of the Bonn coalition between Social and Free Democrats.[77] Of course, one would expect to find a high incidence of conservatism among judges or legal professionals almost anywhere. What is interesting about the background of German judges, however, is the large number who come from civil service families, including high federal judges, especially those on the Federal Supreme Court,[78] all of which adds up to considerable professional inbreeding.

The civil service background of German judges has meaning for the life of the Federal Constitutional Court. If judges perceive themselves as being primarily servants of the state, what is to be said of their attitude toward judicial review or the Constitutional Court? How will German judges respond to a constitutional tribunal vested with authority to strike down legislation and nullify executive acts? These questions are addressed in later chapter.

THE POLITICAL SYSTEM

The Federal Constitutional Court is part of the German political system. It is therefore desirable to describe that system, confining ourselves to those elements of the polity more or less relevant to the operation of the Constitutional Court.

The Basic Law declares West Germany to be a "democratic and social federal state." Bonn's founders sought to ensure the democratic character of the new German system in three ways. First, the Basic Law guarantees certain fundamental rights and freedoms to all persons. These include all the traditional substantive and procedural rights normally associated with the liberal traditions of Western democracy, although the relevant articles of the German Constitution are much longer, less elegant, and hedged by qualifications that do not appear in the American Bill of Rights.[79] Owing to Christian and Socialist influences, the Basic Law specifies still other basic rights and duties. Under Article 6, for example, marriage and the family enjoy the special protection of the state while Article 7 expressly confers on parents the right to decide whether their children shall receive religious instruction in state schools.[80] Although Article 14 guarantees the right to property, Article 15 permits land, natural resources, and the means of production to be transferred to public ownership. Thus the Basic Law ratifies neither a socialist nor a market-oriented economy. Finally, Article 12 gives all Germans the right freely to choose their trade, occupation, or profession, including their place of work. All these rights, incidentally, are judicially secured.

Second, in a radical departure from previous German constitutions, the Basic Law literally sets up a party democracy. Article 21 reads: "Political parties shall participate in forming the political will of the people. They may be freely established. Their internal organization must conform to democratic principles. They must publicly account for the sources of their funds." The Basic Law is not neutral toward all parties, however. Convinced that one Hitler was enough, the founding fathers added a provision to Article 21 asserting that parties which seek to impair or abolish the free democratic basic order or to endanger the existence of the Federal Republic of Germany shall be unconstitutional.

Finally, the Constitution (Article 38) provides for "direct, free, equal, and secret elections." Federal elections of deputies to the lower or popular house of the Federal Parliament (Bundestag) are held every four years. All citizens who have reached the age of eighteen are entitled to vote in federal and state elections. Though the Basic Law seems to underscore the primacy of political parties, Article 38 nevertheless declares that Bundestag deputies "shall be representatives of the whole people, not bound by orders and instructions, and shall be subject only to their conscience."

It is interesting to note that in all three areas—basic rights, political parties, and elections—the Federal Constitutional Court has the final decision as to whether a violation of the Basic Law has occurred. With regard to Article 21, the Constitutional Court is the only agency authorized to declare a political party unconstitutional.

West Germany is also a federal system, consisting at the present time of ten states plus West Berlin with a total population of over 60 million residents. The formal governmental structure additionally includes 30 administrative districts, 564 counties (Kreise), and 24,182 towns and cities. The states vary considerably in territorial size, ranging from Bavaria, covering an area of 70,550 square kilometers, to the small city-states of Bremen and Hamburg. In population, the states range from North Rhine-Westphalia with 17 million to Bremen with around 755,000 inhabitants.[81] Represented in the upper house of Parliament (Bundesrat), where their representatives vote as a bloc, the states are accorded votes based on their population. Each state has at least three votes, while the largest states, with more than 6 million people, have five votes.

In most areas of domestic policy, the states and federal government enjoy concurrent powers. Exclusive powers of the federal government relate mainly to foreign and military policy. Powers not exclusively conferred upon the federal government or which are not a matter of concurrent legislation are reserved to the states. What is most notable about the execution of federal laws is that they are administered by the states. Direct federal administration is confined mainly to foreign service, postal service, and the administration of federal railroads, waterways, and shipping. A bill passed by the Bundstag must be submitted to the Bundesrat, which may delay the measure by demanding its reconsideration by a joint committee of both houses. If the committee amends the original bill, the Bundestag must again act on the measure. If the Bundesrat disapproves again by a majority of its members, the bill must then be passed by an absolute majority of the Bundestag's members in order to become law.

West Germany is also a parliamentary system. There is a federal president, elected by a federal convention composed of members of the Bundestag and an equal number of delegates elected by the state legislatures. The president represents the Federal Republic in international relations, concludes treaties, and signs all public laws, but these functions are largely ceremonial. The effective head of the federal government is the Chancellor who is elected by the Bundestag and assisted by federal ministers whom he appoints and dismisses. The Chancellor is ordinarily the leader of his party in the Bundestag, and one noteworthy feature of the German system is the secure position of the Chancellor. Article 67 of the Basic Law makes a no confidence vote against the Chancellor contingent upon the immediate election of his successor by a majority of the Bundestag, a provision designed to retain the effective power of the Chancellor in times of stress. Doubtless, this arrangement has contributed to political stability in West Germany, for it helped Adenauer survive the crisis set off by the Spiegel affair in 1962-1963, when the Free Democratic Party (FDP) walked out of the coalition, leaving Adenauer momentarily at the head of a minority government.[82]

Equally important as formal constitutional structure in explaining the relative stability of the German political system is the informal sociopolitical structure. Since the early 1950s, Germany has gone through a period of unbounded prosperity. German virtues of hard work, personal sacrifice, and attention to duty mixed very well with market-oriented economic policies to produce the so-called "economic miracle" that within two decades transformed West Germany from a war-ravaged country into one of the most prosperous societies in the world, with a current living standard rivaling that of the United States. The fact that West Germany employs nearly three million foreign workers and enjoys a per capita income higher than most western nations is one manifestation of her material prosperity.

Whether in spite of or because of her economic prosperity, West Germany has evolved into what for all practical pusposes has become a two-party system approximating the American model. Nine political parties were represented in the first Bundstag elected in 1949. Today there are three: The Christian Democratic Union (CDU) and its Bavarian affiliate, the Christian Social Union (CSU); the Social Democratic Party (SPD); and the Free Democratic Party (FDP). One reason for the virtual elimination of splinter parties in Germany is a federal election law—upheld, incidentally, by the Federal Constitutional Court—denying parliamentary representation to any party which fails to receive at least 5% of the national vote.[83] The FDP nearly missed jumping this hurdle in the federal election of 1969, when the party attained only 5.8% of the vote, a precipitous decline in electoral strength from its 1961 high of 12.8%; in 1972, however, the FDP recovered some of its losses by winning 8.4% of the national vote. At all events, about 90% of the German electorate supports the two major parties. Having shed their earlier ideological shells, both CDU/CSU and SPD now compete, on a relatively even basis, to occupy the broad center of the German political stage.

It is important to point out that from 1949 to 1966 the CDU/CSU controlled, although mainly in coalition with the FDP, the federal government. Christian Democrats were at the height of their power after the 1957 election when they gained an absolute majority of deputies in the Bundestag. After the Spiegel affair in the early 1960s, the relationship between the FDP and CDU/CSU, at least at the federal level, visibly cooled. The marriage between the FDP and CDU/CSU was reconstituted after the 1965 election, but one year later it dissolved. In December of 1966, which marked the first major turning point in postwar German politics, the CDU/CSU and SPD formed the "Grand Coalition," giving Social Democrats their first taste of power since the founding of the Federal Republic. Owing, however, to the federal nature of the political system, Social

TABLE 2

ELECTORAL SUPPORT FOR CDU/CSU AND SPD

Federal Election	CDU/CSU	SPD	Total
1949	31.0	29.2	59.2
1953	45.2	28.8	74.0
1957	50.2	31.8	82.0
1961	45.3	36.2	81.5
1965	47.6	39.3	86.9
1969	46.1	42.7	88.8
1972	44.9	45.8	90.7

SOURCE: Werner Kaltefleiter, "Zwischen Konsens und Krise: Eine Analyse der Bundeswahl 1972," *Verfassung und Verfassungswirklichkeit*, Jahrbuch 1973, Teil 1 (Cologne: Carl Heymanns Verlag KG, 1973), p. 133.

Democrats did enjoy a previous power base, governing alone or leading coalitions in several states, notably in Berlin, Bremen, Hamburg, and Hesse. Not until the 1969 federal elections, however, did the SPD take over the controls in Bonn, the Free Democrats having shifted the balance of power to the Social Democrats; together they narrowly elected Willi Brandt as Chancellor, driving Christian Democrats into an unfamiliar opposition role. To many observers, the calm with which this first major transfer of power took place was a sign of the growing maturity of German democracy.

But the new Chancellor, who embarked upon a policy of detente with the Eastern bloc countries, found growing discontent; detente or *Ostpolitik* (Eastern policy), as it was labelled, was founded on proposed treaties with the Soviet Union, Poland, and East Germany. Within two years, Brandt had nearly lost his parliamentary majority, owing mainly to FDP defections over *Ostpolitik*, and, in 1972, he narrowly escaped losing a no confidence vote in the Bundestag. Instead of proceeding with an uncertain majority, he called for new elections, which for many people amounted to a referendum on Brandt's Eastern policy. On November 19, 1972, the SPD/FDP coalition returned to power after an impressive victory which awarded Brandt's government a substantial majority in the Bundstag, thus ensuring continuity in both leadership and policy, further evidence, in the minds of many, of the stability of German politics.

These realities by themselves say little about Germany's political culture or about the average German's attitude toward the Federal Republic's political institutions or constitutional democracy. Opinion surveys, however, show that German attitudes toward democracy and politics have undergone a marked transformation since the 1950s. An early and oft-quoted study of Germany's civic culture found that while Germans exhibited considerable *awareness* of politics and government, they did not hold the political system in high *esteem*; Germans tended to value the economy more than the political system; and although turning out in record high numbers to vote, Germans tended to be politically inert and even uncomfortable with political conversation.[84] A civic culture marked by political lassitude could, of course, pose problems for a constitutional tribunal wishing to inculcate respect for political values and institutions specified and created by the Basic Law. In recent years, however, public opinion polls tend to disclose attitudes significantly more congenial toward politics, democracy, and the institutions of the Federal Republic; and while the number of politically uncommitted persons remains substantial, most Germans do identify with one of the major political parties. German political attitudes do seem to be changing, along with social change and ongoing mutations in the political system. At least for the present, these changes seem to be in the direction of greater democratization of life and politics.[85]

One final observation needs to be made about modern Germany if we are fully to appreciate German politics over the last two decades. That is the division of the German nation into two separate and ideologically opposed states. The Federal Republic and the Democratic Republic of Germany were children of the Cold War. Throughout the 1950s and well into the 1960s, West German politics was militantly anticommunist, influencing both the style of political competition and the substance of foreign and domestic policy. Since the Grand Coalition, the icy relationship between the two German states has undergone a slight thaw. It has melted further since the Four

Power Agreement over Berlin in 1971; West Germany's ratification in 1972 of treaties with Poland and the Soviet Union, and in 1973 with East Germany; and other West German attempts to reestablish economic and cultural ties with Eastern bloc countries. It is of some interest to note, as we conclude this chapter, that the Federal Constitutional Court was drawn into the middle of the conflict over *Ostpolitik*. In 1973, Bavaria petitioned the Court to review the constitutionality of the Intra-German Basic Treaty, asking the Court, in effect, to reverse what many Germans regarded as a historic turn in East-West relations. The Court accepted the case and ruled on the merits of the treaty, demonstrating in the process how vital a role the Constitutional Court plays in the West German political system.

NOTES

1. See, generally, Hermann Mosler, ed., *Constitutional Review in the World Today* (Cologne: Carl Heymanns Verlag KG, 1962). This informative volume, written mostly in German, deals with constitutional review in seventeen different nations. See also Donald P. Kommers, "Cross-National Comparisons of Constitutional Courts: Toward a Theory of Judicial Review" (delivered at the Sixty-Sixth Annual Meeting of the American Political Science Association, Los Angeles, California, September 11, 1970).

2. Marbury v. Madison, 1. Cranch 137 (1803).

3. See Kuzuhiro Hayashida, "Constitutional Court and Supreme Court of Japan," in *Die moderne Demokratie und ihr Recht*, Festschrift für Gerhard Leibholz zum 65. Geburtstag (Tübingen: J.C.B. Mohr [Paul Siebeck] 1966), 2:407-416.

4. See Robert C. Binkley, "The Holy Roman Empire versus the United States: Patterns for Constitution-Making in Central Europe," in Conyers Read, ed., *The Constitution Reconsidered* (New York: Columbia University Press, 1938), p. 274. See also Karl August Betterman, Hans Carl Nipperday, and Ulrich Scheuner, eds., *Die Grundrechte* (Berlin: Duncker and Humboldt, 1959), III (pt. 3): 645-658.

5. See *Dokumente der deutschen Politik und Geschichte von 1848 bis zur Gegenwart* (Berlin: Dokumentaten-Verlag Dr. Herbert Wendler, 1915), p. 5. The practice of taking constitutional disputes to the parliamentary forum was analogous to, and probably originated in, the seventeenth-century requirement that doubts over the interpretation of Imperial Laws be resolved by the

Imperial Council (Reichsrat). More significantly, complaints that Imperial courts had overstepped their constitutional authority could also be taken to the Imperial Council. See Betterman et al., op. cit., pp. 645-646.

6. See Ernst Rudolf Huber, *Deutsche Verfassungsgeschichte seit 1789* (Stuttgart: W. Kohlhammer Verlag, 1957), 1:622.

7. Article 61 should be read together with Articles 54 and 56 of the 1820 Vienna Accords. These provisions appear to have permitted the estates, as well as political subdivisions within the states, to challenge unlawful changes in state constitutions before the Reich Assembly. At any rate, an important historical precedent was set in 1839 when the City of Osnabrück, along with representatives of the Estates Parliament of the Kingdom of Hannover, filed successive constitutional complaints before the Federal Parliament when King Ernst August, upon his succession to the throne in 1837, abrogated the 1833 Hannover Constitution and dissolved Parliament. It was claimed that the King had violated Article 56 of the Vienna Accords by ignoring procedures for constitutional amendment prescribed in the Kingdom's Constitution. The Assembly's ultimate rejection of the complaints did not alter the proceeding's significance for the future development of constitutional review in Germany. The King's proclamation, the constitutional complaints, and the decision of the Reich Assembly are included in Ernst Rudolf Huber, *Dokumente zur deutschen Verfassungsgeschichte* (Stuttgart: W. Kohlhammer Verlag, 1961), 1: 248-252 and 256-259.

8. Constitution of the North German Federation (1864), Article 76.

9. See, for example, the Bavarian Constitution of May 5, 1818, Title X, Article 5 and the Baden Constitution of August 22, 1818, Article 67.

10. Württemberg Constitution of September 25, 1819, Article 196.

11. Kurhesse Constitution of January 5, 1831, Article 154.

12. Bavarian Constitution of August 14, 1919, Article 72. For an excellent discussion of the range of the *Staatsgerichtshof's* authority, see Hans Nowiasky, *Bayerisches Verfassungsrecht* (Munich: J. Schweitzer Verlag, 1923), pp. 452-470.

13. Prussian Constitution of November 30, 1920, Articles 58 and 87.

14. See J.A. Hawgood, "Friedrich von Rönne—A German Tocqueville" in *University of Birmingham Historical Journal*, 3, no. 1 (1951): 79-94. See also Gottfried Dietze, "Robert von Mohl, Germany's de Tocqueville," in Gottfried Dietze (ed.), *Essays on the American Constitution* (Englewood Cliffs, N.J.: Prentice-Hall, 1974), pp. 187-212.

15. Frankfurt Constitution of 1849, Article 126.

16. Georg Jellinek, *Allgemeine Staatslehre* (Berlin: Verlag von Julius Springer, 1929), p. 794. For a good discussion of administrative court

structure during the Weimar period, see Frederick F. Blachly and Miriam E. Oatman, *The Government and Administration of Germany* (Baltimore: Johns Hopkins Press, 1928), pp. 459-513.

17. *Reichsgesetzblatt* 1 (1921): 907, secs. 3 and 31.

18. Ibid., secs. 3, 18, and 31.

19. See Decision of March 23, 1929, *Entscheidungen des Reichsgerichts in Zivilsachen* (hereafter cited as RGZ) 124: 40-50 (Appendix). See also Henrich Triepel, *Die Staatsverfassung und die politischen Parteien* (Berlin: Verlag Liebmann, 1928), pp. 25-32 and Gerhard Leibholz, "Gleichheit und Allgemeinheit der Verhältniswahl nach der Reichsverfassung und die Rechtsprechung des Staatsgerichtshof," *Juristische Wochenschrift* 58 (1929): 3042-3044. The decisions of the *Staatsgerichtshof* do not appear in a separate set of court reports. They were published separately as an appendix to the yearly reports of the *Reichsgericht*. The *Staatsgerichtshof* functioned from 1921 through 1932; its decisions are, accordingly, to be found in appendices to volumes 102 through 139 of the official reports of the *Reichsgericht* (*Entscheidungen des Reichsgerichts in Zivilsachen*). Selected decisions of the *Staatsgerichtshof* appear in Hans-Henrich Lammers and Walter Simons, *Die Rechtsprechung des SGHs für das deutschen Reich und das Reichsgericht auf Grund Art. 13 Abs. 2 der Reichsverfassung,* 3 volumes (Berlin: George Stilke 1929-1931).

20. See Donald P. Kommers, "Politics and Jurisprudence in West Germany: State Financing of Political Parties," *American Journal of Jurisprudence* 16 (1971): 215-241.

21. See Franz W. Jerusalem, *Die Staatsgerichtsbarkeit* (Tübingen: Verlag von J.C.B. Mohr [Paul Siebeck], 1930), pp. 119-120.

22. Ernst Rudolf Huber, *Dokumente zur deutschen Verfassungsgeschichte* (Stuttgart: W. Kohlhammer Verlag, 1966), pp. 269-270.

23. For a discussion of this case, see Hans Spanner, *Die richterliche Prüfung von Gesetzen und Verordnungen* (Vienna: Springer Verlag, 1951), pp. 22-28. See also *Preussen contra Reich vor dem Staatsgerichtshof,* Stenogrammbericht der Behandlungen vor dem Staatsgerichtshof in Leipzig vom 10. bis 14. und vom 17. Oktober 1932 (Berlin: Verlag J.H.W. Dietz Nachf., 1933).

24. Jerusalem, op. cit., pp. 50-51.

25. See Paul Laband, *Das Staatsrecht des deutschen Reiches,* 2nd ed. (Freiburg: Mohr, 1888), 1: 538-549.

26. Robert von Mohl, *Strafrecht, Volkerrecht und Politik* (Tubingen: Buchhandlung Laupp, 1860), 1: 66-95.

27. *Verhandlungen des Dritten Deutschen Juristentages* (Berlin: Druck und

Commissions-Verlag von G. Jansen, 1863), 2: 61.

28. See *Seuffert's Archiv für Entscheidungen der Obersten Gerichte* (Munich: Rudolf Oldenbourg, 1876), 32: 129-131.

29. Decision of February 17, 1883, RGZ 9 (1882): 235. This decision (K v. the Dyke Board of Niedervieland) has been translated in Brinton Coxe, *An Essay on Judicial Power and Unconstitutional Legislation* (Philadelphia, 1893), pp. 99-102.

30. Otto Gierke, "German Constitutional Law in its Relation to the American Constitution," *Harvard Law Review* 23 (1909-1910): 284.

31. The free law school actually began to develop shortly after 1900. For an excellent discussion of its influence and impact upon German law see Albert S. Foulkes, "On the German Free Law School (*Freirechtsschule*)," *Archiv für Rechts-und Sozialphilosophie* 55 (1969): 367-417.

32. See, for example, Carl Schmitt, *Unabhängigkeit der Richter, Gleichheit vor dem Gesetz und Gewährleistung des Privateigentums nach der weimarer Verfassung* (Berlin and Leipzig: Walter de Gruyter, 1926), p. 10.

33. Jellinek reported that a majority on the constitutional committee which considered judicial review was against it. See Walter Jellinek, "Verfassungs-widrige Reichsgesetzes," *Deutsche Juristenzeitung* 26 (1921): 753.

34. See Carl J. Friedrich, "The Issue of Judicial Review in Germany," *Political Science Quarterly* 43 (1928): 190. The implications of judicial review appear not to have been fully comprehended by Weimar's founders. On this point, Friedrich says: "Careful consideration of the various arguments would seem to indicate that there existed no very clear idea as to just what was to be understood by judicial review. There is little doubt that the special significance of the question was realized by only a few in the committee."

35. For an excellent treatment of judicial review as practiced in the Weimar Republic, see J.J. Lenoir, "Judicial Review in Germany under the Weimar Constitution," *Tulane Law Review* 14 (1940): 361-383.

36. Under Article 70 of the Constitution, according to Anschütz, only the president of the Republic had the authority to review the constitutionality of Reich legislation, and even he was limited to reviewing the formal constitutionality of laws. See Gerhard Anschütz, *Die Verfassung des deutschen Reichs* (Berlin: Verlag von Georg Stilke, 1932), p. 367.

37. See Georg Jellinek, *Gesetz und Verordnung* (Tübingen: J.C.B. Mohr, 1919), pp. 395-412; Richard Thoma, "Zur Frage des richterliche Prüfungs-recht," *Deutsche Juristen-Zeitung* 27 (1922): 729; Julius Hatschek, *Deutsches und preussisches Staatsrecht* (Berlin: Verlag von Georg Stilke, 1923), 2: 96-97; Friedrich Giese, *Verfassung der deutschen Reiches* (Berlin: Carl Heymanns Verlag, 1926), pp. 210-211; and Jerusalem, *Staatsgerichtsbarkeit,* p. 28.

38. See Hans Fritz Abraham, "Die Anklage gegen das Reichsgericht," *Deutsche Juristen-Zeitung* (1928): 295; Hans Nawiasky, *Bayerisches Verfassungsrecht* (Munich: J. Schweitzer Verlag, 1923), pp. 368-377; Fritz Poetzsch-Heffter, *Handkommentar der Reichsverfassung* (Berlin: Verlag von Otto Leibmann, 1928), pp. 310-311; Eduard Hubrich, *Demokratisches Verfassungsrecht des deutschen Reiches* (Greifswald: v. Bruncken, 1921), p. 150; Rudolf Stammler, *Der Richter* (Berlin: Tagewerkverlag, 1924), p. 32; Henrich Triepel, Der Weg der Gesetzgebung nach der neuen Reichsverfassung," *Archiv des Oeffentlichen Rechts* 39 (1919): 534.

39. *Sammlung der Entscheidung und Gutachten der Reichsfinanzhof,* 5 (1921): 233-236.

40. Decision of April 28, 1921, 102 RGZ 161-166, 164 (1921). The question before the court in this case was whether a housing law passed by the Reich on May 11, 1920, on the basis of a Bundesrat regulation of September 23, 1918, can have retroactive effect, even if in opposition to Article 153 of the constitution. See also Decision of December 15, 1921, *Entscheidungen des Reichsgerichts in Strafsachen* (hereafter cited as RGS) 56 (1922): 179-191, 182.

41. RGZ 107 (1924): 377-382, 379.

42. Decision of October 21, 1924, *Entscheidungen des Reichsversorgunggerichts* 4 (1925): 168.

43. RGZ 111 (1926): 322-323.

44. RGZ 124 (1927): 173. For other decisions involving judicial review, see Decision of January 19, 1925, RGS 59 (1926): 42-49 and the Decision of May 20, 1926, RGZ 114 (1927): 27-35.

45. The bill provided that if in the course of a judicial proceeding a judge is of the opinion that a certain law or administrative ordinance contravenes the constitution he could refer the constitutional question to the *Staatsgerichtshof* for decision. The bill also provided that doubts or differences of opinion on the constitutionality of laws and ordinances could be submitted for decision to the *Staatsgerichtshof* on the motion of one-third of the members of the Reichstag. See Friedrich, "Issue of Judicial Review," op. cit., pp. 198-199.

46. Walter Simons, "Relation of the German Judiciary to the Executive and Legislative Branches," *American Bar Association Journal* 15 (1929): 762.

47. See Karl Dietrich Bracher, *Die Auflösung der weimarer Republik* (Villingen-Schwarzwald: Ring-Verlag, 1964), p. 193.

48. See Gerhard Anschütz and Richard Thoma, *Handbuch des deutschen Staatsrechts* (Tübingen: J.C.B. Mohr [Paul Siebeck], 1932), 2: 559.

49. See, for example, the Hamburg Administrative Court of Appeals Decision of January 17, 1927, *Juristische Wochenschrift* 56 (1927): 1288-1289.

50. Bavarian Constitution of 1919, Article 72.

51. See Prussian Constitution of January 31, 1850, Article 106. See also Ludwig Waldecker, *Die Verfassung des freistaates Preussen* (Berlin: Verlag von Georg-Stilke, 1928), pp. 187-192.

52. Oldenburg Constitution of June 17, 1919, Article 36.

53. For a clear statement of these principles see Ernst Rudolf Huber, *Verfassungsrecht des grossdeutschen Reiches* (Hamburg, 1939), pp. 194-198. See also Wilhelm Kisch, *Der deutsche Rechtslehrer* (Munich: C.H. Beck'sche Verlagsbuchhandlung, 1939).

54. A good discussion of the reception of Roman Law in Germany is Charles S. Lobingier, "The Reception of the Roman Law in Germany," *Harvard Law Review* 14 (1915-16): 562-569. See also K.W. Ryan, *An Introduction to the Civil Law* (Sydney: Halstead Press, 1962), pp. 19-22.

55. See Fritz Baur's Introduction in *Bibliography of German Law* (Karlsruhe: Verlag C.F. Müller, 1964), p. 16.

56. See Johannes Mattern, *Concepts of State, Sovereignty, and International Law* (Baltimore: Johns Hopkins Press, 1928).

57. Henry Adams, *The Education of Henry Adams* (Boston: Houghton Mifflin, 1918), p. 75.

58. See Philipp Heck, *Gesetzeauslegung und Interessenjurisprudenz* (Tübingen: J.C.B. Mohr, 1914); Foulkes, "Free Law School," pp. 367-417; and Ernst von Hippel, "The Role of Natural Law in the Legal Decisions of the German Federal Republic," *Natural Law Forum* 4 (1959): 1-25.

59. Gerhard Leibholz and H.J. Rinck, *Grundgesetz: Kommentar an Hand der Rechtsprechung des Bundesverfassungsgerichts* (Cologne-Marienburg: Verlag Dr. Otto Schmidt KG, 1966).

60. Christian Starck, *Verfassungsrecht in Fällen: Entscheidungen des Bundesverfassungsgerichts* (Baden-Baden: Nomos Verlagsgesellschaft, KG, 1968-70). These decisions appear in ten small pamphlets organized by subject area.

61. See Martin Kriele, *Entscheidungssammlung für junge Juristen* (Munich: C.H. Beck, 1972).

62. The German court system is fully discussed in Wolfgang Heyde, *The Administration of Justice in the Federal Republic of Germany* (Bonn: Press and Information Office of the Federal Government, 1971).

63. See E.J. Cohn, *Manual of German Law*, rev. ed. (London: British Institute of International and Comparative Law, 1968) 1: 39.

64. Heyde, op. cit., pp. 56-57.

65. *Book of the States 1972-73* (Lexington, KY: Council of State Governments, 1972), p. 125, and *United States Government Organization Manual 1971-72* (Washington, D.C.: Government Printing Office, 1971), pp. 45-47.

66. *Book of States, op. cit.,* p. 125 and *Statistisches Jahrbuch für die Bundesrepublik Deutschland 1972* (Stuttgart and Mainz: Verlag W. Kohlhammer GMBH, 1972), p. 98.

67. See Herbert J. Spiro, *Government by Constitution* (New York: Random House, 1959), pp. 220-221.

68. Heyde, op. cit., p. 52.

69. Hugo Münsterberg, *American Traits: From the Point of View of a German* (Boston: Houghton, Mifflin, 1901), p. 193.

70. For good treatments of German legal education, see Wilhelm Wengler, "Law Studies in Western Germany," *Journal of Legal Education* 18 (1965): 176-183 and Burke Shartel, "Report on German Legal Education," *Journal of Legal Education* 14 (1962): 425-483.

71. Cohn, op. cit., p. 49.

72. Arthur T. von Mehren, "The Judicial Process: A Comparative Analysis," *American Journal of Comparative Law* 5 (1956): 216.

73. Wolf Middendorf, *Der Strafrichter* (Freiburg: Verlag Romback, 1963), p. 52.

74. Quoted in Walther Richter, "Zur Sozialstruktur der deutschen Richterschaft," *Deutsche Richterzeitung* (July 1961), p. 201.

75. Richter, "Zur Sozialstruktur," pp. 199-202; Walter Richter, "Bemerkungen zur Sozialstruktur der Richterschaft," *Deutsche Richterzeitung* (February 1969), pp. 34-38; and Klaus Zwingmann, *Zur Soziologie des Richters in der Bundesrepublik Deutschland* (Berlin: Walter de Gruyter, 1966), p. 21 and Albrecht Wagner, *Der Richter* (Karlsruhe: C.F. Müller Verlag, 1959), pp. 136-137.

76. See Manfred Riegel, "Political Attitudes Towards and Perceptions of the Political System of Judges in West Germany" (delivered at the Ninth World Congress of the International Political Science Association, Montreal, Canada, August 20-25, 1973), pp. 3-4.

77. Ibid., p. 3.

78. Johannes Feest, "Die Bundesrichter" in *Beiträge zur Analyse der deutschen Oberschicht* (Tübingen: Wolfgang Zopf, 1964), pp. 134-149.

79. Basic Law for the Federal Republic of Germany (May 23, 1949, as amended up to May 31, 1971), Articles 1-19.

80. Articles 138 and 139 of the Weimar Constitution, conferring certain rights on religious bodies, were also incorporated into the Basic Law.

81. *Handbook of Statistics,* op. cit., pp. 16-17.

82. See Donald P. Kommers, "The Spiegel Affair: A Case Study in Judicial Politics," in Theodore L. Becker, ed., *Political Trials* (Indianapolis: Bobbs-Merrill, 1971).

83. Bundeswahlgesetz vom 7. Mai 1956, Article 6, sec. 4 *Bundesgesetzblatt* 1 (1956): 383.

84. Gabriel A. Almond and Sidney Verba, *The Civic Culture* (Princeton: Princeton University Press, 1963), p. 102.

85. See generally Elisabeth Noelle and Erich Peter Neumann, *Jahrbuch der Oeffentlichen Meinung 1965-1967* (Allensbach and Bonn: Verlag für Demoskopie, 1967), pp. 149-157 and Werner Kaltefleiter, "Zwischen Konsens und Krise: Eine Analyse der Bundeswahl 1972," *Verfassung und Verfassungswirklichkeit,* Jahrbuch 1973, Teil I (Cologne: Carl Heymanns Verlag KG, 1973), pp. 127-170.

3

INSTITUTION

The German tradition of constitutional review is important to any study of the current structure of judicial review in West Germany. Yet this tradition has not always prevailed. Executive predominance in German national history, the taught tradition of German law, and frequent regime changes over the last century and a half are just some of the reasons why Germany lacks a continuity of constitutional review. Moreover, courts of constitutional review—such as Weimar's *Staatsgerichtshof*—were not permanent tribunals presided over by full-time judges. The Federal Constitutional Court, on the other hand, is a tribunal whose structure and powers are unique in German judicial history. Speaking of the Constitutional Court, Herman Mosler remarked that the Basic Law had created "a system of judicial review of such far-reaching authority that it completely over-shadowed the review of constitutional matters under the Weimar Republic and introduced a significant shift in the balance of power as between the traditional organs of government."[1] It is the purpose of this chapter to describe the origin, organization, and jurisdiction of the structure that houses this authority.

GENESIS

Occupation Policy

The reorganization of the judicial system agreed upon at Potsdam in 1945 was a principal pillar of Allied policy toward the political reconstruction of Germany.[2] Besides the policies of demilitarization and denazification, the military government insisted that any future government of Germany must be federal, democratic, and constitutional. Later, when the military governors commissioned the Germans to draft a constitution for the Western zones of occupation, they made clear that judicial review was implicit in their understanding of an independent judiciary. In an aide-memoire sent to the framers of the Basic Law, they noted: "The constitution should provide for an independent judiciary to review federal legislation, to review the exercise of federal executive power, and to adjudicate conflicts between federal and land authorities as well as between land authorities, and to protect the civil rights and freedom of the individual."[3] Yet it would be a mistake to assume that the military governors forced judicial review upon reluctant Germans. In the first place, the aide-memoire was not released until after the parliamentary council had done most of its work. In the second place, German-Allied correspondence during the time of the parliamentary council shows no disagreement on judicial review. As for its zone of occupation, the U.S. Office of Military Government specified only that "German governmental systems must provide for a judiciary independent of the legislature and executive arms."[4] Except for Allied insistence on a certain fiscal relationship between the states and the federal government, the Basic Law was very much a German product.[5]

The Herrenchiemsee Conference

The ground work for the Basic Law was prepared in a resplendent medieval castle (built by Bavaria's popular King Louis II) on an island in Lake Chiemsee during August of 1948. On the initiative of

Bavaria's Minister-President Hans Ehard, the states in the Allied zones of occupation called upon a group of experts in constitutional law to produce a first draft of a constitution in order to facilitate the task of the forthcoming constituent assembly—the parliamentary council—scheduled to open on September 1. The group—composed of leading scholars and statesmen such as Adolf Süsterhenn, Carlo Schmid, Claus Leusser, Fritz Baade, Theodor Maunz, and Josef Beyerle—favored judicial review and the establishment of a Federal Constitutional Court.[6] The Chiemsee proposals accorded with recommendations previously made in a working paper prepared by Professor Hans Nowiasky, commonly regarded as the father of the Bavarian Constitution, in cooperation with Hans Kelsen. Nowiasky, incidentally, had been a strong advocate of judicial review during the Weimar period, while Kelsen had been one of the creators, in 1920, of the Austrian Constitutional Court. Clause Leusser, an Ehard associate and later a judge of the Federal Constitutional Court, also helped to draft the original proposals considered at Herren-chiemsee.[7]

The Chiemsee Conference looked to German history, especially to the experience of Weimar's *Staatsgerichtshof*, for guidance in writing the judicial provisions of the proposed Basic Law. Constitutional jurisdiction allocated to the *Staatsgerichtshof* and other high German courts under the Weimar Constitution reappeared in the Chiemsee draft. This jurisdiction, specified in Article 98 of the Chiemsee draft, included the authority to decide constitutional disputes among the states, between the states and the federal government, and among the highest organs (president, Bundestag, Bundesrat, federal chancellor) of the federal government. Somewhat new, but not altogether unprecedented in German constitutional jurisprudence, were additional provisions authorizing the Court to decide controversies regarding the unconstitutionality of a political party and the forfeiture of fundamental rights. Most at variance with past practice was the proposal to give the Court express authority to hear the complaint of any person who alleged a violation of his constitutional rights and to decide, on the application of a court, whether a federal or state law violated the Basic Law or whether state law was incompatible with federal law. Finally, the Chiemsee proposals gave broad scope to the rulings of the Federal Constitutional Court; having the force of general law, these rulings were to bind all courts and public officials.[8]

These provisions caused no discord among the conferees at Herrenchiemsee. Disagreement centered mostly on whether the Federal Constitutional Court should be organized as a separate tribunal or whether it should be carved out of one of the high federal courts of appeal. The Chiemsee draft accordingly left the matter open. The conferees did, however, agree (1) that judges of the Federal Constitutional Court be elected in equal numbers by the Bundestag and Bundesrat, (2) that both houses participate in selecting the Court's president, and (3) that one-half of the Court's members be chosen from the judges of the federal courts of appeal and the highest state courts.[9] Beyond these broad principles of judicial recruitment, there was little agreement on the Court's structure and administration. Since the Herrenchiemsee Conference had only fifteen days in which to prepare its report, even minor disagreements on such matters tended to be shunted aside to make way for a document reflecting the widest possible consensus.

Parliamentary Council

In early September 1948, the scene shifted to the West German Constitutional Convention, more commonly known as the parliamentary council. Its delegates, all recruited by political parties, were popularly elected. The council was dominated by the Christian Democratic Party and the Social Democratic Parties, each of which had twenty-seven delegates. In addition, the Free Democrats had five delegates while the German, Communist, and Center Party had two each. (An additional five delegates from Berlin participated as non-voting members.) Because sixty-one percent of the council's membership was made up of current or former state administrative officials, judges, and professors, some people characterized the council as a "Parliament of Civil Servants."[10] Nearly half the delegates had graduated from law school.[11] All told, the delegates were a remarkable group of men; a large number of them, like the council's President, Konrad Adenauer, were destined to play leading roles in the government—and in the Constitutional Court—they were about to create.

Those delegates who assumed leading roles in drafting the Basic Law's judicial provisions should be mentioned here since their names will recur frequently throughout this book. Nearly all of them in later years continued to influence the course of the Federal Constitutional Court's development, particularly in connection with efforts both to staff the Court and to define its structure. They included Georg-August Zinn (SPD), Walter Strauss (CDU), Wilhelm Laforet (CSU), Otto H. Greve (SPD), Herman Höpker-Aschoff (FDP), Carlo Schmid (SPD), Adolf Süsterhenn (CDU), Rudolf Katz (SPD), Walter Menzel (SPD), Thomas Dehler (FDP), and Friedrich W. Wagner (SPD). Höpker-Aschoff was to become the first President of the Federal Constitutional Court, Katz the first Vice President, while Wagner was to succeed Katz as Vice President in 1961. Dehler, as Minister of Justice in Adenauer's first Cabinet, was a principal author of the 1951 Federal Constitutional Court Act, but later emerged as one of Court's bitterest critics, as did Strauss. Zinn, Justice Minister of Hesse, was chairman of the parliamentary council's committee on constitutional court and judiciary; in 1951, he became Hesse's minister-president and during the ensuing twenty years, in part because of his influence in the Bundesrat, exerted unceasing influence over all matters pertaining to the Federal Constitutional Court. Schmid, a distinguished professor of law and one of the SPD's most brilliant spokesmen, headed the council's main committee which included—besides Adenauer and Dehler—Greve, Laforet (also a noted law professor), and Süsterhenn. Greve and Laforet, along with Strauss, were also members of Zinn's committee on the constitutional court; so was Professor Herman von Mangoldt (CDU), who in the years following the council developed a reputation as the Basic Law's most authoritative commentator-historian. Finally, Greve, Laforet, Süsterhenn, Schmidt, and Strauss, though, like Zinn, well beyond middle age, were all to enjoy long parliamentary careers in the course of which they retained an active interest in the court's affairs.

Despite their differing backgrounds and partisan affiliations, these delegates did not stage a great debate about the Federal Constitutional

Court or judicial review; the council accepted the Chiemsee draft proposals almost in their entirety. What controversy did take place concerned details. The political parties tended to leave these matters to their legal experts, for the most part to the persons just mentioned.

The most serious conflict in the parlimentary council was over how much of the constitutional jurisdiction listed in the Basic Law should be vested in the Federal Constitutional Court. Not all the delegates assumed that the Constitutional Court would, or should, exercise all constitutional jurisdiction listed in the fundamental law. In a real sense, the debate was over the nature of the Federal Constitutional Court and its relationship to the regular judiciary. Disagreement arose between those who viewed the Constitutional Court basically as an organ to resolve constitutional conflicts between levels and branches of government—a sort of surrogate for the old *Staatsgerichtshof*—and those who viewed it as a court of general constitutional and judicial review.

The argument was launched by Walter Strauss, leading CDU spokesman, who drew a traditionally sharp line between the spheres of law and politics. He frankly acknowledged the political nature of the Constitutional Court, thereby insisting that the Court's jurisdiction should be limited to constitutional controversies fundamentally political in character. Disputes among the states, between national and state governments, between agencies of government, along with cases involving the legitimacy of political parties, were examples of such controversies. One would assign such disputes to ordinary courts, said Strauss, only at the risk of impairing their credibility. On the other hand, questions fundamentally legal in character, such as those arising from judicial review of legislation, should be the exclusive preserve of the regular judiciary. These cases, he argued, involve the objective process of adjudication. These views—a rather mechanistic approach to the judicial process—were incorporated into what was largely a CDU/CSU-FDP recommendation to establish a separate panel on one of the high federal courts of appeal to decide questions involving the constitutionality of laws, while the Federal Constitutional Court would decide other constitutional controversies.[12]

The principal counterproposal, advocated by Zinn, was to create a single tribunal which would handle all cases and controversies arising under the Constitution and under public law. Zinn envisioned one grand tribunal divided into several panels, each of which would specialize in a separate area of public or constitutional law.[13] This proposal was strenuously opposed by German judges, who regarded any combination of broad constitutional jurisdiction and traditional public law concerns under a simple umbrella as a dangerous mixing of law and politics.[14] The upshot was a compromise that resulted in the establishment of a separate constitutional tribunal with exclusive jurisdiction over all constitutional disputes, including the authority to review the constitutionality of laws.

Deep suspicion of the regular judiciary, especially among Social Democrats, was the main reason why the Constitutional Court became the sole repository for the authority to review the constitutionality of laws. Both Menzel and Schmid mounted heavy assaults on the behavior of judges in the Weimar period. Judicial resistance to Reichstag legislation, said Menzel, "was a political negation of the Weimar system." He pointed out that seventy-six percent of the public prosecutors and judges in the British zone of occupation alone had been members of the Nazi Party; thus, to avoid any recurrence of the Weimar experience he insisted, with the support of most delegates, that judges should be required to submit their doubts about the constitutionality of laws to the Constitutional Court.[15] According to Menzel, reservations about the regular judiciary led to one other change in the Chiemsee draft. This was the decision to confer upon the Federal Constitutional Court authority to dismiss at the request of the Bundestag, federal judges in the event that they infringe the principles of the Basic Law or the constitutional order of a state.[16]

Another subject frequently discussed in the parliamentary council was the problem of protecting minorities inside and outside government. There was a felt need, again mainly but not exclusively among Social Democrats, for a tribunal in which minority groups—especially opposition parties in the Bundestag—might challenge a federal law deemed to be incompatible with the Basic Law. The German Party delegate, Hans C. Seebohm, even proposed that minority groups in state legislatures be given the right to challenge state laws before the Constitutional Court; the main committee rejected the proposal, along with a second German Party recommendation to authorize the federal president to submit proposed emergency legislation to the Constitutional Court for examination in light of its constitutional justification.[17] In a major decision, however, the council granted the Federal Constitutional Court the authority to resolve differences of opinion or doubts about the constitutionality of federal or state law, or doubts about the compatibility of federal and state law, at the request of the federal government, a state government, or one-third of the Bundestag's members. Article 93 of the Basic Law; which expressly confers this authority, also incorporates the Chiemsee recommendation that the Court be vested with authority to decide constitutional conflicts among the highest federal organs.

Christian Democrats, while in the end accepting the provisions of Article 93, found them less palatable than Social Democrats. It is hazardous to talk about party alignments on judicial matters in the parliamentary council. Still, it is fair to remark that Social Democrats tended to support a larger role for the Court in the political system than either Christian or Free Democrats. The reason may be that the latter had a higher number of lawyers and judges in their ranks, prompting them toward a more traditional view of the judicial role. As we shall see in the next section of this chapter, these differing views heavily influenced the attitudes of the political parties toward judicial recruitment.

There was also disagreement over what effect Constitutional Court decisions should have. Should these decisions have the force of general law or should they be limited in application to the immediate parties before the Court? Zinn and Schmid made it clear that they were speaking for the SPD faction when fighting to retain the Chiemsee proposal that judicial decisions voiding a law have the force of general law and be published, along with legislative enactments, in the federal legal gazette. The CDU, speaking through von Mangoldt, wanted to strike the provision.[18] The delegates compromised: Article 94 declares that a federal law will specify the cases in which the Court's decisions shall have the force of general law.

Christian Democrats did envision a large role for the Court in the area of federal-state relations, however. Adolf Süsterhenn remarked: "We [the CDU/CSU] consider that one of the most important organs in a Federal State based on the rule of law is a . . . constitutional court, which shall have the function of protecting the central authority against disobedience and encroachments of the states, and simultaneously of protecting the states against encroachments by the central authority."[19] Remarks by other delegates indicated some differences of opinion as to whether the Court would play a centralizing or federalizing role in the political system. Nevertheless, Article 92, which specifies the Court's authority over federal-state disputes, received the unanimous backing of Christian, Social, and Free Democrats.

It should be reemphasized that very few issues produced sharp cleavages among the council's delegates, who were in a compromising mood. The council was under Allied pressure to produce a constitution as soon as possible; its president, Konrad Adenauer, was equally determined to quicken the council's proceedings. The result was, in some respects, a hastily prepared document. One of the most important and far-reaching recommendations of the Herrenchiemsee Conference—that the Constitutional Court be authorized expressly to hear the complaints of citizens whose rights under the Basic Law are violated—was barely mentioned in the council's deliberations and failed to appear in the final draft of the Basic Law.

The impatience of the delegates to get on with their work was particularly manifest in the council's decision to leave the Court's organization, along with questions of judicial tenure and selection, to legislation. Article 94 of the Basic Law incorporated nearly all the provisions of the Chiemsee draft. One important change was made by the council: Instead of requiring that one-half of the Court's Justices be selected from federal and state courts, Article 94 simply declares that the Constitutional Court "shall consist of federal judges and other members." The time was not yet ripe for doing battle over the Court's structure. Disagreement that did surface in the course of the debate was almost wholly obscured by rhetoric praising the Court as the ultimate symbol of law and constitutionalism.

The Legislative Phase: 1949-1951

The Federal Constitutional Court remained a symbol for nearly two years after the West German government was formed in 1949. Indeed, at the beginning, the Adenauer-led coalition government (CDU/CSU-FDP-DP) seemed in no particular hurry to propose enabling legislation to make the Court a reality. The first move to establish the Court came from the Judiciary Committee of the Ministers-President for the three Allied zones of occupation, which, on July 27, 1949, released a detailed draft of a bill for the Court's organization. The committee stressed the necessity of setting up the Court immediately, on a provisional basis if necessary, and under the authority of the Federal Minister of Justice, pending its formal institutionalization by parliament.[20] The government did not view the matter with equal gravity. None of the high federal courts had yet been established, and it was probably more urgent, in the government's view, to get them off the ground first.

Nevertheless, the Justice Ministry, under Thomas Dehler (FDP), started working on draft legislation in October of 1949. Consultations within the government were still limping along when the SPD came forward with its own bill in December. Over the SPD's objection, the ruling parties ignored the bill, asserting that it was the government's responsibility to initiate such legislation. The government finally produced its own bill, which was considerably at variance with that by the SPD, on March 1, 1950. The Bundesrat responded two weeks later with a series of amendments, and returned the bill to the government. Three weeks later, the government submitted the bill—together with its response to the Bundesrat's amendments—to the Bundestag, which turned it over to the Judiciary Committee on Legal and Constitutional Affairs.[21] The real battle was about to begin, and it was to revolve around the special interests of the government, the Social Democrats, and the Bundesrat.

The conflict was fully expected. After all, the Court's structure was left wholly in the hands of law-makers who enjoyed wide scope in determining how the Court would exercise its jurisdiction, or whether it would exercise it at all. The hazy divisions among delegates at the parliamentary council now crystallized, largely along partisan lines, as competing conceptions of what the Court should do and be became entangled with questions of how it should be structured and how judges should be selected.

To untangle the web and to bring order to the rest of our discussion, we propose to deal here only with those major decisions in parliament which broke the log jam—it lasted a full year—and produced the enabling statute known as the Federal Constitutional Court Act (Gesetz über das Bundesverfassungsgericht). We will confine ourselves to a brief report of the main differences among the three bills and to a description of the politics that moved the conflict to its conclusion. A more detailed consideration of the Court's organization and authority and the formal rules of judicial selection, together with the changes that have taken place since the Constitutional Court Act was passed, will be taken up in other parts of this chapter.

The three bills: In accordance with traditional notions of German court organization, the government bill proposed to establish a constitutional tribunal of twenty-four Justices subject administratively to the Federal Ministry of Justice. To ensure judicial anonymity and to speed judicial proceedings, the bill provided that decisions be made by a panel of nine Justices drawn from the pool of twenty-four on a constantly rotating basis. Twelve Justices were to be chosen from the high federal courts for lifetime terms, while the remaining Justices would serve for six-year terms. In addition, all Justices were to be at least forty years of age and were to have fulfilled the requirements for judicial office or the high civil service. These provisions clearly expressed the government's preference for a bench dominated by career judges. The government bill also provided that Justices be elected by the entire Bundestag, but that the president of the Court be chosen by his fellow Justices. Further, the bill provided for detailed regulation of the Court's jurisdiction, specifying the basis of justiciability, the parties eligible to go before the Court, and the procedures to be followed by the Court in handing down its decisions. In a word, the government proposed a rather faceless, traditionally oriented, closely regulated tribunal.[22]

By contrast, Social Democrats proposed a Court of ten members, only four of whom would be recruited from the high federal courts. No special qualifications were listed for the remaining six Justices, except that they be men of experience who enjoy public trust, have a sense of social awareness, and are committed to the spirit of the Basic Law. The SPD set the eligibility age at thirty-five, provided for compulsory retirement at sixty-five, limited the terms of "federal judges" to seven years and "other members" to coincide with the duration of a legislative term (five years). Instead of letting the judges choose the Court's president, the SPD proposed that he be elected alternately by the Bundestag and Bundesrat. So as to prevent any one party from dominating the selection process, the SPD proposed that the Bundestag, for its part, set up an electoral committee of eight members, chosen from among the house's members by proportional representation, with six votes required to elect. It was proposed also that a two-thirds vote be required in the Bundesrat. Social Democrats, still leary of the judiciary, seemed to be taking no chances, for their proposals provided for a continuing and substantial political check on the Court. Yet the SPD bill allowed the Court much greater flexibility in determining its own standards of review and internal decision-making procedures than did the government bill. It also authorized the Court to give advisory opinions on pending legislation pursuant to a simple motion by the Bundestag, Bundesrat, federal president, or the federal government, underscoring once more the rather active political role for the Court envisioned by the SPD.[23]

The Bundesrat, finally, proposed a structure that included several features of the SPD plan. It, too, advised a single panel Court, except that it would consist of twelve Justices, six of whom would be "federal judges." Proposed also were nine-year terms for all Justices, with one-third to be elected every three years. The Bundesrat's proposal did not include specific qualifications for judges, only that they have a knowledge of law and be experienced in public life. Regarding jurisdictional matters, the Bundesrat bill was largely in accord with the government bill, but was against giving the Court jurisdiction over the constitutional complaints of citizens, maintaining that basic rights would be amply safeguarded by regular and administrative courts. The argument concealed the upper house's fear of giving ordinary citizens a weapon with which to challenge state power.

The Bundesrat also wanted to elevate the Court to a level coordinate with other branches of the federal government and thus defined it as "an independent constitutional organ of the Federation." The government bill had referred to the Court simply as the highest court within the judicial establishment, thereby subordinating it to the administrative jurisdiction of the Federal Ministry of Justice. In short, while the SPD sought to structure a court that would prevent its being controlled by a single party, the Bundesrat sought to prevent its being controlled by the executive branch acting in tandem with the Bundestag.[24]

The politics: For several months, the judiciary committees of both houses of parliament wrestled with the three bills in an effort to resolve their differences. Again, many of the persons at the center of the parliamentary council's deliberations were present here. For example, Laforet (CSU) was now chairman of the Bundestag's Committee on Legal and Constitutional Affairs; Ehard (CSU) and Katz (SPD) were important figures in the Bundesrat. But now other influential men appeared on the scene, chief among whom were Adolf Arndt (SPD), Kurt-Georg Kiesinger (CDU), Willi Geiger, and Josef Wintrich. Arndt was the SPD's top lawyer and vice chairman of the Judiciary Committee; the main author of the SPD bill, he, along with Zinn, led the opposition in the Bundestag. Kiesinger, a member of the Committee on Legal and Constitutional Affairs, emerged as the leading parliamentary spokesman for the government bill. Geiger, one of the original appointees to the Federal Constitutional Court, came on the scene as Dehler's top assistant in the Federal Ministry of Justice; he was a principal author of the government bill. Wintrich, a highly regarded judge of Bavaria's Constitutional Court, was the most influential among the expert witnesses called by the Bundestag.[25] (In 1954 Wintrich succeeded Höpker-Aschoff as president of the Federal Constitutional Court.)

By July of 1950, after weeks of patient negotiation, the Legal and Constitutional Affairs Committee had not come to any agreement on judicial selection or court structure, although some differences on jurisdiction and procedure had been ironed out. This being the case, the committee proceeded to approve, by a vote of fourteen to ten, largely along party lines, a slightly modified version of the government's original plan. At this point, Arndt and the SPD leadership threatened to oppose the entire bill if referred to Parliament in that form. Although Social Democrats were hardly in a position to defeat the coalition parties in any test of strength in the Bundestag, the government would subsequently have to contend with the Bundesrat, where approval was by no means certain.

Under these circumstances the ruling parties decided upon further negotiations. Von Merkatz (DP), who ardently defended the government bill in committee against Social Democratic objections, was of the opinion that nothing less than broad agreement among all parliamentary parties would suffice if the Federal Constitutional Court was to get off to a good start. Everyone agreed. Kiesinger, respected even then for his negotiating skill—as Chancellor in 1966 he engineered the Grand Coalition—proposed the formation of a subcommittee, composed of members of all four parties, to thrash out a compromise.[26]

The idea was unanimously received. Made up of van Merkatz (DP), Neumayer (FDP), Weber (CDU), Wahl (CDU), Ardnt (SDP), Zinn (SPD), and with Kiesinger (CDU) as chairman, the subcommittee spent the next four months in labor, painfully giving birth to a plan that the various parties could live with, all the while remaining in close consultation with the Ministry of Justice—mainly through Geiger—as well as the Bundesrat's Judiciary Committee. Technical experts were called in to ensure the plan's safe delivery. Wintrich was there once again to proffer his advice, as were Karl Lehr and Paul Zurcher, presidents of the Hesse and Baden Constitutional Courts. The product of these efforts was, to shift the metaphor, an arresting tapestry, an interweaving of main threads from the original three designs. The new bill received the unanimous support of the parent committee. A few amendments were added in the Bundestag, but these were minor. On the final vote, all but the Communist Party delegates supported the bill.[27] In the Bundesrat, the Bavarian delegation made a last-ditch attempt to challenge certain parts of the bill, but after a strong plea by the Federal Minister of Justice (Dehler) against any further delays, the house approved.[28] Finally, on March 12, 1951, with the signature of the federal president, the Constitutional Court Act became law.[29]

ORGANIZATION

Status of Federal Constitutional Court

The 1951 act describes the Federal Constitutional Court as "an autonomous court of the Federation independent of all other constitutional organs." Yet, when the Court began to function, the Justices were administratively subject to the supervisory authority of the Federal Ministry of Justice. Finding the insecurity of this situation intolerable, the Justices themselves initiated the decisive battle over the Court's status in the German system. In the very first months of the Court's life, a committee of the Justices, led by Professor Gerhard Leibholz, occupied itself with the status problem. In March 1952, a detailed report was ready for consideration by the Plenum (the Court's full membership).[30] Three months later, on June 27, the Plenum issued a lengthy memorandum, addressed to the federal president, the Chancellor, and the presidents of the Bundestag and Bundesrat, demanding, *inter alia*, immunity from ministerial oversight, suggesting along the way that the superintending authority vested in the Ministry of Justice was in violation of the Basic Law.[31]

The memorandum generated a strong tremor in Bonn; it startled the government, angered the Ministry of Justice, and set off several more years of skirmishing that yielded alignments almost identical to those which formed in the early stages of the parliamentary debate on the 1951 Act. Social Democrats and the Bundesrat generally supported the Court, while the coalition parties in the Bundestag generally opposed the Court. But the real tangle was between the Ministry of Justice and the Constitutional Court, and it featured on occasion unseemly public exchanges between two old FDP comrades who shared experiences in the parliamentary council, Thomas Dehler, Minister of Justice, and Hermann Höpker-Aschoff, the Court's president.

At the same time, the issue of the Court's autonomy generated a high-level debate that focused broadly on the nature of constitutional review in West Germany. Both sides marshalled their forces effectively, the Ministry of Justice calling upon distinguished professors of public law, such as Richard Thoma, to write briefs or advisory opinions (*Gutachten*) in support of its position, while the Court tapped its own esteemed professorial contingent for counter-arguments.[32] These arguments were long and involved, often dealing with such abstract questions as whether certain aspects of constitutional review can logically be absorbed into traditional German teaching on the general theory of the state.

The Constitutional Court's view of its own status was contained in its memorandum of June 27, 1952. Drawing heavily from Justice Leibholz's report, the memorandum contained several propositions, including: The Constitutional Court is a supreme constitutional organ coordinate in rank with the Bundestag, Bundesrat, federal Chancellor, and federal president; .Constitutional Court Justices, therefore, are in no sense civil servants or ordinary federal judges, but rather the supreme guardians of the Basic Law; like the Chancellor, federal president, and members of Parliament, the Justices have the sacred duty to fulfill its grand purposes; indeed, the Court has even a greater duty, which is to ensure that other constitutional organs observe the limits of the Basic Law; at the same time the Constitutional Court is a genuine judicial tribunal whose exclusive function is to *apply* law; the application of the "political law" of the Constitution does not imply that the Court is engaged in a political function; any suggestion to the contrary is plain nonsense; the distinguishing mark of the Federal Constitutional Court is that it is both a constitutional organ of the Federal Republic and a court of law, as was clearly the intent of the men who framed the Basic Law.

The Memorandum concluded with recommendations to confer budgetary autonomy upon the Federal Constitutional Court and to free the Court from any financial dependence upon the Ministry of Justice; to give the Court total control over all internal administrative matters, including the hiring, firing, and supervision of all law clerks and other employees; and to exempt the Justices from all disciplinary regulations applicable to other judges. In sum, the Court was demanding nothing less than the institutional independence enjoyed by Parliament, the federal government, and the federal president.[33]

By 1960, nearly all the above objectives had been achieved. In 1953—shortly after Dehler's departure from the Justice Ministry, incidentally—the Court had already achieved the budgetary independence it wanted, which the Justices continue to regard as one of the Court's most notable victories. At length, the Justices themselves were accorded a status in law corresponding to that of the highest state officials. The president of the Court now earns a salary roughly equivalent to that of a cabinet minister and in Bonn's official ranking order enjoys the fifth-highest position in the Federal Republic, following the federal president, the Chancellor, the president of the Bundesrat, and the president of the Bundestag. As supreme guardians of the Constitution, the remaining judges follow in rank, although their salaries fall somewhat below that of a federal minister. But they enjoy enormous independence, even when compared to high civil servants, like state secretaries. They can work when they please, live where they please, dress as they please, and are subject to no supervisory authority, not even that of the Court's president. Moreover, Parliament may not impeach a Federal Constitutional Court Justice. A Justice can be dismissed only by the federal president, and then only pursuant to a motion filed by the Court itself.[34] In 1961, the Justices achieved still another victory in support of their independence when the disciplinary code regulating the German judiciary (Deutsche Richtergesetz) was amended to read: "The provisions of this law apply to justices of the Federal Constitutional Court only to the extent that they are compatible with their special status under the Basic Law and with the Federal Constitutional Court Act."[35]

A 1968 amendment to the Basic Law, providing for emergency defense measures, was a further and rather clear recognition of the Court's special status in Germany's political system. Article 115g provides that during a state of emergency "the constitutional status and the exercise of the constitutional functions of the Federal Constitutional Court and its judges must not be impaired." Moreover, the Constitutional Court Act of 1951 cannot be amended during such a time unless for the purpose of maintaining the Court's capacity to function. Any such amendment also requires the approval of a two-thirds majority of the Justices present and voting. If a Justice's term of office expires during such an emergency, under Article 115h it shall end six months after the emergency's termination.

It is fitting to note, finally, that the Justices have exercised little modesty in using their own judicial opinions to underscore the high status of the Federal Constitutional Court in Bonn's constitutional democracy.[36] In view of all these developments, any attempt to alter the Court's status would raise serious constitutional questions that the Court itself, if given the opportunity, could ultimately decide. It is fair to conclude that no other judicial tribunal in German history has achieved the status or measure of independence that the Federal Constitutional Court currently enjoys.

The Two-Senate System

The 1951 act established a Court composed of two chambers, called senates, which have become virtually two separate constitutional courts.[37] Justices are specifically elected to either the First or the Second Senate, and they may not sit in the other panel. Jurisdiction between the senates is mutually exclusive. Each senate has its own administrative office for organizing, distributing, and reporting its business. The president of the Court is the administrative head and presiding officer of the First Senate; the vice president the administrative head and presiding officer of the Second Senate. Both "Chief Justices" are wholly independent with respect to judicial matters before their respective senates. The idea of dividing the Court in this way was not at all considered in the early stages of legislative debate on the Constitutional Court Act. The twin-senate idea was in part a compromise between those who wanted a fluid system of twenty-four Justices rotating on a smaller panel and those who wanted a fixed collegial body like that of the U.S. Supreme Court. It was also a compromise between those who viewed the Court in conventional legalistic terms and those who viewed it in wider political terms, one reason why, in the beginning at least, the Second Senate was vested with jurisdiction over "political" cases—i.e., constitutional conflicts between organs and levels of government—while the First received jurisdiction over "law" cases—concrete and abstract norm control together with constitutional complaints—involving what is commonly referred to as "objective constitutional interpretation." The First Senate's concern with "law" cases may explain why more Justices with judicial backgrounds were recruited to it than to the Second Senate.

The original statute provided for two senates with twelve judges each. In 1956, the number was reduced to ten; in 1962, it was further reduced to eight. The total number of judges is now fixed at sixteen. In 1956, the senates were authorized by law to create three-judge committees for the purpose of deciding constitutional complaints. The procedures of these committees, along with their relationship to the full senate, will be discussed at greater length in Chapter 5.

Judicial Qualifications and Terms of Office

To qualify for a seat on the Constitutional Court, persons must be forty years of age, eligible for election to the Bundestag, and possess the qualifications for judicial office stipulated in the German law on judges (*Das Richtergesetz*). This means that prospective Justices must have successfully passed the first and second major state examinations in law. This is a requirement more severe, actually, than the original criteria of the 1951 Act, where, if a person did not qualify for judicial office, he could nevertheless be named to the Court if he satisfied the requirements for high civil service in any state and, in addition, had special knowledge of public law and experience in public life. This alternative was, however, deleted from the statute in 1956. As a member of one constitutional organ, a Justice cannot simultaneously hold office in the government, Bundesrat, Bundestag, or in a corresponding branch of a state government. In addition, the Act specifically provides that all professional activities, with the single exception of teaching law at a German University, are incompatible with the office of Constitutional Court Justice.[38]

The provision allowing Justices to hold on to their professorships during their terms of office has given rise to considerable friction within the Court itself. While only a small number of the Justices were originally recruited from university law faculties, several others accepted positions as honorary professors of law after their appointment to the Federal Constitutional Court. Their outside activities and visibility as university lecturers are viewed with alarm by some Justices and outright disapproval by others who regard the professorial contingent as a privileged caste within the Court. The presiding officers of the two senates have also expressed their disapproval of the professor-Justices, claiming that they do not pull their share of the Court's workload, which of course the professors emphatically deny. In 1970, with the support of the president and vice president, the Court Act was amended, and now stipulates that a Justice's judicial duties shall take precedence over his professorial activity.[39]

Another long-standing cause of concern to law-makers and the Justices was the 1951 Act's tenure provisions. Under these provisions each senate included at least three Justices selected from the high federal courts. (Originally, when each senate had twelve members, the number was four.) These Justices were appointed for the duration of their terms on the federal court, which meant until they reached the compulsory retirement age of sixty-eight. Other members of the Court were chosen for eight-year terms, but were eligible for reelection regardless of age. This provision was changed in 1970 when the Court Act was further amended to provide for twelve-year terms for all Justices, with no possibility of reelection.[40] Now all Justices— "federal" and "other members"—must retire at age sixty-eight.[41] From now on, then, a Justice who has once served on the Court, no matter what his age or how many years may have elapsed since the expiration of his term, may not be returned to the Court, barring, of course, further changes in the law.

Interwoven with the tenure issue was also the question of whether the Justices should be allowed to write and publish dissenting opinions. As early as 1968 law-makers, supported by a majority of the Justices, were prepared to sanction judicial dissent. But the feeling was widespread that Justices could not be expected to speak their minds on the Court if their tenure depended on the continuing pleasure of Parliament. The Justices themselves were in favor of lifetime tenure. A bill submitted originally by the government provided for both dissenting opinions and twelve-year terms for all Justices, but with the possibility of reelection for at least one more twelve-year term. Social Democrats, however, insisted upon a single, fixed term of twelve years, and conditioned their support of the dissenting opinion largely on the acceptance of this proposal. But the question was not hotly contested among the political parties. A single twelve-year term, combined with the dissenting opinion, was generally thought to be an adequate solution to both the problem of judicial independence and the need for a greater measure of judicial creativity within the Constitutional Court.[42]

Selection of Judges: Formal Rules

Here, too, the organic statute represented an amalgam of conflicting positions originally put forth by the coalition parties, the Bundesrat, and the SPD. The Basic Law provides simply that half the Court's members be elected by the Bundestag and half by the Bundesrat. Under the 1951 Act, the Bundestag elects its quota of Justices indirectly through a twelve-man judicial selection committee known as the *Wahlmännerausschuss* (WMA). Party representation on the WMA is proportionate to each party's strength in the Bundestag. Eight votes are required to elect. (Nine votes were required prior to 1956.) The Bundesrat, on the other hand, votes for its quota of judges as a whole, a two-thirds vote being required to elect.[43]

It is important to point out that each house elects four members of each senate. They alternate, however, in selecting the Court's president and vice president. Prior to selecting a "federal judge" to the Constitutional Court, the Minister of Justice is required to compile a list of all federal judges who meet the qualifications for appointment. He is also required to prepare a further list of candidates submitted by the parliamentary parties, the federal government, or a state government. The lists are then delivered to the electoral organs at least one week before they convene. In the event that either house fails to elect a Justice within two months, the chairman of the WMA—the oldest member of the committee—or the president of the Bundesrat, depending on the house involved, must request the Constitutional Court itself to submit a list of names for consideration, three if it concerns the election of a "federal judge," six if it concerns the election of some "other member" of the Court. The Plenum selects the list by a simple majority vote. But Parliament is not obligated ultimately to choose the appointee from this or any other list submitted to it.[44]

A few words more are in order concerning the mechanics involved in selecting the members of the WMA. We would note first that the relationship of this committee to the Bundestag as a whole is unique among Bundestag committees. For one thing, the WMA derives its legitimacy from the Basic Law itself; its decisions are, in effect, the decisions of the Bundestag. For another, only the parliamentary parties may submit lists of committee candidates. Several parliamentary parties may agree on a common list so long as the Bundestag has at least two competing lists to vote for. No changes in these lists are permitted from the floor, and voting is by secret ballot. In addition, committee members may not be removed once elected. The committee's life expires at the end of the parliamentary term. If a member retires or resigns from the committee before the end of the parliamentary term, he is replaced by the person next on the list of candidates originally submitted to the Bundestag. The committee's proceedings are held in closed session.[45]

The number and pattern of appointments to the Federal Constitutional Court during its first twenty-one years can be summarized quickly. By 1972, forty-six Justices had been recruited, twenty-four to the First Senate, twenty-two to the Second Senate. Twenty-three were selected originally by the Bundestag, twenty-three by the Bundesrat. Actually, there have been many more elections than these figures indicate, for the majority of the Justices were reelected to the Court at least once, while thirteen Justices—those chosen from the high federal courts—were elected for life. A 1970 amendment to the Constitutional Court Act limiting judicial tenure to twelve years does not, incidentally, apply to Justices on the Court when the rule was adopted. Hence one judge—Wiltraut Rupp von Brünneck—whose eight-year term expired in August 1971, was reelected to a twelve-year term under the new rule.

Three of the twenty-four Justices elected in 1951 still remain on the Court; nine of them retired, five died in office, and seven resigned. Several of the resignations were occasioned when the Court's membership was reduced in 1956 and again in 1963, the reduction in membership concurring actually with the expirations of their terms. Of the twenty-two Justices selected since 1951, six retired, two resigned, one died in office, and thirteen remain on the Court. Of the thirteen who remain, four were elected for the first time in December 1971, along with two others who were reelected, all for twelve-year terms.

Nonjudicial Internal Administration

When the Court was organized in 1951, it was a logical assumption that the Ministry of Justice would administer its nonjudicial affairs. While the Court might well have the character of a "constitutional organ" with respect to its judicial functions, it was also a judicial institution whose administrative side would be brought within the superintending authority of the highest federal minister responsible for the courts. But the Justices, fully aware of the damage that an unsympathetic minister could do in the name of administration, refused to subscribe to any such distinction. They sought, and eventually received, total administrative autonomy.

Administrative independence has had two notable consequences for the Court's institutional development. First, the Court has been able to plan its own future. It prepares its own budget, bargaining directly with the Ministry of Finance and Parliament. Partly because of its administrative independence the Court has had few problems getting its budget approved. In 1964, for example, the Court's proposal for a resplendent new multi-million-dollar building, which architects and engineers hired by the Court designed, cleared rather speedily the routine parliamentary hurdle. That the Court could have achieved similar success by funneling its request through the ministerial bureaucracy is doubtful.

Second, the administrative authority of the president of the Constitutional Court has been substantially magnified. While the president is only *primus inter pares* in the judicial conference room he is *primus* on most other matters. Most policies having to do with recruitment of nonjudicial personnel, allocation of secretarial assistance and office facilities, provision and supervision of law clerks, decisions on hours and conditions of work, purchase of books and supplies, and use of the Court's transportation pool are made by the president. This authority was granted to the president originally by resolution of the Plenum, although it is not altogether clear whether the Plenum's sanction is needed to vest him with such authority. Gebhard Müller, who presided over the Court from 1959 through 1971, had a reputation for running a very tight ship concerning these matters, always insisting upon exercising his administrative prerogatives as the ranking official within the Court.[46]

In 1969, the internal administration of the Court was reorganized largely to conform to the organization plan depicted in Figure 1. Submitted and approved along with the Court's 1969 budget request, the plan was designed to relieve the president of increasingly burdensome administrative duties.[47] Its major change was the new position of Constitutional Court director. The line of authority, however, is clear. The director is appointed by the president, to whom he is directly responsible. Dr. Walter Rudi Wand, President Müller's top assistant since 1963, was appointed to the post. (In 1970 he became a Federal Constitutional Court Justice.)

The new plan has not resolved all problems of the Court's internal authority. The Federal Constitutional Court still lacks a formal code of procedure (*Geschäftsordung*). This is highly unusual in Germany, where detailed rules specify the precise duties of officials and the decision–making procedures of official agencies. A committee of the Court was originally established to draw up a *Geschäftsordnung*, but it soon dissolved in the face of disagreements over the precise authority of the Court's principal units—namely, the president, the Plenum, and the two senates. The Plenum's decision to give the president control over most of the Court's nonjudicial affairs was a temporary expedient pending adoption of formal rules of procedure. It was hoped that such a code would clarify the precise duties and authority of both president and vice president as well as specify the Court's decision-making procedures. Up to now, the Court's practices and procedures have been a matter of informal agreement and mutual accommodation among the Justices.[48]

In the absence of formal rules governing their procedures, the Justices have been leary of adopting practices which depart substantially from tradition. A good illustration of this pattern was

FIGURE I

FEDERAL CONSTITUTIONAL COURT ORGANIZATION

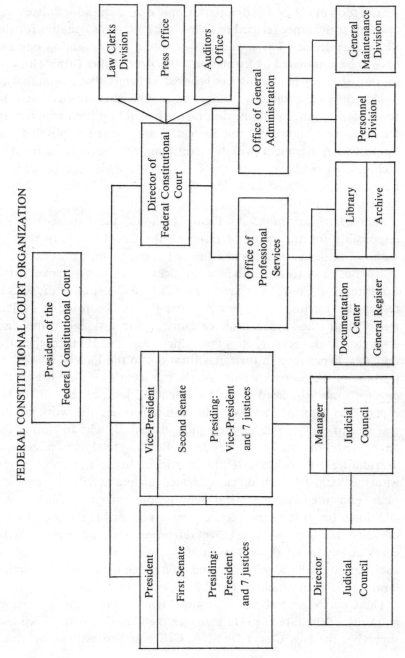

the question of dissenting opinions. Could one senate adopt dissenting opinions if the other refused to follow suit? Was this a matter for the Plenum to decide? The president? Or would the dissenting opinion have to be authorized by legislation? President Müller firmly thought so, though many of the Justices believed as firmly that this authority resided in the Plenum. By 1968, even though most Justices were in favor of dissenting opinions, the practice had not yet been adopted. In the same year, however, the Second Senate began publishing the simple voting alignment (without identifying the respective Justices) in each case, a practice which the First Senate, under the president's chairmanship, refused to follow. The matter was finally settled by legislation in 1970.

Plan of organization: As Figure 1 shows, the two senates are responsible for the administration of the Court's strictly judicial business. Attached to each is a judicial council which processes and distributes cases to the individual Justices. When cases arrive at the Constitutional Court, they are first sent to the Court director, who is responsible for inspecting and classifying them according to subject matter and the procedural category (constitutional complaint, concrete judicial review, etc.) into which they fall. He then channels the cases, depending on their classification, to the judicial council of the First or the Second Senate. As the president's chief assistant, the director is also the head of the First Senate's judicial council. In his capacity as director, however, he also supervises the work of the manager of the Second Senate's judicial council, who in turn is the senior aide of the vice president. Besides readying cases and distributing the workload to the individual Justices in consultation with the "Chief" Justice, each council maintains files of pending cases and prepares statistical reports on current business. An additional function of the Second Senate's council is the preparation of what has become a massive reference work (mimeographed), continuously updated, on the Court's decisional output, actually a codification of all the principles and rulings that the Court has handed down under each article of the Basic Law.

The Court's general administration is also under the immediate authority of the director. He manages the Court's Press Office and supervises the Law Clerks Division, Office of Professional Services, and Office of General Administration. Within the Office of Professional Services are the library, archive, documentation center, and general register. The documentation center maintains files and records of previous cases, all of which are systematically catalogued, year by year. The general register handles all inquiries that are addressed to the Court and also receives from the director any case or complaint that is not filed within the appropriate time period or which is defective on jurisdictional grounds. The civil servant in charge of the general register returns the complaint to the person who filed it, along with a statement of the reasons why it is unacceptable. The Office of General Administration includes the personnel division and the general maintenance division; the first is in charge mainly of security and personnel matters (salaries, social insurance, etc.) relating to all the Court's employees and civil servants; the second is in charge of budgeting and accounting, buildings and grounds, transportation, and supply. All told, the Constitutional Court includes sixteen Justices (*Richter*), fifty-six civil servants (*Beamten*) and other professional assistants (twenty-one of whom are law clerks), forty-one employees (*Angestellten*), and eleven workers (*Arbeiter*), totaling one hundred twenty-four persons.

A final word needs to be said about the Auditor's Office, which is something of an oddity because it is actually an agency of the Federal Accounting Office (*Bundesrechnungshof*) attached to the Constitutional Court. It audits the financial records not only of the Constitutional Court, but also of the Federal Supreme Court, the Attorney General's Office, the Federal Administrative Court, the Federal Finance Court, the High Restitution Court, and the Federal Disciplinary Court.

Law clerks: The Federal Constitutional Court's professional judicial assistants are different in background from those who serve U.S. Supreme Court Justices. The typical Constitutional Court Justice would not hear of hiring someone just out of law school, as is the rule in the Supreme Court. Law clerks at the Federal Constitutional Court are men already embarked upon careers in the judiciary, civil service, or university. Most are younger men who have been out of law school from three to ten years; they are invariably at least in their thirty's, but some are in their forty's and well into mid-career. As Table 3 indicates, it is not unusual for a person to give up a judgeship on a state court or a secure civil service job to accept a position as a law clerk. Most clerks remain at the Court for three years, but some frequently stay longer. A few have remained as long as ten years.

The director of the Constitutional Court is now responsible for recruiting law clerks and assigning them to the Justices. Prior to the Court's administrative reorganization, this was the president's duty. When vacancies now arise, the director solicits applications from

TABLE 3

CAREER PATTERNS OF JUDICIAL ASSISTANTS: 1951-1967
(N = 77)

Prior Position	Number	Position Today	Number
Civil Servant	26	Judge of high federal courts	4
Judge (ordinary courts)	29	Judge of Federal Constitutional Court	4
Judge (state administrative courts)	10	Judge of High State Court	9
Professor	4	Judge of State Trial Court	14
Prosecutor	2	High civil servant (federal)	8
Lawyer	3	High civil servant (state)	9
Unknown	3	Professor	6
		Counsel for corporation	3
		Other	3
		Still at Constitutional Court	20

SOURCE: Law Clerk List (typewritten), Federal Constitutional Court Archive.

administrative and judicial bodies in the various states. Occasionally, clerks are recruited from law school faculties. Applications, which are numerous, are then inspected, ordinarily in consultation with Justices looking for new assistants. A clerk is seldom if ever assigned to a Justice without the latter's approval.

But some Justices prefer to recruit their assistants independently. While the Justices value broad training in constitutional and public law, they also tend to select assistants whose professional interests parallel their own. A Justice preoccupied with tax cases is likely to recruit a tax specialist. Justices from law faculties tend to recruit their former students. It seems, too, that some Justices prefer clerks who share their political convictions and views on constitutional policy. Given some of the tasks performed by clerks, this is not surprising. Their primary function, of course, is to prepare reports on cases received by the Justices. But some of them are asked to prepare drafts of speeches and articles. A few clerks have collaborated with their mentors in writing books about the Court.

Constitutional Court clerks, it is fair to say, are uniformly men of high competence, whatever their political views. A law clerkship is also an avenue to greater opportunity. Rarely has any clerk left the Court to resume his old job. If a clerk returns to the judiciary or to the civil service, and most do, it is ordinarily to assume a position of higher rank than the one he left. Eight former clerks are now on the high federal courts; four have made it to the Federal Constitutional Court itself, some having been assisted along the way by the Justices they formerly served.

Location

Social Democrats wanted originally to establish the Constitutional Court in Berlin as a symbol of national unity. They wanted the Court to occupy the vacant building on Hardenberg Street that once housed the Prussian Administrative Court. It would have been a convenient place to move in 1951, since the library already contained over 60,000 volumes of German law reports. (It was later taken over by the Federal Administrative Court.) From the Social Democratic point of view, Berlin was also a good political choice since the Court would represent an important showcase of constitutional democracy in a city landlocked by a communist dictatorship.

Christian Democrats, true to their original conception of what the Constitutional Court should be, wanted to remove it from centers of political conflict like Bonn or Berlin, preferring to situate the Court in Karlsruhe, the site of the Federal Supreme Court. It was also assumed that many Constitutional Court judges would be recruited from the Federal Supreme Court and that both courts would very likely be dealing with similar matters, making collaboration between them desirable.

Because of the dispute over the Court's location, its site was omitted from the terms of the 1951 Act. Competition among several German cities for the Court's presence was also a factor in making this a subject of separate legislation. On May 4, 1951, however, the Bundestag chose Karlsruhe; the Social Democrats agreed with the majority's choice of the southwestern city in exchange for concessions on several other issues already made by the coalition parties.

Prinz-Max-Palais. Symbolically, at least, the Court was off to a good start. It was to be housed in a charming nineteenth-century villa where one of Germany's most celebrated liberals, Prince Max of Baden, once lived. Partially destroyed by a bombing raid in World War II, the palatial structure was renovated in 1951 for the specific purpose of housing the Constitutional Court. But the weather-beaten baroque exterior sheltered very plain and ordinary facilities that rivaled the simplicity of the Court's own internal operations. Even the main courtroom lacked embellishment. The resplendent red robes worn by the judges in formal public sessions were in sharp contrast to the bare ceiling and plain wooden chairs of a rectangular chamber that looked like an ordinary classroom improvised for a judicial proceeding.

Ceremony was, and is, held to a minimum. As the Justices enter the courtroom single-file from an antechamber, a clerk comes rigidly to attention with a crisp click of the heels and loudly intones, "Das Bundesverfassungsgericht," at which point everyone in the chamber rises and remains standing until the presiding judge signals the proceedings to begin. The "Chief Justice" takes his position at the center of the Court, with the remaining Justices seated left and right according to their seniority. Public proceedings, however, are extremely rare, occurring on the average about four times a year.

Nor is any ritual involved in connection with judicial conferences. In Prinz-Max-Palais, the judges convened in an ordinary meeting room adorned only with the portraits of the Court's previous presidents and vice presidents, along with the colors of the Federal Republic. It is fitting to remark that the Court's atmosphere generally is quiet and restful—like the territory around the Court where Prince Karl Wilhelm once rested after a hunt whereupon, according to legend, he named the new city of his dream "Karls-Ruhe"—with none of the officiousness or stodginess often associated with German institutions.

The new Court. In 1970, the Federal Constitutional Court moved into its new lodgings, a sprawling complex of five modern-styled, low-level, glass-enclosed buildings, arranged in a circle and connected by long corridors looking out on flower beds, well-manicured lawns, and pathways of neatly lined stone. The Court is located on a spacious piece of property situated between the city Museum of Art on the left and Karlsruhe's picturesque and bright golden renaissance-styled castle on the right, with the city's exotic botanical gardens to the rear. One of the buildings, a two-story structure, houses the Justices' comfortable, sun-heated, carpeted offices, a sharp contrast to the dismal quarters in which they formerly worked. Three other buildings house dining facilities and conferences rooms, the library, and the administrative bureaus of the Court. The remaining structure includes the Court's chamber, which is comfortable but plain. Its most striking feature is a towering wood carving of an upright eagle with spread wings—Germany's national symbol—mounted on the wall behind the Justices and overlooking the entire chamber. Its imperious demeanor is an unmistakable reminder that the men who occupy the high black leather chairs behind the elevated bench have the last word on the meaning of the Basic Law. It reinforces the impression that the Federal Constitutional Court is here to stay.

AUTHORITY AND JURISDICTION

Practically all of the Federal Constitutional Court's authority is derived directly from the Basic Law. In addition, the Basic Law authorizes the Court to decide cases otherwise assigned by statute. Until 1969 the right of ordinary citizens to bring constitutional complaints—the largest source, as we shall see, of the Court's business— had been conferred by statute. This right is now anchored in the Constitution. Thus, subject to rare exceptions that will be specified below, all the Court's jurisdiction is protected by fundamental law.[49]

Two Constitutional Courts

The Court's jurisdiction is divided between the two senates, each of which decides different matters. Each has its own judicial personnel and its own administrative machinery; each is presided over by its own "Chief Justice."

The original division of jurisdiction showed that the senates were intended to be very different "courts." The First Senate was accorded jurisdiction over all matters having to do with the basic rights of individuals and groups, its main function being to review legislation (norm control) and other official acts, using procedures largely common to ordinary litigation. Accordingly, the First Senate was given exclusive jurisdiction over (1) the forfeiture of basic rights, (2) the constitutionality of political parties, (3) election complaints, (4) abstract and concrete norm control proceedings, (5) questions concerning the continuing validity of federal law, and (6) constitutional complaints of persons. In short, the First Senate was to serve as a court of judicial review.

The Second Senate's jurisdiction was confined exclusively to intra- and inter-governmental conflicts. It included (1) constitutional disputes between high federal organs, (2) constitutional controversies between the Federation and the states, (3) constitutional disputes within states, (4) complaints by certain governmental agencies against the federal president and federal judges for violations of the Basic Law, and (5) disputes over whether a rule of international law is an integral part of federal law. In short, the Second Senate was designed to perform many of the functions formerly reserved to the *Staatsgerichtshof* of the Weimar Republic.

Largely owing to gross imbalances in the workloads of the two senates, but also partly for political reasons, this division of jurisdiction has undergone considerable modification over the years. The major change took place in 1956 when jurisdiction over forfeiture of basic rights, political parties, and election disputes was shifted to the Second Senate. Henceforth, the Second Senate was also to decide constitutional complaints and concrete norm control proceedings having to do with electoral laws. Subsequent changes, promulgated by the Plenum itself, transferred to the Second Senate constitutional complaints and norm control proceedings involving those rights and guarantees secured by Articles 19 (4), 33, 38, 101, 103, and 104 of the Basic Law. These articles deal mainly with the right of citizens to hold public office, to vote, to be tried in regular courts of law, and to procedural guarantees in trial proceedings.[50] In brief, as Table 4 shows, the First Senate now deals mainly with judicial review of legislation and with the substantive rights of persons, whereas the Second Senate is concerned primarily with the procedural rights of persons along with constitutional disputes between governmental agencies.

It is worth noting that Section 97 of the original Federal Constitutional Court Act conferred upon the Plenum the authority to hand down advisory opinions. Under this section, only the federal president or the Bundestag, Bundesrat, and federal government acting together were authorized to request the Court's opinion on any constitutional question. This jurisdiction was exercised on only two occasions, however, once with regard to a pending tax bill and then again with regard to a pending treaty.[51] The Plenum took a very dim view of these proceedings, indicating in its decision of December 8, 1952, that advisory opinions, though authorized by law, were alien to the judicial function.[52] Owing both to the Court's attitude and the government's fear of a judicial check on its treaty-making power, Section 97 was repealed in 1956, the sole instance so far of any legislative with-

TABLE 4

DIVISION OF JURISDICTION BETWEEN FIRST AND SECOND
SENATES (as of January 1, 1974)

First Senate	Second Senate
1. Concrete Judicial Review (Art. 100, sec. 1) covering Articles 1-17 (Basic Rights)	1. Concrete Judicial Review (Art. 100, sec. 1) covering Articles 19 [4], 33, 101, 103, and 104
2. Constitutional Complaints (Art. 93, secs. 4a and 4b) covering Articles 1-17 (Basic Rights)	2. Constitutional Complaints (Art. 93, secs. 4a and 4b) covering Articles 19 [4], 33, 101, 103, and 104
	3. Forfeiture of Basic Rights (Art. 18)
	4. Political Parties (Art. 21)
	5. Conflicts between high federal organs (Art. 93, sec. 1)
	6. Abstract Judicial Review (Art. 93, sec. 2)
	7. Federal-State conflicts (Art. 93, sec. 3 and Art. 84, sec. 4)
	8. Other Public Law Disputes (Art. 94, sec. 4)
	9. Constitutional Disputes Within States (Art. 99)
	10. International Law Disputes (Art. 100, sec. 2)
	11. State Constitutional Courts (Art. 100, sec. 3)
	12. Complaints Against Federal-President (Art. 61)
	13. Complaints Against Federal-Judges (Art. 98, secs. 2 and 5)
	14. Election Disputes (Art. 41, sec. 2)

drawal of the Court's authority.

Additional jurisdiction is conferred by other statutes, but only to remove doubts about the Court's authority to hear certain controversies. In 1951, for example, when Parliament authorized a referendum to be held on the question of combining the three southwestern states of Baden, Württemberg-Baden, and Württemberg-Hohenzollern into a single state (Baden-Württemberg), it empowered the Federal Constitutional Court to review the validity of the referendum.[53] The Electoral Review Act (*Wahlprüfungsgesetz*) of 1951 reasserts the right of a person denied a seat in the Bundestag to appeal the decision to the Constitutional Court.[54] The Federal Railroad Act of 1951 also removed any doubt that the Court could decide differences of opinion between the federal government and a state on the interpretation of the statute's provisions concerning the relationship of national railroads to the states.[55] Similarly, the Political Parties Act of 1967 certifies that the Court has the authority, pursuant to section 35 of the Federal Constitutional Court Act, to determine how certain prohibitions against unconstitutional parties are to be carried out.[56]

Proceedings and Litigants Before the Federal Constitutional Court

Protecting the democratic order: Only the Constitutional Court is authorized to deny a person the exercise of his fundamental rights under the Basic Law. The legitimate suppression of basic rights may occur in two types of proceedings: actions dealing with the forfeiture of basic rights under Article 18 of the Basic Law and those involving bans on political parties under Article 21. Motions to deprive citizens of their rights may be filed only by the Bundestag, the federal government, or a state government; those against political parties only by the Bundesrat, the Bundestag, or the federal government, although a state government may also move against a party whose organization is confined to the state concerned.[57] Such motions brought by the Bundesrat or Bundestag require a majority vote of its members. A motion brought by the federal or a state government would presumably be a cabinet decision.[58] If in a forfeiture case the motion is found to be valid, the Court will specify which basic rights are to be forfeited, for how long, and in what manner. The Court may also deny a person the right to vote and to hold public office while his rights are suspended. In the event that the Court fails to specify the duration of the suspension, the order can be dissolved or modified pursuant to a motion by the original petitioner or respondent after the lapse of a year.[59] A decision to declare a political party unconstitutional extends to all its branches and surrogate organizations. The Court may also direct that the property of the banned party be turned over to a state or the national government.[60]

Two other jurisdictional categories deal with the unconstitutional behavior of public officials. Under Article 61 of the Basic Law, the Bundestag or the Bundesrat may impeach the federal president before the Constitutional Court for the willful violation of the Basic Law or a federal law. A decision to impeach requires two-thirds of the members of the Bundstag or two-thirds of the votes of the Bundesrat. Under Article 98, the Bundestag may request the Constitutional Court to dismiss, retire, or change the job of a federal judge who is alleged to have infringed the principles of the Basic Law or the constitutional order of a state. Such a decision may be handed down by the Court only by a two-thirds vote.

Constitutional controversies: The Constitutional Court is not authorized to resolve all controversies between organs and levels of government. It enters these conflicts only at the point where an interpretation of the Basic Law is required, and it decides only when there is a real conflict between units of government. At the national level, such conflicts are known as *Organstreit* proceedings. These cases involve constitutional disputes between the highest organs of the Federal Republic. Federal organs eligible to bring cases under this jurisdiction are the federal president, the Bundesrat, the federal government (chancellor and cabinet), the Bundestag, and units of these organs vested with independent rights, by their rules of procedure or the Basic Law. These units include the Standing Committee of the Bundestag (created by Article 45 of the Basic Law) and the parliamentary parties. Thus, a minority party in the Bundestag may bring any *Organstreit* proceeding against the parent body if the party feels that the latter has violated its corporate rights or privileges as a constituent unit of the Bundestag. As a result of a decision by the Plenum in 1954, political parties outside Parliament are also permitted, in certain circumstances, to bring an *Organstreit* proceeding.[61] In the last chapter, we alluded to decisions of Weimar's *Staatsgerichtshof* which regarded political parties as constitutional organs. The Federal Constitutional Court has adopted the same view, holding that political parties, in their capacity as vote-getting agencies or organizers of the electoral process, are constitutional organs of the Federal Republic.[62] Thus, if a party is denied a place on the ballot or if its right to mount electoral activity is infringed by one of the high organs of the Federal Republic, it can, presumably, initiate an *Organstreit* proceeding against the federal organ in question. Such an action is not available, however, to administrative agencies, government corporations, churches, or other corporate bodies with quasi-public status.[63]

A second jurisdictional category is the constitutional controversy between states and the national government. These disputes ordinarily arise out of conflicts over the rights and duties of both levels of government flowing from state enforcement of federal laws and federal supervision of that enforcement. Such conflicts may be brought only by a state government or the federal government acting through its respective cabinet. In addition, the Court may hear "other public law disputes" between the Federation and the states, between different states, or within a state if no other legal recourse is provided. Here again, only the respective governments in question are authorized to bring such suits.

Concrete judicial review: Concrete judicial review arises out of an ordinary lawsuit.[64] If a German court is convinced that a federal or state law under which a case has arisen is unconstitutional, it must certify the constitutional question to the Federal Constitutional Court before the case can be decided. Certification of such questions to the Constitutional Court does not depend upon the litigants or on the issue of constitutionality having been raised by one of the parties. The petition is made solely at the discretion of the Court. If a collegial court is involved, a vote of the majority of its members is necessary to certify the question. The petition must be signed by the judges who vote in favor of certification, and it must contain a statement of the legal provision involved, the provision of the Basic Law that it violates, the extent to which a decision on the constitutional issue is necessary to a decision in the case, along with the record of the case. It is important to note that the Federal Constitutional Court insists that more than judicial doubt be involved in these cases. The Court will dismiss a case if the judges below manifest less than genuine intellectual conviction that a law or provision of law is unconstitutional or if the case can be decided without settling the constitutional question.[65] It is also of interest to note that after a question has been certified the Court is obligated to allow the highest federal organs or a state government to enter the case and also to give the parties involved in the proceding below an opportunity to be heard.[66] Such representations are usually made through written briefs.

Abstract judicial review: While concrete judicial review evolves out of a real lawsuit and is initiated by judges, an abstract judicial review proceeding may be initiated by politicians to secure a decision on the validity of any federal or state law. Review is available merely in the event of genuine differences of opinion or grave doubts regarding the "formal and material compatibility of federal or land law with the Basic Law or the compatibility of land law with other federal law." Such a case may be initiated by the federal government, a state government, or one-third of the members of the Bundestag.[67] Thus, abstract review is not an adversary proceeding in any strict legal sense. But neither are the decisions of the Court in such cases merely advisory opinions; for the question of a law's validity is squarely before the Court, and a decision against its validity renders it null and void.

Constitutional complaints: Individuals. The one exception to the rule that limits access to the Federal Constitutional Court to official agencies of government is the constitutional complaint. Any person who claims that one of his basic rights or one of his rights under Articles 20 (4), 33, 38, 101, 103, or 104 has been violated by public authority may file a constitutional complaint.[68] Ordinarily a person must first exhaust all legal remedies before "appealing" to the Constitutional Court. However, the Court may rule on a constitutional complaint before the exhaustion of remedies if it involves a matter of "general importance" (*allgemeiner Bedeutung*) or if the complainant will suffer serious harm by exhausting his remedies.[69] In any event, the petition must identify the right that is violated, the offending agency or official, and submit any accompanying documents relevant to the case. A constitutional complaint can be brought against any act of government, including administrative and judicial decisions. With regard to the latter, the complainant must file his complaint within a month after the decision has been handed down. A constitutional complaint against a statute not the subject of a judicial proceeding, and concerning which no other legal redress is possible, can be brought within a year after its passage.[70] Juristic persons, such as corporations and labor unions, may also file constitutional complaints. The Court has ruled, however, that political parties are not eligible to file constitutional complaints.[71] Since this is an important matter, it is worth pointing out that a political party can approach the Federal Constitutional Court from two directions only: First, directly through an *Organstreit* proceeding in the event that its right to electoral competition is infringed; second, through an abstract judicial review proceeding initiated by a minority party in the Bundestag or in a state legislative body.

Local governments. The Basic Law also provides that municipalities or associations of municipalities may bring constitutional complaints on the ground that their right to self-government under Article 28 has been violated. Such complaints can only be brought against federal or state laws (not administrative or judicial decisions) and only when such complaints cannot be properly disposed of by state constitutional courts.[72]

Other proceedings: There are three additional kinds of proceedings that may be brought to the Federal Constitutional Court. First are election disputes. A representative who loses his parliamentory seat because of a Bundestag decision concerning the validity of an election or a candidate who has been denied a seat in the Bundestag may file a complaint, within a month of the decision, with the Constitutional Court. However, his petition must either be supported by the signatures of at least one hundred eligible voters in his constituency or by at least one-tenth of the members of the Bundestag. Second, the Court may decide, upon application by the Bundestag, Bundestrat, or federal government, whether a rule of international law is to constitute a part of federal law, thereby creating immediate rights and duties on the part of these organs. Finally, if a state constitutional court, in interpreting the Basic Law, wishes to deviate from a prior decision of the Federal Constitutional Court or another state constitutional court, it must first refer the matter to the Federal Constitutional Court.[73]

NOTES

1. Hermann Mosler (ed.), *Verfassungsgerichtsbarkeit in der Gegenwart* (Cologne: Carl Heymanns Verlag KG, 1962), p. xx.

2. *Germany 1947-1949: The Story in Documents* (Washington, D.C. [U.S. Department of State Publications 3556], 1950), p. 49.

3. Aide-Memoire on German Political Organization Presented by the United States, United Kingdom, and French Military Governors (November 22, 1948), ibid., p. 278.

4. Order of September 30, 1946, ibid., p. 156.

5. See Harold Zink, *The United States in Germany 1944-1955* (Princeton: D. Van Nostrand, 1957), p. 186. Even in the French zone of occupation, state constitutions provided for judicial review of legislation. See Constitution of Rhineland-Palatinate (May 18, 1947), Article 130; Constitution of Baden (May 18, 1947), Article 14; and Constitution of Württemberg-Hohenzollern

(April 22, 1947), Article 65.

6. Bericht über den Verfassungskonvent auf Herrenchiemsee vom 10. bis 23. August 1948 (Munich: Richard Plaum Verlag), pp. 88-91.

7. See Heinz Laufer, *Verfassungsgerichtsbarkeit und politischer Prozess* (Tübingen: J.C.B. Mohr [Paul Siebeck], 1968), pp. 38-39.

8. Bericht über den Verfassungskonvent auf Herrenchiemsee, op. cit., Articles 98-99.

9. Ibid., Article 100.

10. Konrad Mommsen, "Bonn—Ein Beamtenparliament," *Die Wandlung* 4: 250-254 (1949).

11. See Volker Otto, *Das Staatsverständnis des parlamentärischen Rates* (Düsseldorf: Rheinisch-Bergische Druckerei, 1971), p. 44.

12. The debate in the Parliamentary Council is fairly well summarized by Laufer, op. cit., pp. 52-59.

13. *Documents on the Creation of the German Federal Constitution*, prepared by Civil Administration Division, Office of Military Government for Germany (September, 1949), p. 84.

14. *Verhandlungen des Hauptausschusses* 1948-49, Parlamentarischer Rat (Bonn, 1950), p. 275. (mimeographed).

15. Ibid., p. 31. See also *Documents on Creation*, op. cit., pp. 83-84.

16. Ibid., p. 84.

17. *Verhandlungen des Hauptausschusses*, op. cit., p. 275.

18. Ibid., pp. 276-277.

19. See *Documents on Creation*, op. cit., p. 82.

20. *Bericht des Verfassungsausschusses der Ministerpräsidentenkonferenz der westlichen Besatzungszonen* (Verlag Richard Pflaum).

21. For an excellent discussion of the genesis of the government bill see Willi Geiger, *Gesetz über das Bundesverfassungsgericht* (Berlin: Verlag für Rechtswissenschaft vorm. Franz Vahlen GMBH, 1951), pp. III-XXV.

22. Bundestag Drucksache Nr. 788 (Government Draft), March 28, 1950.

23. Bundestag Drucksache Nr. 328 (SPD Draft), December 14, 1949.

24. Bundesrat Drucksache Nr. 189/50 (Bundesrat Draft), March 17, 1950.

25. This section on the politics of the Court's organization draws almost exclusively upon the debates and proceedings of the Legal and Constitutional Affairs Committee of the Bundestag. The protocols are included in *Die Verhandlungen des (23.) Ausschusses für Rechtswesen und Verfassungsrecht über das Gesetz über das Bundesverfassungsgericht* (mimeographed), Deutscher Bundestag, 1. Wahlperiode. Good summaries of these proceedings may be found in Geiger, op. cit., pp. III-XXV and Laufer, op. cit., pp. 97-139. See also Wolfgang Kralewski and Karl Heinz Neunreiter, *Opposi-*

tionelles Verhalten im ersten deutschen Bundestag 1949-1953 (Cologne and Opladen: Westdeutscher Verlag, 1963), pp. 192-204.

26. Kralewski and Neunreiter, Ibid., p. 193.

27. *Verhandlungen des deutschen Bundestages*, 1. Wahlperiode 1949, Sten. Ber., 116, Sitzung (February 1, 1951), p. 4419B.

28. Deutscher Bundesrat, 49. Sitzung (February 9, 1951), pp. 91-92.

29. Gesetz über das Bundesverfassungsgericht vom 12. Marz 1951, BGBI. I, p. 243 (Hereafter cited as BVerfGG).

30. "Bericht an das Plenum des Bundesverfassungsgerichts zur 'Status Frage' " (March 21, 1952) in *Jahrbuch des Oeffentlichen Rechts* 6:120-137 (1957).

31. "Denkschrift des Bundesverfassungsgerichts" (June 27, 1952), Ibid., pp. 144-148.

32. Richard Thoma, "Rechtsgutachten betreffend die Stellung des Bundesverfassungsgerichts" (March 15, 1952), Ibid., pp. 161-194.

33. "Denkschrift," Ibid., p. 148.

34. BVerfGG, sec. 105.

35. Deutsches Richtergesetz vom 8. September 1961 (BGBI. I, p. 1665), sec. 92.

36. See Gerhard Leibholz and Reinhard Rupprecht, *Bundesverfassungsgerichtsgesetz* (Cologne-Marienburg: Verlag Dr. Otto Schmidt KG, 1968), pp. 1-21.

37. There have been four major amendments to the Federal Constitutional Court Act of 1951. These were the amendments of July 21, 1956 (BGBI. I., p. 297); August 3, 1963 (BGBI. I., p. 589); and December 21, 1970 (BGBI. I., p. 1765). All of these changes appear in the revised statute of 1971. See Neufassung des Gesetzes über das Bundesverfassungsgericht vom 3. Februar 1971 (BGBI. I., p. 105). All further references to the Constitutional Court Act (BVerfGG) are based on the revised statute.

38. BVerfGG, sec. 3 (4).

39. Ibid.

40. Ibid., sec. 4 (1).

41. Ibid., sec. 4 (3).

42. Ibid., sec. 30 (2).

43. Ibid., secs, 6 and 7.

44. Ibid., sec. 7a (2).

45. Hans Trossmann, *Parlamentsrecht und Praxis des deutschen Bundestages* (Bonn: Wilhelm Stollfuss Verlag, 1968), pp. 284-287.

46. For a discussion of the Plenum's administrative authority see Willi Geiger, *Gesetz über das Bundesverfassungsgericht: Kommentar* (Frankfurt/M,

1952), pp. 52-53.

47. Gesetz über die Feststellung des Bundeshaushaltsplans für das Rechnungsjahr 1969, BGBI. II. (1969), p. 793.

48. See Laufer, op. cit., pp. 329-334.

49. See BVerfGG, sec. 13.

50. The 1956 amendment to the Federal Constitutional Court Act authorized the Plenum itself to redistribute the workloads between the senates if necessary to relieve one of the senates of an excessively burdensome docket. Such decisions of the Plenum have the force of law.

51. Decision of November 22, 1951 (Plenum), BVerfGE 1: 76 (1952) and Decision of June 16, 1954 (Plenum), BVerfGE 3: 407 (1954).

52. See Decision of December 8, 1952 (Plenum), BVerfGE 2: 79, 86 (1952).

53. See BGB1. I. (1951), sec. 9, p. 285. A similar provision was contained in other authorized changes in state boundaries. See Gesetz über Volksbehehren und Volksentscheid bei Neugliederung des Bundesgebiets nach Artikel 29 Absatz 2. bis 6. des Grundgesetzes vom 23. Dezember 1955, BGB1. I., p. 835 and Gesetz über die Eingliederung des Saarlandes vom 23. Dezember 1956 (BGB1. I., p. 1011).

54. Wahlprüfungsgesetz vom 12. Marz 1951, BGB1, I, p. 166.

55. Bundesbahngesetz vom 13. Dezember 1951, BGB1 I. p. 955, sec. 52 (2).

56. Gesetz über die Politischen Parteien vom 26. Juli 1967, BGB1. I., p. 773, scc. 32 (3).

57. BVerfGG, secs. 36 and 43.

58. Leibholz and Rupprecht, op. cit., pp. 138-139.

59. BVerfGG, sec. 46.

60. Ibid., sec. 46.

61. Decision of July 20, 1954, BVerfGE 4: 27 (1956).

62. See Party Subvention Case II, Decision of July 19, 1966 (Second Senate), BVerfGE 20: 56, 98 (1967).

63. For a general discussion of the Court's jurisdiction over constitutional controversies involving the highest organs of the Federal Republic, see Leibholz and Rupprecht, op. cit., pp. 169-207. See also Julius Federer, "Aufbau, Zuständigkeit, und Verfahren des Bundesverfassungsgerichts" in Das Bundesverfassungsgericht 1951-1971 (Karlsruhe: Verlag C.F. Müller, 1971), pp. 64-66.

64. BVerfGG, sec. 80 (2).

65. See Leibholz and Rupprecht, op. cit., p. 295.

66. BVerfGG, sec. 82.

67. Ibid., sec. 76.

68. Ibid., sec. 90.

69. Ibid., sec. 90 (2).

70. Ibid., sec. 93.

71. Decision of September 3, 1957 (Second Senate), BVerfGE 7: 99, 103 (1958).

72. See Leibholz and Rupprecht, op. cit., pp. 394-397.

73. BVerfGG, secs. 48, 83, and 85.

4

ACTORS

In the last chapter we described the far-reaching authority of the Federal Constitutional Court. For this reason a seat on the Court is a high political reward. Its occupant enjoys high status, social prestige, and a measure of influence over the direction of constitutional policy. Who becomes a justice of the Federal Constitutional Court, and why, are therefore questions of considerable importance. Accordingly, this chapter seeks mainly (1) to describe the process of judicial selection and (2) to identify judicial background characteristics along with the Justices' personal values and attitudes.[1]

RECRUITMENT

Informal Rules of Judicial Selection

The formal rules of judicial selection, discussed earlier, have been justified on two grounds: that they are likely to produce the best men for the job of Constitutional Court Justice, and that parliamentary selection, in contrast to judicial recruitment by the executive, accords "democratic legitimacy" to the election of Justices.[2] Yet the rules themselves could hardly be more calculated to politicize the judicial selection process. Partly because of the rule requiring a two-thirds vote for the election of a Justice, appointments to the Federal Constitutional Court are the subject of intensive bargaining. The selection system ensures that political parties will play the decisive role in the recruitment of Justices and that the Court will be widely representative of parliamentary interests.[3]

Bundestag: Who are the choosers? Let us start with the *Wahlmännerauschuss,* or Judicial Selection Committee (JSC), of the Bundestag, which elects half the members of the Constitutional Court. This is no ordinary standing committee, but one staffed mainly by party leaders. If a committee member is not a party leader, he invariably is a person of prominence and influence in judicial matters or a person who enjoys high regard among his party associates and often among members of the opposition parties.

Ideally, the JSC functions as an independent decision-maker. But the parliamentary parties do seek to influence the selection of Justices through the lists they put forward when the committee is chosen by the whole house. The members of the committee in fact represent their respective parties, although the parties may not legally instruct the JSC members how to vote. Still there is close collaboration between party contingents on the JSC and the parliamentary party leadership. As just noted, this leadership actually dominates JSC membership. In fact, election to the JSC is now a signal that the committee member himself may be in line for a seat on the Constitutional Court.

Table 5 is an overview of the party alignment on the JSC at the beginning of each legislative period. In every period the parties in the governing coalition agreed on a common list of JSC candidates. Even so, no single party or governing coalition in the JSC has ever attained sufficient strength to elect a Justice over the objections of the opposition party. It is this situation which mandates negotiations among all parties in the JSC. Yet, if politics must direct the search for qualified Constitutional Court Justices it would be hard to find a group of twelve men anywhere who have as much negotiating skill or who

TABLE 5

PARTY STRENGTH IN THE BUNDESTAG AND JUDICIAL SELECTION
COMMITTEE 1951-1972, BY LEGISLATIVE PERIOD
(in percentages)

| Legislative Period | | | Party Members | | | | | | | Number of Judges Chosen |
| | CDU/CSU | | SPD | | FDP | | DP | | Other | |
	BT	JSC	BT	JSC	BT	JSC	BT	JSC	BT	JSC	
First (1949-53)	35	42	33	42	13	8	4	8	15	—	12
Second (1953-57)	51	58	31	33	10	9	4	—	4	—	2
Third (1957-61)	52	50	36	34	8	7	5	7	—	—	1
Fourth (1961-65)	49	50	37	42	12	8	—	—	2	—	2
Fifth (1965-69)	48	50	39	42	9	8	—	—	4	—	3
Sixth (1969-72)	49	50	45	42	6	8	—	—	—	—	3

SOURCE: *Amtliches Handbuch des deutschen Bundestages* for the First, Second, Third, Fourth, Fifth, and Sixth Legislative Periods.

combine as much political experience with as many legal qualifications as JSC members.

The elite character of the JSC is indicated by the concurrent positions held by the forty-four persons who have served on the committee since 1951. Eighteen were committee chairmen, nineteen were members of their party executive committees, thirty-two were members of the Judiciary Committee, and twenty-five were members of the Federal Judges' Committee. It is also noteworthy that thirty-five have been lawyers, many of whom have specialized in judicial and legal matters during their legislative careers.[4] As Gerhard Loewenberg has observed, specialization is highly valued in the Bundestag, and the skilled lawyer is apt to end up on the "prestigious" Judiciary Committee.[5] Thus, there seems to be a rather firm link between the Judiciary Committee and the JSC. The link is underscored by the fact that so far in each legislative period the chairman of the Judiciary Committee has also been a member of the JSC.

Equally interesting is the link between the JSC and the Bundestag's Federal Judges' Committee (FJC), which is responsible for recruiting all federal judges other than Constitutional Court Justices. The FJC, incidentally, is not made up exclusively of Bundestag members. Besides eleven members of the Bundestag, also chosen by proportional representation, its membership includes the federal and state ministers within whose competence a federal judge is being selected.[6] Thus, if a judge of the Federal Labor Court is being chosen, the FJC includes the labor ministers of both federal and state governments. No fewer than eighteen members of the JSC have simultaneously been members of both the Judiciary Committee and FJC (usually as a full member of one and an alternate member of the other). Members of the JSC who have not served simultaneously on either of the other two committees have invariably been members of their respective parliamentary party executive committees.

Thus, the three committees are interlocked in membership. Their relationship in the selection of federal judges, including Constitutional Court Justices, is one of cooperation and mutual adjustment. Collaboration is of course necessary to avoid duplicate selections. But occasionally a person chosen as judge of one of the federal courts will be headed eventually, by prearrangement, to the Constitutional Court. In 1971, the Federal Judges' Committee even elected a sitting Federal Constitutional Court Justice as president of the Federal Administrative Court. In this connection, incidentally, it is worth mentioning that among federal judgeships a seat on the Constitutional Court may no longer be as desirable as some positions on the other high federal courts. For one thing, the emoluments of a president or senate president of a high federal court are more attractive than an ordinary seat on the Constitutional Court. For another, tenure on the high federal courts expires when a judge reaches retirement at age 68. Ironically, Justices forced to leave the Federal Constitutional Court under the new twelve-year rule are, if not of retirement age, likely to be prime candidates for selection to some other high federal court.

The activity of the JSC varies from one legislative period to the next, depending on the number of vacancies to be filled on the Federal Constitutional Court. Actually, the committee has chosen only eleven Justices since the selection of the original twelve Justices in 1951, two in the second legislative period (1953-1957), one in the third (1957-1961), two in the fourth (1961-1965), three in the fifth (1965-1969), and three in the sixth period (1969-1972). The JSC had no vacancies to fill between 1972 and 1975.

Bundesrat: The Basic Law provides for the direct election of Constitutional Court Justices in the Bundesrat. It has never quite worked this way, however. The role of the Bundesrat as a whole is one of ratifying choices made elsewhere. Just as in the JSC the parties in the Bundesrat are forced to bargain. But negotiation with the JSC is also necessary. For one thing, the Bundesrat must ensure that it is not about to designate a Justice already under consideration by the Bundestag. For another, the JSC and the Bundesrat alternate in choosing the Court's president and vice president from among Justices already appointed. Moreover, the Justice who becomes president or vice president is usually elected as Associate Justice by one electoral organ and then selected, simultaneously, to one of these offices by the other. The recent election of Ernst Benda exemplifies this. The JSC chose him as an Associate Justice while the Bundesrat, simultaneously, in an independent proceeding, elected him president. If the Bundesrat had made its own decision in the matter, it would not have selected Benda as president. Though it was the Bundesrat's turn to name the president, the JSC or, more accurately, the Christian Democrats in the Bundestag, wanted Benda. He was accepted by the Bundesrat, and by Social Democrats, as part of a package deal which we will discuss later, involving four new Justices of the Constitutional Court.

The Bundesrat, like the JSC, has elected only eleven new Justices since 1951. But it is essential to point out that in the Bundesrat the states, many of which have coalition governments, vote as a bloc. Thus, the votes themselves say little about the influence of the various parties. Table 6 identifies the governing coalitions in the Bundesrat along with the number of votes they represented when the Justices were elected. A few minor parties, like the German Party (DP), German Refugee Party (BHE), and the Center Party (Z), which were involved in some very early coalitions, have been excluded. As the table shows, no one party or governing coalition has come close to achieving two-thirds strength in the Bundesrat.

From the beginning the Bundesrat's negotiations with the JSC have

TABLE 6

RULING PARTIES (COALITIONS) AND
SELECTION OF JUSTICES BY THE BUNDESRAT*

Year	Total BR Votes	CDU	CDU FDP	CDU FDP SPD	CDU SPD	SPD	SPD CDU FDP	SPD FDP	SPD CDU	SPD other	Judges Elected
1951	43	8	8	3	5	7	—	7	—	5	12
1952	38	5	8	—	5	10	—	5	—	5	1
1955	38	—	21	5	—	7	—	5	—	—	1
1958	41	5	13	8	—	4	3	3	5	—	1
1961	41	5	21	—	—	4	—	11	—	—	1
1963	41	5	21	—	—	4	—	11	—	—	2
1967	41	5	11	—	5	7	—	8	5	—	2
1970	41	8	8	—	5	5	—	15	—	—	1
1971	41	8	8	—	5	5	—	15	—	—	2

*In 1951 there were eleven West German states. In 1952 the southwestern states of Baden, Württemberg-Baden, and Württemberg-Hohenzollern were united to form the single state of Baden-Württemberg. In 1957 Saarland reverted to Germany, becoming the tenth state. The ten states now have a total of forty-one votes in the Bundesrat. Each state's vote in the Bundesrat is determined by population. Baden-Württemberg, Bavaria, Lower Saxony, and North Rhine-Westphalia have five votes each; Hesse, Rhineland-Palatinate, and Schleswig-Holstein four each; Bremen, Hamburg, and Saarland three each. Berlin, which is not a voting member of the Bundesrat, is excluded from the table. The leading party in each coalition appears at the head of each list.

been handled by a special *ad hoc* committee made up largely of the justice ministers of the individual states. The *ad hoc* committee is drawn mainly from members of the Bundesrat's Judiciary Committee. As a rule, the committee recruits Justices from the Bundesrat's own state constituencies. Moreover, the states, particularly the larger ones, have informally agreed to divide the judgeships among themselves. In any case, the recommendations of the *ad hoc* committee are usually unanimously accepted by the Bundesrat as a whole.

Yet it is open to question whether even the *ad hoc* committee makes its own decisions. Since each state casts a bloc vote, justice ministers invariably consult with their respective governments before "voting" in committee. In coalition governments, a decision may require consultation among the ruling parties. In some states, the minister-president takes full command of the selection process. Ministers-president have concluded informal pacts among themselves relative to the order in which their states shall claim a Constitutional Court judgeship. In these cases, the minister-president whose state is up for a judgeship can, if he wishes, usually name his own man to the Constitutional Court.

Hesse's Georg-August Zinn needs to be singled out for special attention, for his influence reached far beyond Hesse's boundaries. A man of immense prestige and impeccable background—he was in the resistance movement and suffered under the Nazis—he served as Hesse's minister of justice from 1947 to 1951 when he became minister-president, holding that post until his death in 1970. He was a powerful member of the Judiciary Committee and frequently served as chairman of the *ad hoc* committee. Twice president of the Bundesrat, he was himself frequently mentioned as a prospective Constitutional Court Justice, but he preferred to remain in the background as a maker of Justices. His name was mentioned repeatedly in interviews with journalists and parliamentarians familiar with the politics of judicial recruitment in the Bundesrat. Indeed, several Justices of the Federal Constitutional Court have openly admitted that he was at least partially responsible for their recruitment.

Yet, no one person is in a position to control all electoral outcomes. Many interests have to be considered. Party interests are important, but state interests seem equally critical. Then, too, the Bundesrat has to deal with the JSC, the point at which negotiations are most likely to break down. Finally, the Bundesrat is itself made up of many powerful and distinguished men, several of whom may themselves be candidates for the Federal Constitutional Court. Erwin Stein (Hesse), Gebhard Müller (Baden-Württemberg), and Rudolf Katz (Schleswig-Holstein), to name just three, were chosen from the Bundesrat's own membership. No political party or single coalition of political parties has ever commanded enough votes, as Table 6 shows, to name its own Justice. The partisan adjustments necessitated by this general situation are undoubtedly one reason why the Bundesrat has commonly looked to its own members as a principal source of judgeships.

Politics of Judicial Selection: 1951

This section on the recruitment process is based mainly on newspaper reports, along with interviews with Bonn politicians and the Justices themselves. In this regard, we would inject a word of caution. Although many of the Justices were willing to discuss the circumstances of their own recruitment, they are probably not the most reliable sources of information. On the other hand, some members of the Judicial Selection Committee, though willing to discuss general procedures of recruitment, are not at liberty to disclose the nature of negotiations concerning particular Justices; they are in fact legally bound to secrecy. Newspaper reports by Bonn journalists close to the Court's heartbeat are helpful, but they too leave some questions unanswered. Still, when these sources of information are added to what we do know about the objective political circumstances out of which particular persons emerged as Justices of the Constitutional Court, together with their formal ties to the recruiters themselves, we are able rather clearly to demonstrate why certain men have been elected to the Court.

The search for the original twenty-four Justices commenced when the Constitutional Court Act was being forged in Parliament. At that time, each party came forward with its own list of candidates for all available seats. The CDU's list reputedly included members of the coalition parties, but no member of the SPD. The SPD list, while heavily weighted with party faithful, included both Christian and Free Democrats. The FDP and DP also submitted candidate lists. The Court's presidency was first offered to Gebhart Müller, popular minister-president of Württemberg-Hohenzollern. Following his refusal and subsequent talks among Adenauer, Ollenhauer and FDP leaders, Hermann Höpker-Aschoff emerged as the unanimous choice to head the Court, but five months of further negotiation among the parliamentary parties failed to produce further agreement on a common list of candidates.

At an impasse, party leaders adopted the following formula in constructing the common list. The coalition parties and the SPD were each to select eight Justices; the remaining eight seats were to go to persons unaffiliated with any party. These "neutral" Justices, however, were also recruited by Bonn politicians and, like the other Justices, had to be acceptable to all parties. Still, it is interesting to note that even in the first years of the Court's existence these so-called neutral seats were rather easily identified, by the press and others, as being CDU or SPD "controlled." Besides partisan political parity, the recruiters sought to achieve religious equilibrium on the Court as well as some balance among Justices with centralistic and those with federalistic views. In addition, three other criteria governed the selection process. First, and most importantly, the Justices had to be "clean," as some interviewees put it; they had to be untainted by Nazism. Second, they had to be persons with wide experience in public life; within this frame, the recruiters sought to achieve further balance among Justices drawn from state justice ministries, the general civil service, and the federal courts. Finally, a portion of the seats was to be assigned to persons of Jewish ancestry.

The job of recruiting such persons was assigned to a joint subcommittee composed of representatives of the Bundestag—all of whom were on the JSC—and the Bundesrat. The subcommittee worked in tandem with the government, which was represented mainly by Federal Justice Minister Dehler (FDP), who enjoyed the confidence of Adenauer. Federal Supreme Court President Hermann Weinkauff also appears to have played a critical role; he had strong ties to Christian Democrats in the Bundestag who sought his advice on Justices to be chosen from the high federal courts. Seven of the eight Justices ultimately recruited from the federal courts were chosen from his Court.

Within weeks, the common subcommittee had composed the three lists, due regard having been given to the partisan, professional, ideological, religious, and geographical considerations involved in their composition. That the various interests were well served was exemplified by the prompt approval of the three lists. Unfortunately, there is no official record of these lists. Still it was a fairly easy matter to reconstruct them from newspaper articles and interviews. All the evidence points to the lists below. The selections were well planned. Bundesrat and Bundestag divided the lists equally.

BUNDESTAG	BUNDESRAT

Coalition Parties

Höpker-Aschoff	Ritterspach
Scholtissek	Stein
Kurt Zweigert	Geiger
Roediger	Leusser

SPD

Lehmann	Drath
Heiland	Ellinghaus
Klaas	Wessel
Rupp	Katz

Nonpartisan

Konrad Zweigert	Scheffler
Federer	Friesenhahn
Henneka	Fröhlich
Leibholz	Wolff

Unlike the first two lists, the nonpartisan group was made up almost exclusively of former judges and law professors. Not one of them had ever been actively engaged in partisan politics, although by looking at their sources of support, backgrounds, and off-the-bench writings and speeches, it is possible to position them rather nearer the CDU or the SPD, which we shall do further on in this chapter. In every case, they were known personally by and often were personal friends of members of the recruiting committees. It is also an interesting coincidence that the "nonpartisan" Justices split evenly between Catholics and Protestants. With regard to the Jewish representation on the Court, only one of the Justices was actively of the Jewish faith—Rudolf Katz, the Court's vice president. Gerhard Leibholz, though of Jewish ancestry, was a devout Christian and active in lay evangelical circles. The background data on Georg Fröhlich and Bernhard Wolff do not reveal their ancestry, but in interviews they were often mentioned in tandem with Katz and Leibholz, although Fröhlich was a practicing Catholic and Wolff a Protestant. What Fröhlich and Wolff did have in common with Katz and Leibholz—the only four members of the original Court who shared the experience—was that they were forced to flee Nazi Germany. Fröhlich lost his job in the civil service in 1933, when he fled to Holland, and later lost his son in a concentration camp. Wolff left Germany in 1938, remaining in England until the war's end.

But these were not the only Justices with "clean" backgrounds. In addition to the four refugees, nine of the Justices had been dismissed from public service or hindered in their careers for opposition to Nazism. Three, including Höpker-Aschoff, resigned from government service and sat out the Nazi period as private citizens. The remaining Justices, if in public life at all, had positions of minor importance. Several were drafted into military service. Finally, nearly all of the Justices did have experience in public life, most having established their reputations in the immediate postwar period, between 1945 and 1951. Many were present at the founding of the states and the new German federal government.

If the Bundestag had planned to pick a president who combined the splendor of Prussia's grand tradition of government service with an abiding faith in Bonn's new democracy it could scarcely have done better than its selection of Hermann Höpker-Aschoff. He was an easy choice, as noted earlier, and in demeanor and style even invited comparison with Adenauer. His features were rocklike, his bearing dignified, his mind firm, his leadership resolute. Brought up in a disciplined Protestant family, he was trained for Prussian judicial service but went on to distinguish himself mainly in finance and economics. A German liberal and democrat, he participated in the creation of both the Weimar and Bonn Republics. He was Prussia's finance minister between 1925 and 1931 and a member of the Reichstag from 1930 to 1933 when he withdrew altogether from public life, preferring, like Adenauer, to sit out the Nazi period in private seclusion. In 1946, he emerged as finance minister of North

Rhine-Westfalia and, after serving in the parliamentary council, was elected to the Bundestag. It was from his position as chairman of the powerful Finance and Taxation Committee and as one of the top leaders of the Free Democratic Party that he emerged as president of the Constitutional Court. Doubtless, he was helped by his deep and lifelong friendship with Theodore Heuss, the first president of the Federal Republic and former head of the FDP. He was also respected by Adenauer, who credited him with authorship of the Basic Law's financial provisions in the area of federal-state relations.[7] It is not inappropriate to note that Höpker-Aschoff also commanded the high respect of his colleagues on the Constitutional Court, for he gave the Court the strong leadership that any fledgling institution needs at its birth. His public defenses of the Court were ardent, and he frequently identified the Court's work with the fate of German freedom.

Rudolf Katz, elected by the Bundesrat, had equally impressive credentials as vice president, in which capacity he presided over the Second Senate. He had personal attributes and political qualities that offset those of Höpker-Aschoff. He was Jewish, an emigree, and a leading figure in the Social Democratic Party. Active in SPD politics since 1924, he left Germany in 1933, served for a brief time as an adviser to the League of Nations, lectured at Columbia University from 1930 to 1938, and edited the New York German language newspaper *Neue Volkszeitung* from 1938 to 1946. He then returned to Germany, renewed his contracts with SPD leaders, became minister of justice in Schleswig-Holstein, was elected to the parliamentary council, and became chairman of the Judiciary Committee of the Bundesrat in 1949.

Katz was a man of immense charm, deep religious convictions (he was the son of a cantor), personal courage (he had defended many communists in German courts during 1929-1933), and was respected for his intellectual capabilities. He renounced his membership in the SPD upon election to the Constitutional Court and skillfully led the Second Senate until his death in 1961. While a judicial pragmatist, he was uncompromising—like Höpker-Aschoff—in his defense of the Constitutional Court. He had no reservations about responding publicly to the Court's critics, even when they turned out to be former SPD colleagues.

The remaining twenty-two Justices were also recruited, for the most part, from high positions in German public life or were found to have had strong links to powerful politicians in Bonn or to state officials with influence in the Bundesrat. In surveying the recruitment of these Justices, we find that many of them emerged out of broadly identifiable groups—or loose friendship networks—allied to certain centers of power within or at the fringes of the major parties. We underscore the importance of these groups here because they continued to be principal sources of recruitment long after the first twenty-four Justices were selected.

The first group we shall call the "Zinn circle." Zinn's influence is attributable in part to his powerful position at the head of the largest and most powerful state (Hesse) controlled by the Social Democratic Party and, in part, to the respect he commanded from all parties in the Bundesrat. Zinn was a power in the Bundesrat's Judiciary Committee and conducted nearly all of the upper house's negotiations with the Bundestag. In coordinating party interests, he worked closely with Dr. Adolf Arndt, Zinn's former associate, incidentally, in the Hesse Justice Ministry and principal SPD recruiter in the JSC. Drath, Wessel, Wolff, and Stein were all within Zinn's circle of close acquaintances. Drath had served with him for a short time in 1948 as a high government administrator. Wessel was the secretary of the Bundesrat's Judiciary Committee. Wolff was a high civil servant in Hesse. Stein, though a member of the CDU, was also a close friend of Zinn; he was Hesse's Minister of Culture from 1947 to 1951 when Zinn was justice minister. Zinn was minister-president when the Bundesrat elected Stein in late 1951.

A second group, which might be referred to as the "Bamberg circle," was dedicated to preserving Bavaria's interests on the Federal Constitutional Court. Primarily Catholic and largely conservative, it formed originally around Minister-President Hans Ehard. The group's influence was predominant in the Bundestag. Besides Ehard, the circle included Laforet (chairman of the JSC), Dehler (federal minister of justice), Geiger (Dehler's former assistant and now, at the time of recruitment, a Federal Supreme Court judge), and Weinkauff (president of the Federal Supreme Court). Geiger, Laforet, Dehler, and Weinkauff were close friends and, coincidentally, all from the city of Bamberg. No fewer than five Justices on the coalition list emerged out of the "Bamberg circle." Ritterspach, Leusser, and Geiger himself were all Catholic, conservative, Bavarian federalists, and associates of Ehard. Henneka also emerged out of this group. Like Geiger, he moved from the Federal Supreme Court to the Constitutional Court and indeed attributed his elevation to Weinkauff's backing. Kurt Zweigert, although not a Bavarian, was also recruited from the Federal Supreme Court with the apparent backing of Weinkauff.

Yet a third circle needs to be mentioned. In terms of its visibility, the appearance of this group was somewhat murky when the first twenty-four Justices were selected, but it began to take shape with the selection of Leibholz and became increasingly influential in subsequent years. The group is not marked by the internal cohesion or self-consciousness of the other two groups, but it is no less real. To some extent it might be regarded as the Protestant equivalent of the Bamberg circle. Though mainly Christian Democratic in composition, it includes Social Democrats highly active in Evangelical affairs. Arndt, for example, was extremely active in the church as a member of the Society for Evangelical Theology. Leibholz, on the other hand, was associated with a select circle of upper-class German Protestants who were partly responsible for the postwar establishment of the Christian Democratic Party. This circle, which included Eugen Gerstenmaier, later president of the Bundestag and, for a time, a member of the JSC, had its origin in the Protestant resistance movement that included Leibholz's brother-in-law, the renowned Pastor Dietrich Bonhoeffer whom the Nazis executed in 1945. What we wish to suggest here, apart from this historical note, is that more than coincidence is involved in the selection of numerous Protestant Justices with strong Church affiliations. Throughout this chapter we shall refer to the group responsible for their selection as the "third circle."

At the outset, Christian Democrats had to share the eight seats allocated to the coalition parties with the FDP and the DP. Thus, they had to be content with fewer actual seats than were accorded the SPD. Höpker-Aschoff was clearly the choice of the FDP. The other party in the coalition was the German Party (DP). The DP seems not to have insisted on putting one of its own politicians on the Court, but is generally assumed to have supported Conrad Roediger, who was actually recruited by an FDP representative. Roediger had spent his life in the foreign service and was involved in the first phase of the negotiations on the European Defense Community when Adenauer suddenly replaced him with Theodore Blank, later minister of defense, at which point Roediger resigned from the foreign service and retired. By Roediger's own account, he was approached originally by Karl Georg Pfleiderer (FDP), an old foreign service colleague who was now in the Bundestag. Pfleiderer is reputed to have indicated the need for a Justice learned in international law, and Roediger fit the bill. With his acceptance, Roediger was put on the coalition list with no objection from any quarter. Scholtissek was recruited with the support of the Christian Democratic Union in North Rhine-Westfalia, where he was a leading member of the state legislature from 1947 to 1951. Ritterspach, Stein, Geiger, Leusser, and Zweigert (Kurt), already mentioned, rounded out the coalition list.

The SPD list included five Justices (Drath, Ellinghaus, Wessel, Katz, and Heiland) who had solid credentials as party activists. Rupp, a protege of Carlo Schmidt, had been a high civil servant in Württemberg-Hohenzollern and was recruited directly from the Federal Supreme Court. Lehmann, with no partisan background as such, had been a lawyer and civil servant, and, at the time of his selection, a legal adviser in the *Bundespräsidialamt*. Interestingly, Klaas was actually a member of the FDP. After the war, British Occupation authorities appointed him president of the Criminal Division of Hamburg's Central Legal Office. When this office was dissolved in 1950, he served in various capacities in Hamburg's state administration. A centralist and a liberal, Klaas had the support of both Hamburg and the SPD.

The nonpartisan list included three university professors (Leibholz, Friesenhahn, and Konrad Zweigert), four career judges (Federer, Henneka, Scheffler, and Fröhlich), and one civil servant (Wolff) who spent a year as a judge of the Federal Finance Court before his appointment to the Constitutional Court. It is worth noting that Erna Scheffler was the only woman among the twenty-four Justices. She first gained public attention at the 1950 *Juristentag* (Law Day)—a yearly conference attended by the elite of the legal profession—where she gave a stirring address on women's rights. The wife of a Federal Supreme Court judge, she was herself Director of the Düsseldorf Administrative Court when appointed to the Constitutional Court. Her candidacy was supported by North Rhine-Westfalia and the SPD. As mentioned earlier, the eight Justices on the nonpartisan list were evenly divided between Catholics and Protestants.

Few people in Germany found fault with the new Court. The Bundestag as a whole received the announcement of the lists with hardly a grumble. Although the selection process did not receive as much attention as one might have expected, the public reaction, as measured by press reports, was generally supportive. In the Bundesrat, there was but one discordant note; Bavaria objected to the election of Rudolf Katz as the Court's vice president on the ground that he, like the Court's president, was a fervent centralist, making the point that at least one of these offices ought to go to a federalist.[8] Bavaria abstained from voting in the final balloting, which was otherwise unanimous. In short, not much fanfare attended Parliament's approval of the new Justices. News of the event was received simply in the calm satisfaction that a very difficult hurdle in the way of the Court's establishment had been successfully removed.

Politics of Judicial Selection: 1952-1972

It was not until after the Court had begun to function that politicians seemed actually to realize that it would become an extremely important factor in the life of the nation. That is one reason it is hard to separate the subsequent process of judicial recruitment from the actual work of the Court. Since we will be dealing with the Court's work and Parliament's relation to the Court later in this book, we shall keep these considerations to a minimum, however.

Figure 2 reveals a trend that in one respect helped to simplify judicial recruitment after 1951. Once a political party had "possession" of a seat, the party held onto it. There has only been one real break in this pattern, and that was when Geller (CDU) succeeded

Klass (SPD) in 1963. But that was an unusual year, as we shall see. There was no real break when Wintrich (CDU) succeeded Höpker-Aschoff (FDP), for it was generally understood in Bonn that the president's chair was the "property" of the CDU and when Wand (CDU) succeeded Kutscher (SPD) in 1970 it was also clear that the partisan balance on the Second Senate would be restored in 1971 by the CDU's concession to the SPD of both the Geller and Leibholz seats. In turn, the SPD conceded one of these to the FDP (Rottmann) as a reward for participation in the coalition government. In each case, however, agreement by the other party was necessary. In addition to all this, the recruitment process was simplified further by the practice of keeping sitting judges on the Court, obviating the necessity for renewed battle at the expiration of each term.

At this point we might reveal the basis of the partisan identifications in Figure 2. These identifications are helpful mostly for what they tell us about the politics of judicial recruitment. Whether they constitute a valid basis for evaluating the Court's output is a question to be taken up later. In most instances, a Justice's party identification was a well known fact prior to his elevation to the Constitutional Court. Justices recruited from political life were invariably party members. If a Justice had not actually been a member of a political party, he had nevertheless been identified with the party responsible for his recruitment. In doubtful cases—which were few—the writer based the party identification of a Justice on information the latter revealed about himself, on newspaper reports of his activities and associations, and on the opinions of people close to the recruitment process. This information was checked against the Justice's career and the general political environment out of which he emerged. For instance, a Justice with no prior background in partisan politics was nevertheless identified with the CDU if he owed his rise in state government to the CDU or was recommended for a seat on the Court by a CDU controlled state or its Minister-President.

We should hasten to remark that, after the original twenty-four Justices were selected, there were no more pretensions about recruiting so-called nonpartisan Justices. In every case but one— Justice Karl Heck—it was relatively easy to position the Justices in one party camp or another. In recent years, actually, a rising crescendo of

FIGURE II

FEDERAL CONSTITUTIONAL COURT JUSTICES: 1951-1973

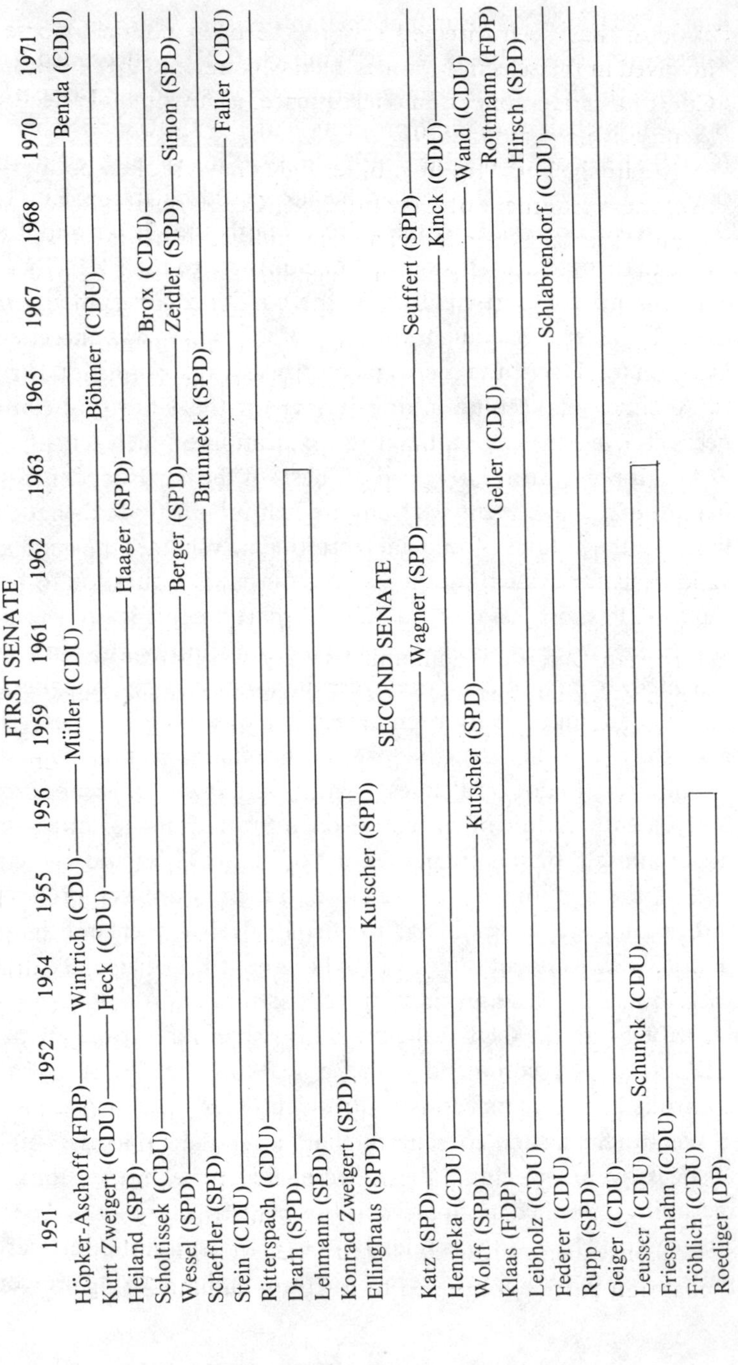

criticism has been directed toward the open political horse-trading involved in the selection process, many commentators feeling that the Court has undergone, as a consequence, a measureable decline in the quality of its personnel.[9]

Despite the horse-trading, bitter fights have broken out periodically over the recruitment of Constitutional Court Justices. Most occurred against the backdrop of changing political circumstances in West Germany. As we discuss the highlights of these controversies, it should be borne in mind that the practice of assigning seats to "members" of certain political parties was not the product of a happy handshake following a gentlemen's agreement. It was a hard pill that the parties—especially the CDU/CSU—had to swallow if Germany was to have a Constitutional Court peopled with live Justices.

Round one: 1952-1956. The first major post-1951 skirmish over judicial recruitment began with the resignation of Kurt Zweigert on February 14, 1952. Apparently for financial reasons, he left the Court after only five months to accept a judgeship on the Administrative Court of Appeals in Berlin, where he resided.[10] At the time, the European Defense Community Treaty was before the First Senate, which Zweigert vacated. The SPD, opposed to German rearmament, was contesting the validity of the pending treaty, a cornerstone of Adenauer's foreign policy, in a case before the Federal Constitutional Court. Many people thought that Zweigert's departure gave the SPD or, perhaps more accurately, the anti-treaty bloc in the First Senate, a six to five majority. Hence, in the government's view, Zweigert needed to be replaced, fast, in order to restore the balance. The CDU blandly assumed that since the SPD accepted Zweigert originally as part of the coalition package, there would be no SPD opposition to his being replaced by the coalition parties. It was not to be. The coalition parties soon found out that they were in a brand new ball game, and that it was going to be roughly played.

During the controversy—and throughout the 1950s—because the SPD appeared to "control" the First Senate and the CDU the Second, reference was commonly made to the "Red" and "Black" senates. At all events, the government worried while the press speculated about the consequences of the "Red" Senate's rejection of EDC. The coalition parties continued to insist on naming Zweigert's successor, unabashedly putting forth candidates outspokenly in favor of EDC.[11] Christian Democratic newspapers and the conservative press linked up behind the coalition parties, viciously attacking the SPD and particularly Arndt for blocking the selection of Zweigert's successor, intimating along the line that the SPD was sabotaging West German foreign policy. The newspaper assault was of sufficient gravity to prompt Arndt to write an open letter to the president of the Federal Constitutional Court deploring these intimations and rejecting the contention that the SPD was responsible for holding up the election.[12] In an earlier letter to the president of the Federal Republic, Arndt put the blame squarely on Laforet, chairman of the JSC, for failing to call a committee meeting.[13] It bears notice that Arndt was also the SPD's attorney in the case before the Constitutional Court. It was partly for this reason that he resigned from the Judicial Selection Committee in July of 1952, using the occasion once more to blast the obstructive tactics of Laforet and the CDU, and to express his dismay over the very idea of partisan quotas on the Federal Constitutional Court. Owing to the tactics of the Christian Democrats, he announced that he could no longer cooperate with the JSC.[14] But the deadlock continued, Zweigert's seat remaining vacant for two more years. Suddenly, on January 15, 1954, Höpker-Aschoff died, leaving a second vacancy on the First Senate. A month later, although the EDC controversy had long since been settled, there was still no agreement on the replacements for Zweigert or Höpker-Aschoff.

Meanwhile, new federal elections had taken place, increasing the CDU-FDP majority in the Bundestag. It was at this stage that Christian Democrats, now having difficulty electing a new president, strove hard to change the rules of judicial selection. With a nine out of twelve requirement on the JSC, it was impossible to overcome SPD opposition to any judicial nominee. The government wanted to reduce that number to a committee majority, and even talked of changing the method of judicial selection. The government had the votes in the Bundestag to do it. Fuming, the SPD accused Christian Democrats of making plans to pack the Court and of undermining the rule of law.[15] It was the Bundesrat, however, that grounded the plan, for the upper house would not agree to any change in judicial selection methods, although it was prepared to reduce the number of votes required to elect a Justice in the JSC, but only from nine to eight votes. It should also be noted that the Bundesrat was, at this time, at odds with the Bundestag over which body was entitled to elect the Court's new president.

In March 1954, realizing that it would be impossible to change the rules of judicial selection and responding to harsh press criticism for their failure to elect new Justices, the parties broke the log jam and got down to the serious business of choosing a new president, along with Zweigert's successor. Meanwhile, the Bundesrat conceded the Bundestag's right formally to designate the Court's president, but his selection was actually a joint decision.

A committee made up for four members of the JSC and the Bundesrat's Zinn went to work on picking the new Justices.[16] Several prominent names were considered for the Court's presidency, the leading candidates being Dehler, Katz, Weinkauff, Müller, and Wintrich. The committee's first choice was once again Gebhard Müller, able and respected CDU minister-president of Baden-Württemberg, who had been on good terms with all parties.[17] A firm believer in creating broad public support of his political leadership, he was the first CDU minister-president in Germany to take the SPD into a coalition government, even though it was unnecessary to do so. Müller rejected the offer, however, claiming that he was still needed in Baden-Württemberg.[18] Weinkauff (a member of the "Bamberg circle"), supported reluctantly by the SPD, also withdrew from the competition, preferring to remain president of the Federal Supreme Court.[19] Eventually, after some haggling, the committee settled on Josef Wintrich, although he, too, had reluctant SPD support.[20] A few days later, Zweigert's successor, Karl Heck, was also chosen. Obviously the parties were weary of battle and, in this instance, chose two professional judges with no visible party ties.

Nevertheless, Wintrich was a product of the "Bamberg circle," and he contrasted sharply with Höpker-Aschoff. Catholic, Bavarian, scholarly, deeply religious, measured in judgment, a man of culture and refinement, he was one of Germany's most respected jurists. He began his early career as a judge, later became a prosecutor in Munich, taught church law at the Bavarian Academy of Public

Administration, and was briefly a member of the Bavarian People's Party. An opponent of Nazism, he left public office in 1933 and never again engaged in active politics. In 1947, he became a judge of Munich's Court of Appeals and its president in 1953. He was also one of the founders of Bavaria's constitutional court and was an expert witness in connection with the drafting of the Federal Constitutional Court Act. He was not, however, a strong president, like Höpker-Aschoff before him or Gebhard Muller after him. He was fundamentally an intellectual, and in the famous Communist Party Case, over which he presided, had a Hamlet-like tendency toward indecision. Still, he was articulate in his defense of the Court as a protector of basic rights, his main interest, and for which at his death four years later he received an outpouring of praise from his Socialist colleague, Rudolf Katz.

Karl Heck was selected along with and as a balance to Wintrich, as he came from Baden-Württemburg, where the major parties were still in coalition. He had influential friends at the top of both political parties. One was Kurt Kiesinger (CDU), a member of the JSC; another was Carlo Schmidt (SPD), a power among Social Democrats. He was also a good friend of Constitutional Court Justice Franz Wessel, originally of the SPD, whom he credits with talking him into taking the seat. Recruited from the Federal Supreme Court, Heck was known for his liberal views; the SPD proposed to put him on the Court to offset the well-known conservatism of Wintrich.

The first vacancy on the Second Senate was easy to fill, partly because the Bundesrat made the selection. Egon Schunck replaced Leusser, who resigned in 1952 to accept an administrative post in Bavaria, on the recommendation of the CDU government of Rhineland-Palatinate. Hans Kutscher was also an easy choice for the Bundesrat. Filling the vacancy left by the retirement of Ellinghaus in 1955, he was secretary of its Judiciary Committee and in the "Zinn circle." The terms of several Justices, incidentally, were about to expire in 1955, at a time when the Bundestag was considering a bill to reduce the Court's membership. As a stop-gap measure, all these Justices were reelected, but only for a term of one year, pending the outcome of the bill.[21] Other changes in the Constitutional Court Act were being considered against the background of the government's anger over the First Senate's reluctance to decide its petition for a declaration of unconstitutionality against the Communist Party (KPD).

Because of its problems with the Court, the federal government initiated a second major effort to change the method of judicial selection and to reorganize the Court.[22] The Bundesrat, however, once again proved to be the stumbling block, as nearly all the ministers-president and state ministers of justice opposed any attempt to abolish or modify the principle of parliamentary selection.[23] An earlier government proposal to reduce the Court's membership by almost half generated speculation that the Chancellor and his aides wanted to get rid of at least six Justices up for reelection in 1956, several of whom were believed to have opposed Adenauer on German rearmament.[24] The Justices most frequently named in this connection were Drath, Friesenhahn, Leibholz, and Conrad Zweigert, all professors. Indeed, Friesenhahn had publicly rebuked Justice Minister Dehler for his attacks on the Court over the EDC affair.[25] Leibholz, too, lashed out at the Court's critics, virtually identifying them as enemies of West Germany's new constitutional democracy.[26] In the course of the following year, newspapers supporting the government wrote, occasionally disparagingly, about the Court's "professorial contingent," while Arndt and the SPD leaped to the Justices' defense.[27] The "cold war" between Bonn and Karlsruhe, as *Die Zeit* described the fray, had turned hot.[28]

It cooled down, as usual, with a compromise. The parties agreed to reduce the Court to ten Justices per senate—to reduce it still further to eight Justices in 1963—and to allow the JSC to elect Justices by eight votes, still short of what the coalition parties originally wanted or would need unilaterally to pack the Court.[29] The likelihood of a purge in 1956 was reduced by several voluntary resignations. In the Second Senate, three Justices—Wolff, Fröhlich, and Roediger—resigned, because of age, as their terms expired. Konrad Zweigert of the First Senate also resigned, preferring to return to the university. Kutscher was reelected and, to even the senates at ten Justices each, transferred to the Second Senate. All other Justices whose terms had expired were reelected for full terms. Thus, something approaching a sitting judge tradition was beginning to establish itself.

From 1956 to 1963 a modus vivendi prevailed between the political parties. By now, seats on the Court were clearly labelled "SPD" or "CDU." These each party conceded to the other, reserving the right to veto the other party's choice. Moreover, tempers had a chance to cool owing to the lapse of two and a half years before another occasion arose to select a Justice. In any case, four new Justices were elected in the absence of any major frictions among the parties. Three vacancies had been created by the deaths of President Wintrich, Vice President Katz, and Justice Wessel; they were promptly filled, respectively, by Gebhard Müller, Friedrich Wilhelm Wagner, and Hugo Berger. The presidency was once again in the hands of the CDU, the vice presidency of the SPD. Berger was recruited from the "Zinn circle." Karl Haager, a protege of Adolf Arndt, succeeded Heiland in 1962.

Round two: 1963. In the spring of 1963, new storm clouds gathered as the Court was scheduled for a further reduction in membership, effective September 1, coincident with the expiration of the terms of no less than nine Justices. The political context deepened the conflict. By now the Court had decided a large number of important and very controversial cases, some resulting in bitter defeats for the government. In Bonn's high circles, the air was heavy with talk about bringing the Court down to size and curtailing its jurisdiction if necessary.[30] By this time, however, the Court's own power and prestige had reached the point of making any such frontal assault on the Court politically inadvisable. Thus, the battle was fought at the level of judicial recruitment.

Terms about to expire were those of Müller, Drath, Lehmann, and Scheffler on the First Senate, and those of Kutscher, Klaas, Leibholz, Friesenhahn, and Schunk on the Second. Scheffler and Schunck used the occasion to announce their retirement, while Friesenhahn decided to return to his chair at Bonn University. The remaining six let it be known that they were available for reelection, but there was only room for five. Müller, Leibholz, and Kutscher were reelected without difficulty. But Klaas, Lehmann, and Drath were removed and replaced by two new Justices, Wiltraut von Brünneck and Gregor Geller. If the judicial recruiters had removed Klaas or Lehmann, leaving Drath, there would hardly have been a whimper. But Drath was controversial, and the ensuing conflict focused mainly on him.

Actually, the public phase of the conflict did not erupt until after the decision had been made and announced. On August 19, 1963, the SPD Press Service made public a lengthy statement by Adolf Arndt entitled "Shadows over Karlsruhe." Bristling with anger, Arndt recounted the political circumstances surrounding Drath's defeat, in the course of which he charged the CDU with violating confidential understandings regarding judicial elections. His was the first public disclosure of an agreement between government and opposition that sitting Justices were customarily to be reelected and that any reduction in the Court's membership would not be at the expense of a sitting Justice. He noted that the pact was observed in 1956. But now he blamed the CDU for seeking to purge the Court of SPD members and for spreading false rumors about Drath. Two of these rumors, Arndt revealed, were particularly damaging to Drath. First, he accused President Müller himself of trying to "dump" Drath for not doing his work on the Court. Second, he asserted that a high official in the Bavarian Ministry of Justice had informed the Bundesrat that Drath had undertaken a lecture tour in East Germany, and had held discussions with top communist officials in East Berlin.[31] Drath might easily have been harmed by the latter rumor. Long a target of Germany's right-wing press, he was a man of strong leftward convictions. Active in the SPD since his youth, he was involved in the political reconstruction of Thuringia (in the East Zone) after the war. He taught law at Jena University and later in East Berlin, where he was alleged to have joined the Socialist Unity Party (SED) before joining the staff of West Berlin's new Free University. He had never been able to still whispers that his early ties in East Germany were more than mere accidents of time and circumstance. On top of all this, the question of his professional qualifications was once more resurrected. After his original appointment in 1951, mainly on Zinn's recommendation, questions of propriety were raised about his quick promotion to professor of law at Jena. Particularly damaging was the lack of any record showing that he had taken his major state examinations in law. Within this context, questions about his workmanship on the Court, not to mention those concerning his political links, proved fatal to his reelection, at least in Drath's own assessment of the situation. These rumors, which cast doubt upon his political reliability and judicial competence, reached the point where the Federal Constitutional Court itself felt impelled to speak out in his defense. On November 29, 1963, the Plenum made a brief statement that Drath enjoyed, during his tenure on the Court, the complete confidence of his colleagues, and that rumors of his political unrealiability were totally false.[32] The Court's statement came too late to do Drath any good, however, for he had already been denied reelection.

Arndt's original charges ("Shadows over Karlsruhe"), which led to all these disclosures and rumors, were of course highly partisan. They aroused a storm of protest among Christian Democrats, who accused him not only of making false charges, but also of violating the rule of silence that obligates legislators, under the Constitutional Court Act, not to disclose the political circumstances involved in the selection of Justices.[33] They pointed out in their defense that the Court's membership was reduced with the support of both the SPD and the Federal Constitutional Court. Moreover, they maintained that the SPD had itself cashiered Drath. There seems to be some truth to this allegation, since the "Zinn circle" appears at least in part to have been the cause of Drath's downfall.

The story of the Klaas-Lehmann-Drath removals was a complicated one that appeared to cut across party lines, with personal, professional, and state interests intruding. Further, the decisions were made in the Bundesrat, where Zinn surfaces again as the head of the ad hoc committee charged with the search for new Justices. Despite the Berlin Senate's support of Drath's reelection, the committee chose instead Wiltraut von Brünneck, whom Zinn claimed was a compromise candidate.[34] Actually, Zinn pressed fervently for von Brünneck's election. She was in fact one of his proteges. An extremely able woman, she served with distinction in the Hesse Ministry of Justice and was one of Zinn's top assistants in the state chancery and, for a time, was an alternate member of the Bundesrat's Judiciary Committee. What is also of interest is that she was chosen not to succeed Drath, whose seat was left simply to expire, but Mrs. Scheffler, and thus it could be maintained, somewhat plausibly, that her selection was intended to retain the tradition of having a woman represented on the high bench. Klaas' removal caused no stir, for he was already of retirement age. A CDU-affiliated Justice took his place mainly because it was North Rhine-Westfalia's turn to put a man on the Court. Minister-President Franz Meyers chose Gregor Geller, who was also a long-time friend of Gustav Heinemann, later president of the Federal Republic.

Not until 1971 was there to be another open controversy over judicial nominees. Eight new Justices were elected between 1963 and 1971, all filling vacancies left by an unusual number of retirements and resignations. The recruitment of these Justices proceeded without a hitch and followed a familiar pattern, reflecting partisan, religious, and geographical balances, except that now one witnesses also the beginning of a trend to recruit former assistants of Federal Constitutional Court Justices, in a few cases with the active support of the Justices themselves.

Justice Heck was one of the first to manifest an interest in his successor. Before his retirement, he wrote a lengthy paper seeking to justify the selection of a Justice from the Federal Administrative Court,[35] and privately favored Werner Böhmer, whose candidacy the president of the Federal Administrative Court also supported. Böhmer succeeded Heck in 1965. With Wagner's retirement in 1967, Walter Seuffert became the Court's third vice president and seemed a perfect choice since both major parties were now embracing each other in Bonn's Grand Coalition. For the third time, the vice presidency was awarded to a Social Democrat. The JSC elected Fabian von Schlabrendorff and Hans Brox following Federer's resignation, because of ill health, and Scholtissek's retirement. Both were recruited by Christian Democrats. Brox, a professor of civil law, Catholic, and politically liberal, was a perfect balance to Schlabrendorff, who, with the support of Justice Leibholz and Eugen Gerstenmaier (president of the Bundestag), emerged clearly from the "third circle." Although born a nobleman, active in high Evangelical circles, and a former member of the Prussian officer corps, Schlabrendorff was most well known for his active participation in the plot to overthrow Hitler.[36] Hans Justus Rinck was also a Leibholz protege. He was Leibholz's law clerk and close associate for ten years.[37] Wolfgang Zeidler, who replaced Berger, was formerly the clerk of Justice Scheffler; his selection, however, was mainly the work of Burgermeister Herbert Weichmann (SPD), Hamburg's top man in the Bundesrat. Zeidler resigned in 1970 to accept the presidency of the Federal Administrative Court and was replaced by Helmut Simon, whose support was derived mainly from the SPD in North Rhine-Westphalia. Active in the Synod of the Evangelical Church, he appears to have been linked, although tenuously, to the "third circle." Finally, Rudi Wand succeeded Kutscher when the latter resigned in 1970 to accept a position on the European Court in Luxembourg. Like Rinck, he had spent most of his professional life inside the Court, first as the president's clerk and then as the Court's administrative director. Years before Wand's election, it was rumored that Müller was grooming him for a place on the Court. Wand was chosen to fill out Kutscher's term, due to expire, along with the terms of five other Justices, in August 1971.

Round three: 1971. The first sign that there might be trouble in electing Justices in 1971 was the Bundesrat's failure to replace Stein, one of the original 1951 appointees, when his term expired in March. The Bundestag's JSC, however, held up the election, pending a package agreement with the Bundesrat on all Justices to be selected in 1971. Müller, Geller, and Leibholz, like Stein, having reached the age of 68, would retire upon the expiration of their terms in August. Wand and von Brünneck, whose terms also expired in August, were eventually reelected out of respect for the sitting judge tradition. Round three was fought over the vacancies created by the four retiring Justices.

By 1971, the German political scene had changed significantly. Social Democrats, in coalition with the FDP, were at the helm in Bonn, with a slim parliamentary majority over the CDU/CSU. In the Bundesrat, as a result of similar shifts of power in several states, the Christian Democratic majority had been shaved to one vote. At first, impatient with the standoff over Stein's seat, SPD leaders themselves seemed content now to wait for a four-Justice package deal. Earlier, the press had speculated that the SPD wanted to change the rules of judicial selection.[38] SPD leaders might have been able to do so had the May 1971 election in Schleswig-Holstein turned out in their favor. A SPD victory would have overcome the Christian Democratic majority in the Bundesrat; in that event, with a majority in both houses of Parliament, the SPD-FDP could technically have changed the rules of judicial selection, as the CDU/CSU tried to do in 1956. The CDU, however, won an impressive victory in Schleswig-Holstein, killing any court-packing plan that the SPD might have had in mind.

Once again the political parties would be forced to compromise. Now that Social Democrats were on top in Bonn, speculation was adrift that the SPD would try to wrench the presidency away from the CDU. There was an even chance, too, that an FDP man might fill the post; as a coalition partner, the FDP was in a position to name at least one of the four Justices. Two Justices were to be selected by the Bundestag and two by the Bundesrat. In addition, the Bundesrat was this time to designate the president, which would require close collaboration with the Bundestag, since the JSC was to elect the Justice whom the Bundesrat would then, simultaneously, elect as president.

From September to the end of December, the German press closely followed, mostly deploring, the political skirmish in Bonn. Until the end of October, the parties had been quietly negotiating behind the scenes, the negotiations having been handled by a joint committee of the Bundestag and the Bundesrat. Not until late October, however, was any agreement reached on the Court's presidency. Dieter Posser (SPD minister of federal affairs in North Rhine-Westfalia) blamed Christian Democrats for the delay. At the time, Rainer Barzel and Helmut Kohl were in a power struggle for the chairmanship of the CDU and, reportedly, they favored different candidates for president.[39] At length, in late October—after Barzel's party victory—the JSC appeared finally to have agreed on Ernst Benda (CDU)—Barzel's candidate, by the way—for president, while Martin Hirsch (SPD) was slated to succeed Leibholz and, eventually, after Seuffert's retirement in 1975, to attain the vice presidency itself. It bears notice that both Benda and Hirsch were members of the JSC. While such blatant cooptation by the JSC of its own members did not go unnoticed or uncriticized in the German press, both men were nevertheless widely recognized as the top lawyers in their respective parliamentary parties.

Following a JSC meeting on November 3, 1971, however, owing to what now appeared to be an FDP-SPD feud, the SPD announced its choice of Emmy Diemer-Nicolaus, the FDP's representative on the JSC, instead of Hirsch. The CDU immediately objected, accusing the SPD of breaking the covenant which produced the Benda-Hirsch combination. SPD leaders retaliated by announcing that they would block Benda's election if the CDU refused to accept Diemer-Nicolaus.[40] The CDU held firm, and Benda's election as president remained a question mark for over a month.

The Diemer-Nicolaus case, to the embarrassment of the SPD, was reminiscent of the Carswell episode in the United States, although without the racial issue. Christian Democrats might eventually have opposed Diemer-Nicolaus on the basis of her extremely liberal views on social and cultural matters, but they chose to base their opposition on her qualifications, which were not manifestly impressive. Although she held a doctoral degree in law, she had published nothing since her dissertation, nor had she attained any real distinction as a practicing attorney, a role she combined with that of housewife. At 62 years of age, her clearest claim to recognition, besides her role in the Bundestag, was two decades of unstinting service to the Free Democratic Party. Wolfgang Mischnik, FDP parliamentary chief, ardently defended this "liberal personality and courageous woman," as he described her, but in the meantime the SPD's ardor for Diemer-Nicolaus had visibly shrunk.[41] In mid-November Diemer-Nicolaus herself broke the logjam by withdrawing her name from consideration, whereupon Benda and Hirsch emerged again as the JSC's top choices to succeed Müller and Leibholz.

The Bundesrat's choice for the Geller seat was Joachim Rottmann (FDP), a high civil servant in the Interior Ministry whom the SPD had, all along, preferred over Diemer-Nicolaus. Rottmann was strongly supported by Federal Interior Minister Hans-Dieter Genscher (FDP). The remaining seat, "belonging" to the CDU, was a source of some friction between CDU Minister-President Hans Filbinger (Baden-Württemberg) who preferred the appointment of his aide, Paul Feuchte, and other Christian Democrats who preferred Hans Faller, a judge of the Federal Supreme Court. What finally tipped the scale in favor of Faller was the "intervention" of the Federal Constitutional Court itself. In a statement signed by a majority of the Justices, the Court noted that Stein's successor must be chosen from the federal bench, a highly dubious legal position in view of the fact that there were already three Justices on the First Senate who had been recruited directly from the federal courts.[42] Nevertheless, the Bundesrat accepted the Court's view and Faller became the fourth former law clerk to be elected to the Federal Constitutional Court.

A few more words might be said about Benda who, at the age of 46, became the fourth president of the Federal Constitutional Court. His rise in the CDU was meteoric. From 1947 to 1955, he was heavily engaged in student affairs and the study of law at the University of Berlin. During much of this time, he was also chairman of the Young Christian Democrats in Berlin. In 1957, he was elected to the Bundestag and, in recognition of his legal ability, the CDU appointed him to its prestigious Judiciary Committee, where he soon established himself as the party's top legal authority. From April to October 1968, he was federal minister of the interior. A conservative and hard-liner on questions of internal security, he was a principal author of the controversial Emergency Laws of 1968. Still, more lawyer than Christian Democrat, he was acceptable to Social Democrats, mainly because he had always dealt with them in a fair, reasonable, and forthright manner. Benda's political aplomb was manifested by his statesmanlike refusal to say anything or to grant any interviews during the long time that his nomination was pending.

In reviewing the politics of judicial recruitment since 1951, several patterns are increasingly to be observed. First, judges chosen by the Bundesrat are ordinarily high civil servants who have distinguished themselves in state administration. Second, the Bundestag is inclined to recruit Justices from the high courts and from among active politicians. Third, there is a growing tendency in both Bundestag and Bundesrat to select Justices from among their own members. If the route to the Federal Constitutional Court is through the Bundesrat, the leading candidates are justice ministers or high civil servants associated with the Bundesrat's Judiciary Committee. If the route is through the Bundestag, the leading candidates are top party leaders who are often members of the JSC. (In 1971, Hirsch, Benda, and Diemer-Nicolaus were all members of the JSC.) Finally, Federal Constitutional Court Justices are themselves becoming active in the recruitment process, especially if the candidate has had prior

experience as a law clerk and is to be recruited from the Federal
Supreme Court.

BACKGROUND CHARACTERISTICS
AND PERSONAL VALUES

Background Characteristics

Information on the Justices' backgrounds was culled from a variety
of sources, including biographical directories, necrologies, and
newspaper reports about the Justices at the time of their selection.
Missing information was often cheerfully supplied by the Justices
themselves, twenty-five of whom agreed to fill out a background
questionnaire supplied by the writer. The data below, presented in
Table 7, are therefore fairly complete.

TABLE 7

JUDICIAL BACKGROUND CHARACTERISTICS

Characteristic	Chosen by:				Appointed to:				Total	
	Bundestag N = 23		Bundesrat N = 23		First Senate N = 24		Second Senate N = 22		Total	
	No.	%	No.	%	No.	%	No.	%	No.	%
Age										
40-49	6	26.09	9	39.13	8	33.33	7	31.82	15	32.61
50-59	11	47.83	5	21.74	11	45.83	5	22.73	16	34.78
60-65	4	17.39	6	26.09	4	16.67	6	27.27	10	21.74
Over 65	2	8.70	3	13.04	1	4.17	4	18.18	5	10.87
Parental Occupation										
Civil Servant	7	30.43	4	17.39	5	20.83	6	27.27	11	23.91
Teacher or Professor	3	13.04	4	17.39	3	12.50	4	18.18	7	15.22
Judge or Lawyer	1	4.35	2	8.70	1	4.17	2	9.09	3	6.52

TABLE 7 (continued)

| Characteristic | Chosen by: | | | | Appointed to: | | | | Total | |
	Bundestag N = 23		Bundesrat N = 23		First Senate N = 24		Second Senate N = 22			
Other										
Professional	4	17.39	4	17.39	4	16.67	4	18.18	8	17.39
Businessman	5	21.74	3	13.04	6	25.00	2	9.09	8	17.39
Landowner	0	0.00	3	13.04	2	8.33	1	4.55	3	6.52
Worker	1	4.35	1	4.35	1	4.17	1	4.55	2	4.35
Unknown	2	8.70	2	8.70	2	8.33	2	9.09	4	8.70
Birthplace										
W. Germany	13	56.52	13	56.52	13	54.17	13	59.09	26	56.52
Berlin	3	13.04	1	4.35	2	8.33	2	9.09	4	8.70
E. Germany	4	17.39	3	13.04	4	16.67	3	13.64	7	15.22
Polish Administered Territory	3	13.04	5	21.74	5	20.83	3	13.64	8	17.39
USA	0	0.00	1	4.35	0	0.00	1	4.55	1	2.17
Legal Education										
Empire	7	30.43	6	26.09	6	25.00	7	31.82	13	28.26
Weimar	7	30.43	11	47.83	9	37.50	9	40.91	18	39.13
Third Reich	4	17.39	3	13.04	5	20.83	2	9.09	7	15.22
Occupation	2	8.70	1	4.35	2	8.33	1	4.55	3	6.52
Federal Republic	2	8.70	2	8.70	2	8.33	2	9.09	4	8.70
No Record	1	4.35	0	0.00	0	0.00	1	4.55	1	2.17
Prior Occupation										
Civil Service	6	26.09	7	30.43	6	25.00	7	31.82	13	28.26
Judge	9	39.13	10	43.48	11	45.83	8	36.36	19	41.30
Professor	3	13.04	2	8.70	3	12.50	2	9.09	5	10.87
Legislator	4	17.39	4	17.39	4	16.67	4	18.18	8	17.39
Lawyer	1	4.35	0	0.00	0	0.00	1	4.55	1	2.17
Religion										
Protestant	15	65.22	10	43.48	16	66.67	9	40.91	25	54.35
Catholic	8	34.78	9	39.13	7	29.17	10	45.45	17	36.96
Other	1	4.35	3	13.04	1	4.17	3	13.64	4	8.70
Party Identification										
CDU/CSU	14	60.87	9	39.13	11	45.83	12	54.55	23	50.00

TABLE 7 (continued)

| Characteristic | Chosen by: | | | | Appointed to: | | | | Total | |
	Bundestag N=23		Bundesrat N=23		First Senate N=24		Second Senate N=22			
SPD	7	30.43	13	56.52	12	50.00	8	36.36	20	43.48
FDP	1	4.35	1	4.35	1	4.17	1	4.55	2	4.35
DP	1	4.35	0	0.00	1	4.17	1	4.55	1	2.17
State of Residence										
Bavaria	4	17.39	4	17.39	3	12.50	5	22.73	8	17.39
No. Rhine-Westfalia	3	13.04	6	26.09	6	25.00	3	13.64	9	19.57
Hesse	2	8.70	4	17.39	4	16.67	2	9.09	6	13.04
Rhineland-Palatinate	1	4.35	2	8.70	0	0.00	3	13.64	3	6.52
Baden-Württemberg	8	34.78	2	8.70	6	25.00	4	18.18	10	21.74
Lower-Saxony	2	8.70	1	4.35	1	4.17	2	9.09	3	6.52
Berlin	2	8.70	2	8.70	3	12.50	1	4.55	4	8.70
Hamburg	1	4.35	1	4.35	1	4.17	1	4.55	2	4.35
Schleswig-Holstein	0	0.00	1	4.35	0	0.00	1	4.55	1	2.17
Bremen	0	0.00	0	0.00	0	0.00	0	0.00	0	0.00
Saar	0	0.00	0	0.00	0	0.00	0	0.00	0	0.00

All Justices must be at least forty years old to be elected to the Constitutional Court. This rule and the practice of recruiting justices from high governmental positions means that they are well advanced in career, the median age being 53 at the time of election.

Close to half the Justices were born outside the territory of what is now West Germany. Birthplace is of some importance, since it is very often related to the Justices' religious affiliation and partisan background. Seventeen of twenty Justices born outside the Federal Republic are Protestant and, of these, eleven have been identified with the SPD and one with the FDP. Seuffert, whose father worked as a chemist for a German-owned company in New Jersey, was born in the United States, but at age four he returned to Germany with his parents shortly after the company's seizure by the American government at the outset of World War I. Like Seuffert, nearly all the Justices were born into middle- or upper-middle-class families. Their fathers, many of whom were among the privileged few with university training, were businessmen, landowners, teachers, or highly placed officials in public careers closely allied to law. In addition, two Justices were the sons of Protestant ministers, two of physicians, one of a high army officer, and one of a renowned professor of law. Only two Justices had working-class backgrounds.

Geographical residence seems to be a conscious factor in judicial recruitment, especially by the Bundesrat. The distribution of seats among the various states is in rough accord with their population and political importance. The large number of Justices recruited from Baden-Württemberg (with half the population of North Rhine-Westfalia) is explained by the presence there, in Karlsruhe, of the Federal Supreme Court, from which most of the "federal judges" on the Constitutional Court have been chosen. Many were originally appointed to the Federal Supreme Court in 1950. No Justice has so far been recruited from Bremen or the Saar, the two smallest states. Actually, except for Bavaria and perhaps Berlin, the German states are no longer marked by distinct cultures or interests that would prompt them to demand representation on the Constitutional Court. On the other hand, were we to divide West Germany regionally into its four more or less integrated geographical sectors—namely, Bavaria, the Rhineland (including the Ruhr), the Northeast (including Berlin and Hesse), and Southwestern Germany (the former states of Baden and Württemberg)—we would find the justices fairly evenly distributed among them.

Legal education, as pointed out in Chapter 2, has always been rather uniform in Germany. Yet judicial values are likely to be influenced by the political structure of the state. Table 7 identifies the regimes in which the Justices received their legal training. Most Justices finished their studies prior to 1933. Ten took their legal training in overlapping periods, but the classification in Table 7 is based on the period in which a Justice received most of his formal law school training prior to taking the first state examination. Still, legal training is probably less important in the formation of individual values than the factors to be discussed below.

The first of these factors is religion. Judicial recruiters have attempted to achieve a balance between Catholic and Protestant representation on the Court. This has produced a deep philosophical cleavage among the Justices. Relative to their numbers in the population, however, Catholics are actually underrepresented on the Federal Constitutional Court. One reason for this is that Social Democrats have not sought to achieve a religious balance among the "members" of their party elected to the Court; as a consequence, vice president Seuffert is the only Catholic among Justices affiliated with the SPD. Hence, Catholics are recruited within the framework of the CDU. But here seats are shared by Catholics and Protestants. Even so, the large majority of CDU seats—sixteen out of twenty-three— have gone to Catholics.

The second factor is party identification. So far, the major parties have recruited approximately an equal number of Justices. The slight advantage of the CDU/CSU is owing merely to the larger number of deaths and resignations of judges occupying "CDU seats." The totals, however, are somewhat deceptive, because the parties have been nearly equal in strength on the Court as a whole. But the parties have not always had equal representation on the individual senates, in part owing to the adjustments and compromises made on the two occasions when the Court's membership was reduced. Today the parties are perfectly balanced in both senates.

Finally, what distinguishes Federal Constitutional Court Justices as a whole from other German judges is the wide variety of life experiences they represent. German judges generally, as noted in Chapter 2, are very much alike in attitude and background, and their experience is confined mainly to the conservative social milieu of the judicial establishment. Constitutional Court Justices, on the other hand, have been drawn from a variety of professions and career backgrounds. The data in Table 7 show only the occupations in which the Justices were engaged immediately prior to their selection. The large number of those with judicial backgrounds stems partly from the requirement that one-fourth of the Justices be recruited from the federal courts. Of the thirteen federal judges so far chosen under this mandate, ten have been recruited from the Federal Supreme Court and one each from the Federal Administrative Court, the Federal Finance Court, and the Federal Labor Court. Six other justices have also been recruited from the courts, five from high state tribunals and one (Simon) from the Federal Supreme Court. Justices recruited from high civil service positions include two persons with substantial experience in foreign affairs, several high ministerial officials in Bonn, a number of state cabinet ministers, a minister-president, and a former director of the Federal Constitutional Court.

The large majority of Justices have had varied careers. Only twelve Justices have had careers confined exclusively to civil service or the judiciary. Twenty-eight have held high civil service positions in state or national government. Ten have had legislative experience. Nine Justices spent most of their professional lives practicing law. Five had careers as professors of law, while three others held professorships at one time or another. Many were involved in the work of the Parliamentary Council and in the constitutional conventions of the German states. A few served on state constitutional courts, while others authored authoritative commentaries on their state constitutions.

It is important to mention that at least ten Justices have had considerable experience traveling and studying abroad. Five were refugees (Fröhlich, Katz, Wagner, Wolff, and Leibholz), four having gone to England or the United States, where they acquired considerable familiarity with Anglo-American law. Justice Rupp spent 1935-1937 at Harvard University studying law under Roscoe Pound, and in recent years has occasionally been a visiting professor of comparative constitutional law at the University of Michigan; Zeidler studied at Harvard's International Legal Studies Center during 1960-1961; Benda, the new president, studied political science at the University of Wisconsin in 1951; Roediger was in the foreign service and has spent most of his life in London and Paris; Geller spent several years in Geneva, first with the International Labor Organization and later as chief of the Legal and Personnel Division of the Intergovernmental Committee for European Migration. In short, the Justices of the Federal Constitutional Court are a very mixed group.

Personal Values

Men with mixed professional backgrounds and varied experiences are likely to hold different views on law and politics. This seems also to be the case with the Justices of the Federal Constitutional Court. Unfortunately, the attitudes or values of individual Justices are not as yet deducible from judicial decisions. Judicial dissents have been available since 1971, but not in numbers sufficient to tell us very much about individual *judicial* values. From interview data and off-the-bench lectures, speeches, letters, and publications of several Justices, however, it is possible to gain some insight into their *personal* values. Specifically, what this information discloses are value conflicts along broad philosophical lines.

It was clear from the writer's interviews that an overarching philosophical disagreement among the Justices occurred largely but not exclusively on the basis of religious affiliation. One Justice, a Protestant, spoke of a "Catholic *Kulturpolitik*" inside the Court, indicating that the Justices were split along religious lines in matters relating to education, cultural affairs, and family law. The Justice complained that several of the Court's members "have a Thomistic *Weltanschauung* that is beyond penetration." The internal cleavage over *Kulturpolitik* should occasion no surprise given Germany's divided religious culture and the religious factor at work in the process of judicial recruitment.

The Catholic Justices include several persons who are not only extremely devout members of their faith, but also important jurists and intellectual leaders in their own right. Wintrich was a leading Catholic jurist long before he became president of the Constitutional Court in 1954. So was Professor Friesenhahn. Many of the Catholic Justices were—and are—open adherents of natural law jurisprudence, a commitment which is of some interest since the natural law school is wholly outside the mainstream of German legal philosophy. Federer, on his accession to the Court in 1951, solemnly proclaimed: "If you want to know what my juristic inclinations are I will tell you. I am a moderate supporter of natural law."[43] Wintrich's ardor for natural law was even deeper. He frequently spoke of law and morality in the same breath. As Vice President Katz eulogized: "President Wintrich was deeply schooled in the work of Thomas Aquinas. . . . [For him] justice was part of the moral order which limits political power."[44] President Müller, who presided over the Court from 1958 to 1972, frequently condemned judicial positivism and reminded his public audiences of the inseparable link between freedom and Christianity.[45] Geiger, one of the most active Catholics on the Court, has sounded the same theme in scores of lectures and articles.[46] Scholtissek, once knighted by the Vatican, has emphasized the responsibility of all Christians to saturate public life with Christian principles.[47] Other Catholic Justices, such as Ritterspach and Henneka, were known to share many of these views.

A Christian-oriented jurisprudence, however, is not the exclusive property of the Court's Catholic members. Gerhard Leibholz, the most prominent Protestant Justice and one of the Court's most influential members, has spent much of his life writing and thinking about the relationship among law, politics, and theology. Leibholz's view of law and the state is more deeply rooted in Christian belief, actually, than that of his Catholic colleagues who premise their arguments on reason and natural morality more than on any religious doctrine as such. Leibholz has tried to formulate what he calls a "Christian alternative" to natural law. Clearly influenced by Reinhold Niebuhr, he advocates what he calls "theonomic thinking" in politics; if natural law principles are to have any validity at all, he writes, they must "not be separated from their dependence on the eternal and sacred justice which has been revealed by God."[48] Indeed, the whole complicated structure of Leibholz's thought, including his theory of parliamentary democracy, is based on Christian revelation and the Christian experience as he sees it. If democracy is to be informed by Christian principles, he writes, it must reject positivism and liberalism at the point where these begin to question the supposition on which democracy rests. These ideas appear to be associated juridically with the concept of West Germany as a "fighting democracy," a notion that appears frequently in the Court's decisions. Another Protestant Justice, Erwin Stein, has publicly deplored the pure "philosophical humanism" which he felt was creeping into German textbooks after the war, and suggested that deeper faith is necessary for the preservation of freedom and democracy.[49] Heiland, too, was described by one of his colleagues as a justice with a "strong Christian *Weltanschauung.*"

These Justices are to be identified with the Christian Democratic Party. But they are an articulate minority within the Christian Democratic contingent on the Court. Many other Justices, including several Christian Democrats, have simply not expressed their views on such broad questions of political order. But those who have—such as Drath, Geller, Höpker-Aschoff, Katz, Kutscher, Rupp, Schunck, and Konrad Zweigert—do not seek to justify this order in natural law or religious terms. They insist upon the distinction between the political and religious spheres of life, although in Germany this has in no sense led to an acceptance of anything approximating the American doctrine of separation of church and state. For them liberty and order are to be secured by the *Rechtsstaat* and by the law of the Constitution. They look to the Basic Law itself, rather than to sources outside it, for norms of constitutional interpretation. In this sense, these Justices are intellectually at ease with a positivistic jurisprudence.

One must not conclude, however, that religious affiliation or party identification is a fully reliable guide to attitudes on issues concerning which we were able to discern other differences of opinion among the Justices. With regard to civil liberties, for instance, especially in the areas of free speech and censorship, the Justices seem to distribute themselves in a way that defies classification along religious or party lines. This might be illustrated by reference to the Justices of the First Senate, which decides most cases involving free speech claims. These claims have, in several cases, been rejected in the interest of preserving political order, community values, or the personal honor of individuals. Still, the Justices are deeply divided over the limits of free speech, a rift that was manifest in the 1966 Spiegel Seizure Case. There, in a wholly unprecedented step, four Justices published an unsigned dissenting opinion challenging the constitutionality of the government's seizure of a popular news magazine for reasons of military security.[50] While the general public battle over the Spiegel affair was largely a CDU-SPD encounter, it appeared that the Court's decision was not strictly along party lines. The writer's impression substantiated rumors that the Senate was split between a "conservative bloc" headed by President Müller and a "liberal bloc" headed by his CDU colleagues Scholtissek and Stein. That the rumors had some foundation was affirmed five years later—after the introduction of dissenting opinions—by the blistering dissents of Justices Stein and von Brünneck in another landmark free speech decision.[51] If the votes in the latter case are a guide to how the Justices voted in the Spiegel case, at least one Justice associated with the Social Democratic Party would have had to have joined Müller in support of the government. In any event, it was clear from the writer's interviews with seven of the eight Justices who participated in the Spiegel case that party identification has little to do with whether a Justice, in talking about free speech, tends to emphasize the values of authority and responsibility or those of freedom and liberty.

That Christian Democrats on the First Senate are in fact deeply divided on the free speech question is substantiated further by the off-the-bench activities of both Müller and Stein. For instance, President Müller's public speeches are heavily accented by references to community norms and moral values that limit speech. Even on the formal occasion of his retirement from the Court in 1971, he reminded his colleagues and the nation of the perils of a permissive society that tolerated an upsurge of pornography and the degradation of women.[52] Stein, on the other hand, as outspoken in Germany as Justice Douglas in America, makes no bones about doing public battle with those whom he regards as enemies of free speech. One incident brought him into open conflict with the mayor of Baden-Baden, where Stein makes his home. In 1962, the mayor forbade the showing of a film based on a Brecht play because it was produced by a person with links to East Germany. Stein wrote an open letter to the mayor reminding him that the value placed on freedom of art under the Basic Law is of higher worth than the protection of the community, whereupon he concluded: "Therefore, it follows that you also, Mr. Mayor, are directly bound by Article 5 of the Basic Law, and must observe it."[53] Scholtissek's public remarks also disclose a mind sensitive to the claims of speech.[54] Indeed, he was the reporter in the Spiegel case, and is reputed to have recommended a decision against the government. It is noteworthy that in an interview Scholtissek expressed deep misgivings about the condition of German democracy, in part because of the emphasis upon authority in German public life.

Still another value cleavage is evident in the general area of socioeconomic equality, although the depth of the cleavage should not be exaggerated. When asked to describe the major function of the Court in the German political system, a large number of Justices, both Christian and Social Democrats, emphasized the protection of the individual against the state in the socioeconomic field. They were particularly interested in making sure that the state did not erect barriers to equal opportunity in employment. The Justices, Social Democrats included, also turned out to be fiercely individualistic in their views on how far the state should go in distributing the socioeconomic rewards of society. Still, opinions were sufficiently divergent at the poles to warrant notice. At one end was a small core of CDU Justices who saw the levelling of modern society, with its attendant organization, as a positive danger to democracy and individual freedom. Stein and Müller, incidentally, antagonists on the issue of free speech, were in agreement here. Müller has even publicly attacked compulsory insurance and certain aspects of the social security laws as a rejection of personal responsibility and free choice, for which he was roundly criticized in the Social Democratic press.[55] These Justices equally feared the danger to personal freedom posed by large private associations exercising quasi-public authority over the individual. Stein, for instance, is fearful of the extent to which organized groups are beginning to "refeudalize" the social structure, which in his view is also a threat to parliamentary democracy, since it is no longer certain who represents whom in parliament.[56] At the other end of the pole are those Justices, mostly Social Democrats, who believe that the state has a constitutional duty to enhance the social welfare of the individual. For them, the state is a positive good and an agency for the liberation of man.

Finally, there is a cleavage on the issue of federalism. In cultural, educational, and tax questions, Social Democrats and Free Democrats tend to be heavily oriented toward the national government. The centralistic views of Katz and Höpker-Aschoff were well known, for instance. But the Court's membership has also included a minority of hardy federalists, among them Scholtissek, Böhmer, Leusser, Ritterspach, and Geiger. Geiger particularly has written extensively and cogently about federalism and is unquestionably the Court's leading theoretician of a strong federal state.[57] He was one of the original appointees in 1951, and he is still a member of the Second Senate, where most federal-state conflicts are decided.

To sum up, party affiliation does appear to be related to attitudes on religion in public life and questions of social welfare. But that is all. In discussions with the Justices about a variety of public issues, the writer did not find Justices identified with the Social Democratic Party differing significantly from those identified with the Christian Democratic Party on other broad matters likely to affect the distribution of opinion on specific questions coming before the Court. Social Democrats seem far from the egalitarian philosophy that once characterized Socialist political thought in Germany. Politically most are middle-of-the-roaders, although in the context of German politics that would be a good centimeter or two to the left of an American liberal Democrat.

Regarding free speech the two sets of Justices turned out to be equally moderate. Twenty-one Justices (eleven CDU, ten SPD) were specifically asked whether there should be far more controversial and political discussion on radio and television in Germany, in the expectation that their replies would reveal something about their attitude toward the value of free speech. Most expressed agreement with the statement, but hedged their replies with qualifications. Only six expressed strong affirmative views in reply to the question and, interestingly, three were Christian and three Social Democrats.

This chapter has shown that the Justices, as a whole, are a very mixed group, not easily classifiable. Some are liberal, some conservative, but their liberalism or conservatism varies from issue to issue, which seems to depend more on personality and general experience than on any single background characteristic. Yet their backgrounds, taken together, seem to explain the attitudinal mix that the Justices, as a group, represent. They are, collectively, well-bred, university-educated, law-trained, middle-aged people who, before going to the Constitutional Court, had achieved, usually after a varied career in government or politics, a high position in the civil service, judiciary, or legislature of a state or the national government. Politically, the Justices are middle-of-the-roaders; socially, they are middle- to upper-middle-class; ideologically, they evince little or no tendency toward dogmatism; juristically, they seem rather pragmatic and, almost universally, are aware of and sensitive to the political nature of their work as Constitutional Court Justices.

NOTES

1. This chapter, along with Chapter 5, relies heavily upon interviews with politicians, journalists, court clerks, and the Justices themselves. It should be noted that twenty-eight current and former Justices consented to be interviewed at length concerning the circumstances of their recruitment, the nature of their work and roles on the Court, and their relationship to fellow Justices. Each Justice was given assurance of confidentiality; hence, the anonymity of the Justices will be preserved unless a matter under discussion is also in the public record. Members of the Judicial Selection Committee of the Bundestag were extremely reluctant to talk about the circumstances involving the recruitment of particular Justices. Indeed, they are legally bound to hold this information confidential. The judicial selection process, however, is closely followed by German newspapers, whose reports turned out to be fairly well consistent with what the writer learned in interviews. Personal data on the Justices were secured from various biographical directories, necrologies, newspaper articles, and the results of a background questionnaire prepared by the writer.

2. See Theodor Maunz et. al., *Bundesverfassungsgerichtsgesetz: Kommentar* (Munich: C.H. Beck'sche Verlagsbuchhandlung, 1972), Sec. 4 (2).

3. For further details on the mechanics of judicial selection, see Hans Trossmann, *Parlamentsrecht und Praxis des deutschen Bundstages* (Bonn: Wilhelm Stollfuss Verlag, 1971), pp. 284-287.

4. In the first three legislative periods, non-lawyers held four of the twelve committee seats. In recent years, fewer non-lawyers have been elected; for example, in the Sixth Legislative Period, Herbert Wehner was the Judicial Selection Committee's only non-lawyer. Next to Willi Brandt, he was the most powerful Social Democrat in the Bundestag.

5. See Gerhard Loewenberg, *Parliament in the German Political System* (Ithica: Cornell University Press, 1967), p. 195.

6. Richterwahlgesetz vom 25. August 1950, BGBI. I, p. 368 (Sec. 3). See also Glenn A. Schram, "The Recruitment of Judges for the West German Federal Courts," *American Journal of Comparative Law* 21: 691-711 (1973).

7. See *Das Parlament*, January 27, 1954.

8. Deutscher Bundesrat, Sitzungsberichte, 66. Sitzung (September 6, 1951), pp. 597-598.

9. See, for example, Hans Schueler, "Bonner Kuhhandel," *Die Zeit*, November 16, 1971, p. 21 and Friedrich Karl Fromme, "Der Gefährliche Kuhhandel ums Bundesverfassungsgericht," *Frankfurter Allgemeine Zeitung*, November 4, 1971, p. 2.

10. *Süddeutscher Zeitung*, March 18, 1954.

11. *Badische Allgemeine Zeitung*, September 9, 1954.

12. Letter from Dr. Adolf Arndt to Dr. Hermann Höpker-Aschoff, president of Federal Constitutional Court, December 15, 1952 (mimeographed).

13. Letter from Dr. Adolf Arndt to Dr. Theodor Heuss, June 28, 1952 (mimeographed).

14. *Verhandlungen des Deutschen Bundestag*, 52. Sitzung, Sten. Ber., July 17, 1952, p. 10.

15. See *Frankfurter Allgemeine Zeitung*, January 21, 1954.

16. *Süddeutsche Zeitung*, February 19, 1954.

17. Ibid.

18. *Badische Neueste Nachrichten*, February 17, 1954.

19. *Christ und Welt*, February 25, 1954.

20. Ibid.

21. See Gesetz über die im September 1955 fällige Wahl von Richtern des Bundesverfassungsgericht vom 5. August 1955, BGBI. I. p. 473.

22. Specifically, the government sought (1) to abolish the twin senate system, (2) to reduce the Court's membership to twelve Justices, and (3) to "depoliticize" the process of judicial recruitment by selecting all Justices from a list of nominees chosen by a special committee composed of the presidents of two high federal courts, two law professors, and three presidents of state constitutional courts. Months earlier Gebhard Müller, who became president of the Federal Constitutional Court in 1958, suggested a similar plan, proposing the selection of Justices by the federal president from a list of nominees submitted by a committee appointed by him and composed of high court judges and law professors. See *Stuttgarter Zeitung*, June 29, 1955.

23. *Süddeutsche Zeitung*, July 12, 1956.

24. *Neue Zurcher Zeitung*, June 29, 1955.

25. *Stuttgarter Nachrichten*, December 19, 1952.

26. *Salzburger Nachrichten*, July 5, 1955.

27. *Deutsche Zeitung*, June 15, 1955 and *SPD-Pressedienst*, July 3, 1956 (P/XI/150).

28. *Die Zeit*, July 12, 1956.

29. The government originally proposed to reduce the number of votes needed to elect a Justice in the Judicial Selection Committee from nine to eight, subject to the proviso that if the JSC would still be deadlocked after two months a vote of seven, a simple majority, would be sufficient to elect. See Bundesrat Drucksache 178/55 (June 3, 1955).

30. *Süddeutsche Zeitung,* May 17, 1963.

31. Adolf Arndt, "Shadows over Karlsruhe," *SPD-Pressedienst,* Sonderausgabe, (P/XVIII/156), August 19, 1963 (mimeographed).

32. Verlautbarung der Pressestelle des Bundesverfassungsgerichts, November 29, 1963 (mimeographed).

33. *Frankfurter Allgemeine Zeitung*, August 22, 1963.

34. *Süddeutsche Zeitung*, August 23, 1963.

35. Dr. Heck, paper prepared for the Justices of the Federal Constitutional Court, March 24, 1965 (mimeographed).

36. See Fabian von Schlabrendorf, *They Almost Killed Hitler* (New York: Macmillan, 1947) and *The Secret War Against Hitler* (New York: Pitman, 1965).

37. Rinck and Leibholz collaborated on a massive commentary on the Basic Law. See *Grundgesetz: Kommentar an Hand der Rechtsprechung des Bundesverfassungsgerichts*, 4th edition (Cologne-Marienburg: Verlag Dr. Otto Schmidt KG, 1971).

38. *Frankfurter Allgemeine Zeitung*, April 23, 1971.

39. *Süddeutsche Zeitung*, September 30, 1971.

40. See *Süddeutsche Zeitung*, November 13/14, 1971.

41. Ibid. See also *Frankfurter Allgemeine Zeitung*, November 3, 1971.

42. *Die Welt*, November 13, 1971.

43. *Die Neue Zeitung*, December 27, 1951.

44. Rudolf Katz, "Ansprache bei der Trauerfeier für den Prasidenten des Bundesverfassungsgerichts Dr. Joseph Wintrich," November 6, 1958 (mimeographed).

45. See a report of a public speech by President Müller in *Stuttgarter Zeitung*, July 4, 1961. See also Gebhard Müller, "Katholik in dieser Zeit," Festreda beim 150—Jahr Jubilaum der St. Eberhardsgemeinde in Stuttgart am 29. Oktober 1961 (mimeographed).

46. See, for example, Willi Geiger, "Freiheit and Autorität in der Kirche," *Der Fels* 9: 270-273 (1970). See also "Gebot, Gewissen, Freiheit," in Erich Klausener, *Katholik in Freiheit und Verantwortung* (Berlin: Marus-Verlag, 1966), pp. 9-32. For his general views on the relationship between authority and freedom, see "Authority and Freedom in Modern Western Democracy,"

in George N. Shuster (ed.), *Freedom and Authority in the West* (Notre Dame: University of Notre Dame Press, 1967), pp. 55-68.

47. See *Badische Allgemeine Zeitung,* July 13, 1961.

48. Quoted in Paul Lehmann, "A Christian Alternative to Natural Law," in Bracher et al., *Die Moderne Demokratie und ihr Recht,* Festschrift für Gerhard Leibholz zum 65. Geburtstag (Tübingen: J.C.B. Mohr (Paul Siebeck), 1966), I: 518. For a fuller expression of Leibholz's views on the relationship between politics and Christianity see *Politics and Law* (Layden: A.W. Sythoff, 1965), pp. 91-138.

49. See report of speech by Stein in *Badische Neueste Nachrichten*, June 28, 1960.

50. Decision of August 5, 1966 (First Senate, BVerfGE 20: 162, 191-230 (1967).

51. The Mephisto Case, Decision of February 24, 1971 (First Senate), BVerfGE 30: 173, 200-226 (1971).

52. *Das Bundesverfassungsgericht 8. Dezember 1971: Festakt* (Karlsruhe: Verlag C.F. Müller, 1972), p. 36.

53. *Badisches Tagblatt,* January 16, 1962.

54. See *Badische Neueste Nachrichten*, March 21, 1959 and *Saarbrücker Zeitung*, January 19, 1958.

55. These views were expressed in a speech entitled "Soziale Sicherheit in einer democratische Gesellschaft," reported in *Stuttgarter Nachrichten*, December 9, 1959. President Müller reiterated his views in another speech on the "total social state." See *Badische Neueste Nachrichten*, October 11, 1961. Müller's remarks came under attach in *Volks-Wirtschaft*, Sozialdemodratischer Pressedienst, October 23, 1961.

56. *Stuttgarter Zeitung*, November 29, 1966. See also *Badische Neueste Nachrichten*, December 5, 1964.

57. See, for example, Willi Geiger, "Bedeutung und Funktion des Föderalismus in der Bundesrepublik Deutschland," *Bayerische Verwaltungsblätter* 3: 65-69 (1964).

5

PROCESS

In this chapter, we will consider the flow of cases through the Federal Constitutional Court. We shall also deal with the decision-making process, where our main interest is in the Court as a human group organized to settle certain kinds of disputes. Like any enduring collegial decision-making body, the Court might be regarded internally as a system of interactions made up of norms, practices, and roles in terms of which business is transacted. Thus, some of the questions we wish to answer here are: Who goes to the Federal Constitutional Court? What, generally, is the Court called upon to decide and how frequently? How has the Court's workload affected its capacity and manner of processing cases? What workways has the Court adopted? What purposes do they serve? How do the justices interact with one another? What roles do they play individually? In a phrase, how are decisions made? Consideration of substantive policy decisions that have emerged from the decisional process will be taken up in the next chapter.

THE BUSINESS OF THE
CONSTITUTIONAL COURT

General Overview

The establishment of the Federal Constitutional Court raised several questions concerning its future capacity to function as an authoritative institution in the German political system. Initially there was some danger that the Court might not transact enough business to justify its existence. The constitutional complaint allowing ordinary citizens to invoke the Court's jurisdiction was prescribed by law and might have been abolished at any time. Other cases were to be initiated, as seen earlier, by specified public officials and agencies of government. But would Germany's tradition of executive predominance prompt public officials to find other than judicial means to resolve constitutional controversies? More importantly, would a legal culture previously unreceptive to judicial review dampen the willingness of ordinary judges to certify constitutional questions to the Court's keeping?

On the other hand, there was a possibility of judicial overload, what Easton would call "volume stress."[1] Notwithstanding a weak tradition of judicial review, German society places high value, as we have also seen, on legal rules and judicial resolution of conflicts. Once new legal remedies are created, a litigious people is apt to use them. Would Germans flood the Court with constitutional complaints regardless of their gravity? Would trivial litigation interfere with the Court's capacity to establish itself as an authoritative institution in German public life? That German politicians would themselves overburden the Court with politically charged constitutional disputes was still another possibility. Many people predicted that the institution of abstract judicial review would be used to channel into the judicial forum legislative conflicts which were fundamentally political in character.[2] Resort to the judicial process in such controversies, it was feared, would transpose the Court into a super-legislature and thus blunt the full blossoming of German democracy.

Table 8 shows that these fears were misplaced. The Court certainly has not languished from lack of activity. At the same time, its boundaries have not been porous. The Court has received an average yearly input of 1,181 cases, enough of a workload to keep the Justices extremely busy, but not enough to threaten the Court's institutional stability. (In recent years, the Court's annual caseload has far exceeded this average.) Of interest, in view of Germany's tradition of constitutional review, is the relatively few direct federal-state conflicts. Federal and state governments are not rushing to the Constitutional Court in pursuit of judicial solutions to their problems.

TABLE 8

WORKLOAD OF FEDERAL CONSTITUTIONAL COURT
FROM SEPTEMBER 1, 1951 TO DECEMBER 31, 1972

Proceeding	Cases Filed	Cases Decided	Cases Terminated Without Decision	Unfinished Cases
Forfeiture of Basic Rights	2	1	0	1
Prohibition of parties	2	2	0	0
Election disputes	38	29	6	3
Presidential impeachment	0	0	0	0
Conflicts between high federal organs	35	18	17	0
Abstract judicial review	53	38	14	1
Federal-state conflicts	13	9	4	0
Other public law conflicts	19	10	8	1
Judicial removals	0	0	0	0
Constitutional disputes within states	8	6	2	0
Concrete judicial review	1379	552	657	170
International law disputes	6	4	2	0
State constitutional court certifications	7	3	3	1
Disputes concerning the continued validity of federal law	151	22	129	0
Constitutional complaints	25,040	20,577	3,781	682
Interlocutory orders and other proceedings	139	68	71	0

SOURCE: *Das Bundesverfassungsgericht 1951-1971* (Karlsruhe: Verlag C.F. Müller, 1971), pp. 204-209 and unpublished statistical summaries prepared by the judicial councils of the two senates for the years 1971 and 1972.

By the end of 1972, thirteen direct federal-state conflicts involving rights and duties growing out of the execution of federal law had been taken to the Court, only nine of which were decided. Of the latter, the states initiated six and the federal government three. In view of the peculiar nature of German federalism—legislation concentrated in the federal parliament and administration concentrated in state bureaucracies, with all the friction that such divided responsibility is likely to bring—it is a wonder that more federal-state conflicts have not come before the Court.

Actually, the most important federal-state conflicts have arisen under the Court's abstract judicial review procedure. It will be recalled that this procedure is available to the federal government, a state government, or one-third of the members of the Bundestag in the event of differences of opinion or doubts about the compatibility between federal and state laws or between these laws and the Basic Law. The large majority of the 38 cases involving abstract judicial review were brought by state governments challenging provisions of federal law. It is noteworthy that these cases have dwindled appreciably in recent years. All thirteen cases cited in Table 8 were taken to the Court prior to 1963. Since then there has been only one direct federal-state conflict—namely, Bavaria's 1973 suit against the federal government challenging the validity of the Intra-German Basic Treaty (discussed at length in Chapter 7). There are three reasons why so few cases have come to the Court in the last decade. First, the mid-1960s and after marked the high point of coalition governments in state capitals, only to be capped by the Grand Coalition itself in 1966, lasting through 1969, reducing considerably the polarity between federal and state regimes. Second, the Federal Constitutional Court's own prior decisions seem to have made Bonn politicians exceedingly cautious of journeying to Karlsruhe to settle their differences with the states. Third, and in the view of one German law professor who has argued several cases before the Court on behalf of the federal government, the two levels of government simply prefer to settle their disputes by negotiation.[3]

A further word needs to be said about the parties involved in the Court's proceedings on abstract judicial review. We noted above that state governments challenging federal laws are most apt to resort to such proceedings. Contrary to original expectations, the federal government and the Bundestag have rarely petitioned the Court. At the same time, the Court's own rules of entry and treatment of these cases may have reduced their inflow to a trickle. For one thing, the Court has ruled that only a formal law, not pending legislation, will be considered on abstract judicial review.[4] For another, the Court sometimes sits on these cases for years without deciding them, a strategy that is actually calculated to drain controversies of their urgency. Occasionally, the strategy has worked. It is a useful strategy because the petitioner has the option of withdrawing the case any time prior to decision. One Justice interviewed by the writer frankly admitted that he was letting one politically charged case "sleep" in the expectation that the petitioner—a political party—would withdraw it.

The Court has often taken the same attitude toward separation-of-powers conflicts (*Organstreitigkeiten*), concerning which it has decided an average of one case a year. What is interesting about these controversies is that in nearly every case the action was not brought by one of the main branches of the federal government, but by a political party against one of these branches. In about half the cases, a minority party in the Bundestag challenged some parliamentary decision. Hence, these cases have not been separation-of-powers conflicts in any strict sense; there is yet to be a case involving a direct constitutional conflict between the high organs or branches of the federal government.

The cases so far discussed constitute a small portion of the Court's work, although occasionally they have taken up much of its time. The remaining categories of jurisdiction, exclusive of constitutional complaints and cases arising under concrete judicial review, do not add substantially to the Court's workload; yet, though small in number, they are extremely important, for some of them, such as the Party Prohibition Cases, have helped to shape the postwar pattern of West German politics.

Concrete Judicial Review

Concrete judicial review makes up the second largest category of cases disposed of by the Federal Constitutional Court. Recall that the Court receives such cases in the form of constitutional questions certified by other courts. In the last decade the Court has received annually about fifty-five cases—about five percent of all cases filed—from lower court judges, not much when it is considered that in all of West Germany there are 1,128 courts presided over by some 13,000 judges. Whether these figures express the judiciary's general confidence in law's subservience to the Basic Law or its lack of confidence in, or indifference toward, the Federal Constitutional Court is hard to say.

On the other hand, it is not altogether an easy matter to get such questions decided by the Constitutional Court, in view of the rules of entry that the Court has laid down. Review in these cases is limited to formal statutes and permitted only when the lower court is absolutely convinced that the law in question, on the basis of which a case *must* be decided, is unconstitutional; if the petition of the lower court contains language suggesting that only constitutional *doubts* are involved it will be rejected.[5] Nor is it permissible to certify a constitutional question to decide a difference of opinion between two or more courts concerning the validity of a law. The constitutional question must be the central issue before the Court, but if there are competing interpretations of a constitutional provision, one validating a law and the other invalidating it, the lower court must accept the favorable construction.[6] Finally, the certification of a constitutional question requires the approval of a majority of the judges sitting on the court below. A higher court, it must be added, cannot overrule a lower court's decision to certify a constitutional question. The large majority of the 1,379 petitions that courts have sent to Karlsruhe were disposed of without decision. In most cases the lower court itself withdrew the petition. The Constitutional Court rejected many others for violating the rules of entry just mentioned. In the last decade, the full senates have been deciding, on the merits, an average of twenty-one such cases per year.

Constitutional Complaints

Constitutional complaints need to be considered in greater detail, not only because of their general importance in the German scheme of constitutional government, but also because of their substantial impact upon the internal order and workways of the Federal Constitutional Court. Table 9 marks the increase in constitutional complaints over the twenty-year period, although the flow pattern, dipping at various times, is uneven. Still, the relative growth and consistency of the year-to-year figures underscore in an important way the institutional stability of the Court. Constitutional complaints make up a full ninety-six percent of all docketed cases. But only fifty-five percent of the Court's published opinions have their source in constitutional complaints. Still, many Justices find the constitutional complaints of citizens exceedingly burdensome.

A remedy was introduced in 1956 following an amendment to the Constitutional Court Act. Until then, each complaint was heard and decided by the full senate. Now the senates were able to establish

TABLE 9

CONSTITUTIONAL COMPLAINTS IN THE FEDERAL
CONSTITUTIONAL COURT 1951-1972

Year	Complaints	Year	Complaints
1951	423	1962	1377
1952	822	1963	1349
1953	591	1964	1569
1954	453	1965	1440
1955	389	1966	1520
1956	686	1967	1526
1957	779	1968	1549
1958	1004	1969	1556
1959	1160	1970	1606
1960	1054	1971	1453
1961	993	1972	1641

SOURCE: Same as Table 8.

three-judge committees, each senate being authorized to create as many of these committees as needed.[7] Each senate has customarily chosen three such committees among which the complaints are divided. A committee originally had the authority unanimously to refuse a complaint in the name of the Court if it was "inadmissible" or "patently unfounded." Failing unanimity, the question of the complaint's rejection was then to be decided by a majority of the full senate. No justification was necessary to buttress the Court's refusal to accept a complaint if the reporter in the case had previously notified the complainant in writing concerning the Court's doubts about the admissibility of his claim. All other cases in which the complaint was rejected had to be supported by a reasoned argument.

This policy was followed until 1963, when, under the stress of a one hundred percent increase in constitutional complaints, the law was again amended, at the same time that the Court's membership was reduced, to further lighten the judicial burden. The new statutory ruling broadened, but only slightly, the discretionary authority of three-judge committees to reject complaints. The law's language now reads that a complaint may be refused acceptance "if it is inadmissible or for other reasons cannot satisfactorily be resolved." But a majority of the full senate is no longer able to kill a complaint that has survived committee consideration. If at least two Justices "are of the opinion that a decision in the matter would clarify a constitutional question or a failure to decide would result in a heavy hardship for the complainant," the petition is accepted and the case decided by the full senate.[8]

It is also relatively easy for a constitutional complaint to get past the Court's gates. All that is required is a letter and postage stamp. The large majority of complaints are handwritten and mailed although, occasionally, a petitioner will show up at the Court in person to hand-deliver his complaint. Most are prepared without the aid of a lawyer. In 1967, for example, only 257 out of the 763 complaints filed with the First Senate were prepared with legal counsel. Moreover, it does not cost anything to file a complaint, although the Constitutional Court is authorized by law to levy a fine against the complainant ranging from about $8 to $400 if the petitioner abuses the privilege of filing a constitutional complaint. But the Court is not very punitive in this respect, having assessed in 1970 a total of $3,600; in 1971, the charges totaled $2,700.[9]

When complaints first arrive at the Court they do not go directly to the Justices. They are first examined by the director of the Constitutional Court for jurisdictional and other formal errors. In the event of a serious error or omission, the complaint is forwarded to the General Register which returns the complaint to the petitioner with an accompanying letter explaining why it has been refused. (In 1971, 292 complaints fell into this category.) However, if the complainant objects or writes back insisting that his complaint be heard, it is then channeled to a three-judge committee.

Actually, only a very small number of constitutional complaints survives committee consideration. From 1956 through 1971, three-judge committees turned down 16,284 constitutional complaints.[10] A mere handful—628 or 3.8%—were admitted to full senate consideration. Complaints disposed of by the full senate ranged from a low of 20 in 1958 to a high of 59 in 1970. The Second Senate's records for 1971 are illustrative of what happens to constitutional complaints after arriving at the Court. Of 992 complaints received, 715 were disposed of in the committees. Of these, 315 were summarily dismissed without any written justification.[11] In 352 cases, however, a written opinion accompanied the dismissal of the case, even though the committees were no longer legally required to justify their refusals of constitutional complaints. These opinions, which occasionally run several pages in length, are not published. They are written mainly for the benefit of lawyers filing the complaints on behalf of their clients in the belief that lawyers have a right to know the reasons why their cases are turned down.

One example of a committee refusal to accept a complaint was the decision handed down on March 16, 1960. The complainant, an engineer, had difficulties with the Heidelberg Housing Authority over the registration of personal property. In the course of time, after losing several lawsuits, he publicly accused a number of judges, civil servants, and state prosecutors of "bending the law, undermining the Constitution, crimes against humanity, and communist intrigues."[12] A Heidelberg Court convicted him of recklessly defaming public officials and sentenced him to six months in prison. On procedural grounds, the Federal Supreme Court reversed, remanding the case for a new trial. At this point, the defendant filed a constitutional complaint invoking his rights under fourteen articles of the Basic Law and under the European Convention for the Protection of Human Rights. The committee, composed of Justices Henneka, Leibholz, and Rupp rejected the petition on the following grounds:

(1) It was inadmissible because of late filing;
(2) it was unacceptable in the measure that it rested on the Convention of Human Rights;
(3) it did not specify how the judgment of the Federal Supreme Court violated the petitioner's basic rights;
(4) the court decision did not manifestly offend the Basic Law;
(5) no clarification of a constitutional question could be expected from a decision in this case; and
(6) a denial of decision in the case would not cause the petitioner irreversible harm.

The committee than levied a $35 "fine" against the complainant for misusing his right to make a constitutional complaint. As this decision shows, committee jurisdiction is limited to a decision on whether to decide.

Besides certain statutory limitations on the Court's constitutional complaint jurisdiction, such as filing a complaint within a specified time period, the Court has erected a few barriers of its own. It refuses, for instance, to accept complaints arising out of offenses that occurred before April 17, 1951, the date on which the Court began operating; it will not deal with attacks on administrative regulations or other official directives that do not directly impinge upon individual rights; it will hear only concrete cases in which individuals allege an immediate and direct violation of constitutional rights; thus, it will not accept complaints brought by organizations or associations on behalf of their members.[13]

Who, then, brings constitutional complaints, for what reasons, and against what or whom? This information is not ordinarily available. Not even the Court's published opinions identify the complainants. However, the writer was permitted to look at certain data in the records of all 1,526 constitutional complaints brought to the Court in 1967. Coincidentally, each senate received the same number of complaints—763—in that year. The data included: (1) the name and address of the complainant; (2) the case number and classification; (3) the constitutional provisions invoked by the complainant; (4) the object of the complaint; and (5) the justice to whom the case was referred. From the data, we were able roughly to establish at least broad categories of people who make constitutional complaints; this task was simplified by the typical German's habit of recording his title, and very often his occupation, along with his name.

TABLE 10

PERSONS FILING CONSTITUTIONAL COMPLAINTS, 1967

Complainant	First Senate	Second Senate	Total
Corporate institutions	68	27	95
Professionals persons and businessmen	215	158	373
Inmates of state institutions	49	22	71
Ordinary citizens (including criminal defendants)	417	550	967
Foreign residents	14	6	20
Total	763	763	1526

We constructed Table 10 out of these data. The large majority of constitutional complaints—967 or sixty-three percent—comes from rank and file citizens. Civil servants in the judicial council of each senate estimate that about half this number comes from criminal defendants, alleging some violation of the fair trial provisions under Article 103 of the Basic Law. The remaining half are challenges to substantive rulings handed down by the civil courts. (These estimates appear generally to be supported by Table 12, which discloses the number of complaints against civil and criminal court judgments.) Only slightly more than six percent of complaints are filed by corporate persons such as business firms, labor unions, civic societies, and other institutions. A few of these are government units and community associations claiming a violation of their right to self-government under Article 28. It is also clear from the data that a substantial number of petitions are brought by persons confined to prisons, detention homes, mental hospitals, and other closed institutions. Frequently, these petitioners invoked no specific provision of the Basic Law, an omission that the Court's gatewatchers appear willingly to overlook when inmates or prisoners are involved. Actually, the number of petitioners from closed institutions is probably far greater than the figures in Table 10 indicate, since many complaints are filed by persons legally authorized to represent the complainant. A small number of complaints was brought by foreign residents. Our data included a San Francisco lawyer, a Kentucky businessman, a Canadian doctor, and an Ecuadorian professor. Most of the foreign residents, however, were women, obviously widows. Several were apprently married to German citizens and had gone to the Constitutional Court to contest, on equal protection grounds, administrative decisions relative to social security and widows' benefits.

A very substantial number of the petitioners are businessmen and professional people such as doctors, dentists, engineers, architects, teachers, lawyers, and government officials who commonly plead either a violation of the Basic Law's equal protection provision (Article 3) or a denial of a fair hearing in an administrative proceeding relating to their business or occupation. In many cases, however, it was not possible to tell what provision of the Basic Law the petitioner was mainly relying on, for the German constitutional complainant likes to hedge his bet by invoking as many provisions of the Basic Law as possible. Then there are the so-called *Quarrelanten* or habitual complainers who never cease sending petitions to the Court. In 1967, it was not unusual to find the same person sending in five or more complaints.

Besides illustrating the differences in the subject matter before the two senates, Table 11 shows the frequency with which certain articles of the Basic Law were invoked in the 763 cases before each Senate in 1967. Practically all complaints involving procedural issues come before the Second Senate, which of course is the reason for the high number of "Article 103" cases; many of these appear to involve

TABLE 11

ARTICLES OF THE BASIC LAW CITED IN
CONSTITUTIONAL COMPLAINTS, 1967

Provision of Basic Law	Number of Cases in Which Cited
First Senate	
Article 3 (Equality under law)	463
Article 2 (Right to life, liberty, and development of personality)	216
Article 1 (Protection of human dignity)	155
Article 14 (Right to property)	140
Article 6 (Family rights)	70
Article 12 (Right to choose trade or profession)	48
Article 5 (Freedom of expression)	40
Article 4 (Freedom of religion)	4
Article 9 (Freedom of association)	2
Others (21 additional articles)	282
Second Senate	
Article 103 (Fair hearing)	514
Article 3 (Equality under law)	265
Article 1 (Protection of human dignity)	148
Article 101 (Ban on special courts)	139
Article 19 (Restriction of basic rights)	97
Article 80 (Issuance of legal ordinances)	90
Article 104 (Legal guarantees during deprivation of liberty)	82
Article 20 (Constitutional order)	65
Other (37 additional articles)	299

criminal defendants. The overwhelming majority of constitutional complaints outside the criminal field appear to deal with claims to various social rights. What is striking about the data is the relatively few complaints against what Americans would regard as preferred freedoms—namely, freedom of religion, expression, and association. The articles of the Basic Law specifically guaranteeing these freedoms (Articles 4, 5, and 9) were raised in only 79 of the 1,526 complaints filed in both senates; the religious freedom clauses were invoked in 13 complaints, the free expression clauses in 60, and the free association clauses in 5. This contrasts with the 443 cases in which complainants challenged public acts as violative of the right to property, the right to choose an occupation, and the right to rear a family (Articles 14, 12, and 6); family rights were raised in 95 complaints; property rights in 177; and occupational rights in 71.

Furthermore, constitutional complaints against ordinances or statutes are permitted only in those cases where prompt judicial redress is not possible. When comparing the number of complaints against judicial decisions with the number of cases judges forward for constitutional review, it might seem that German citizens take a wider view of their rights under the Basic Law than do German judges. But the more likely explanation is a utilitarian one; German citizens are prone to take every legal break the law affords, and for the losing litigant it is relatively easy and inexpensive—not even legal counsel is

TABLE 12

OFFICIAL ACTIONS CHALLENGED IN
CONSTITUTIONAL COMPLAINTS, 1967

Action Against	Number of Complaints	
	First Senate	Second Senate
Ordinary Court Decisions	474	560
Civil cases	(204)	(275)
Criminal cases	(248)	(276)
Non-contentious proceedings (probate, guardianships, etc.)	(22)	(5)
Administrative court decisions	103	69
Patent court decisions	1	2
Finance court decisions	59	14
Labor court decisions	10	19
Social court decisions	53	36
Constitutional court (state) decisions	3	3
Decisions of other courts	5	15
Laws and Legal ordinances	45	15
Election decisions	0	1
Acts of high federal officials	0	5
Acts of high state officials	0	20
Other official acts	14	4

SOURCE: Records of First and Second Senate Judicial Councils for 1967. See also Hans Rupp, "Die Verfassungsbeschwerde in Rechtsmittelsystem," 82 *Zeitschrift für Zivilprozess* (January 1969), p. 11.

required—to write a complaint even if the odds are fifty to one against its acceptance by the Court.

JUDICIAL WORKWAYS AND PROCEDURES

Formal Rules of Procedure

Very few of the Court's decision-making procedures are prescribed in the Constitutional Court Act. They are largely the product of customs borrowed from other German courts, together with innovations the Constitutional Court has adopted in the course of its own trial and error experience. The Constitutional Court Act does include special procedural provisions governing each separate proceeding (party prohibition cases, federal-state conflicts, concrete judicial review, etc.) in the Constitutional Court, but these are technical matters specifying the periods for filing cases, the rights of petitioners or litigants, and the form in which the decision is to be handed down. Other provisions deal with (1) conditions under which a Justice may be excluded from a case, (2) the general process by which decisions are to be arrived at and announced, (3) the special rules accompanying the issuance of interlocutory orders, and (4) the obligations of public officials and courts to cooperate with the Constitutional Court in disposing of certain cases.[14]

Two of these items warrant brief attention. First, a Justice must exclude himself if he has been personally involved in a case or is related to one of the participants. A decision to exclude is not wholly left to the discretion of the individual Justice, however. If a Justice does not, pursuant to a challenge by one of the parties, exclude himself voluntarily from a case, the question of his exclusion is to be decided by his colleagues in the absence of the Justice concerned. A decision to exclude must be supported in writing and is included among the Court's published opinions. (Only two Justices have been excluded involuntarily from participating in a case, Justice Leibholz in the Party Subvention Case of 1966 and Justice Rottmann in the Intra-German Basic Treaty Case of 1973, both moments of high tension within the Court.) Second, the Court's decisions are to be made in closed session and on the basis of the record before the Court. Decisions are to be in writing, justified by supporting arguments, and signed by the participating Justices. If the case involves oral arguments in public session before the Court, the decision must be publicly announced within three months of the proceeding, unless the Court votes to extend the period for three additional months.[15]

Assignment

After classifying entering cases on the basis of the jurisdictional category into which they fall, the Court director forwards them to the repective senates where they are, in turn, distributed to the individual Justices under the supervision of the presiding officer, assisted by his senior aide in the judicial council. Cases outside the constitutional complaint category are not randomly distributed but are allocated to the Justices on the basis of their particular interests and specializations, matters worked out by mutual agreement and in consultation with the senate's presiding officer. If a new Justice has no specialty, he is ordinarily expected to develop an expertise in a given subject area. He may develop an interest in one or two articles of the Basic Law or prefer to work in a substantive field of law (e.g., taxation or labor law) that might involve any number of constitutional provisions.

At the initial stage of the judicial process, cases are not collectively considered, as they are by American Supreme Court Justices. The Justice receiving the case is known as the *Berichterstatter*, or the reporter, and it is his independent responsibility to ready the case for discussion by his colleagues and to recommend a decision. His report is known as a *votum*. Whatever the reaction to the votum or however the case is decided, the reporter must also write the opinion in the case. Owing to their large number, constitutional complaints are, for the most part, distributed randomly among the Justices. Assisted by his law clerk, each Justice prepares a short memorandum—a mini-votum—on each case for the benefit of his two colleagues on the three-judge committee. If the complaint survives senate consideration, then the case is assigned to a reporter in accordance with the "rule of specialization."

The workload of the Justices is fairly evenly distributed except that the presiding officers—the president and vice president—assign very few cases to themselves. In 1967, the year for which such data were made available to the writer, each Justice, excluding the presiding officers, was assigned, on the average, 108 cases. Altogether, the two presiding Justices reserved to themselves only a handful of cases. But their relatively light caseloads, a sore point with some of the Justices, can be attributed to their many administrative duties and to the fact that they are responsible for guiding the weekly conference to a decision in each pending case.

The Votum

The preparation of the votum is a crucial stage in the decisional process. Quite simply, the votum is a detailed research report on all aspects of a case. The reporting Justice prepares a statement of the relevant facts and issues, including arguments on both sides of the question, with full citation to court decisions and published commentary, and concludes with his own personal recommendation as to how the case should be decided. A votum may take weeks, even months, to prepare. Often it turns out to be a weighty document, running from fifty to two hundred pages. A votum is one measure of the skill and ingenuity of its author, occasionally representing an intellectual tour de force.

An example of a votum is the one prepared by Justice Hans Kutscher in a 1968 case involving aliens.[16] Under the West German Equalization of Burdens Act, property was taxed to raise revenue for the purpose of compensating German refugees from the East for suffering and hardship arising out of the war. In 1963, citizens of Finland, Saudi Arabia, and the United States filed constitutional complaints alleging that the act violated international law. The petitioners argued that under international law a state may not shift the burden of its own illegal warlike acts to the citizens of foreign states not a party to such acts. The question was raised here because Article 25 of the Basic Law makes the general rules of international law a part of, and indeed even superior to, federal law. The complaints were brought against several court decisions, including one by the Federal Finance Court, denying the alien claims. Because the petitions raised important questions of international law, the case was assigned to Justice Hans Kutscher, the Second Senate's authority in that field.

The votum was dated April 10, 1968—five years after the case had been filed. A fifty-five page document, the votum was extremely impressive for its craftsmanship and meticulous attention to detail. It began with a discussion of threshold problems of jurisdiction, continued with a summary of the legal issues in the case, cited relevant laws, foreign statutes, treaties, judicial decisions, United Nations resolutions, and constitutional provisions, and concluded with the opinion that the constitutional complaint was well grounded and properly before the Court. There followed a review of previous Constitutional Court decisions bearing on the issues in dispute, along with an analysis of the tax policy under review. The votum then proceeded—in the main body of the report—systematically to consider various judicial authorities, divergent opinions represented in leading international law commentaries, the brief against the petitioners filed by the Federal Minister of Finance, and an advisory opinion (*Gutachten*) in support of petitions submitted by Professor Inez Seidl-Hohenveldern, one of West Germany's top international law experts. Finally, the votum included a summary of the reporter's own views, with these concluding words: "I recommend the following decision: that the constitutional complaint be rejected." A copy of the votum was sent to each Justice for perusal and study prior to the judicial conference.

`There is no deadline for the submission of a votum. Each justice works pretty much at his own pace. The full senate could, if it wanted, set a deadline for the consideration of a votum or, if necessary, reassign the case to another Justice, but this is rarely done. As one member of the Second Senate noted, each Justice has his own priorities and any pressure from the vice president or colleagues to bring up a case would be deeply resisted. Occasionally, however, before the end of a term, the Justices will meet in conference and agree informally upon a priority list, but there is no compulsion in this respect.

Conference

The presiding officer of each senate schedules a weekly conference in order to decide cases and dispose of other business. The vice president, for instance, sets conference dates for the Second Senate six months in advance, scheduling sessions from four to six times a month, excluding August and September, when the Justices go on vacation. Meetings are normally held every Tuesday and frequently spill over into Wednesday. The main items of business on the agenda are vota and draft opinions of cases already decided. When a votum is being considered, the presiding officer calls upon the reporter who summarizes the case and states reasons for his recommendation as to how it should be decided. He then entertains questions and comments, after which the presiding officer calls for a vote by a simple show of hands. Here, of course, the presiding officer can play an extremely important role. He guides the discussion after the reporter has summarized the case and, if no clear consensus emerges, he formulates the questions on which votes are to be taken.

A vote on the reporter's recommendations commences the next stage of the decisional process. The reporter now proceeds to draft the opinion in the case. He does so even though his colleagues may have rejected his final recommendation. If the reporter feels very strongly about his dissenting views, he may request that the writing of the opinion be assigned to another Justice. This rarely happens, however, for the reporter is expected to express the general consensus of the *group*, although he may, and often does, take into account the minority views expressed in conference.

Once the opinion is drafted, it too is considered in conference, where it may undergo pruning, deletion, and amendment. Several Justices have talked of excruciating sessions in which an opinion is gone over line by line, until a satisfactory result is achieved. (In one case, a Justice reports, the Second Senate deliberated in this fashion for eight full days.) This was common operating procedure prior to the adoption and publication of dissenting opinions in 1971. While unanimity is still valued by the Justices, there is no longer any need to resort to such a cumbersome procedure for relieving stress growing out of the inability to dissent publicly.

Oral Argument and Other Processes

Oral argument does not play the important role in the proceedings of the Federal Constitutional Court as it does in the American Supreme Court. Up to July 27, 1971, only 151 cases had been decided after oral argument. This averages out to four such cases annually per senate. In its first four years, the Court decided one-third of its cases—that is, those which resulted in full opinions—after oral argument, but in recent years public hearings before the Constitutional Court have been rarely held, occurring no more than once or twice a year, and only in the most important cases. Oral argument may, of course, be waived if both the Court and the parties consent; they invariably do, often with the Court's encouragement.[17] Indeed, several Justices, including one presiding officer, frankly admitted to the writer that oral arguments are a waste of time, since in their view such arguments do not yield information not already in the printed record. The main function of oral argument, it seems, is not to refine legal issues, but to uncover additional facts that bear upon the issues. Oral arguments may also be used on occasion to add legitimacy to a proceeding by giving all sides, especially in disputes involving the highest organs of government, an opportunity to make their cases in an open forum.

In the two oral proceedings that the writer attended in 1968, it was interesting to observe that the reporter did most of the questioning, with the remaining Justices simply looking on, creating the impression that only the reporter had really done his homework. The proceedings strengthened the writer's impression that the Justices rely far more heavily on the expertise of their colleagues than they do on the arguments of counsel appearing before the Court.

A brief word might be said about the procedures of three-judge committees. How a committee proceeds depends on its members. Some committees meet once a month and consider as many as fifty to seventy constitutional complaints in a single sitting. The members of other committees do not meet at all. Rather, a Justice will circulate his memos on cases to his two colleagues, who simply check their approval or disapproval of his recommendation. Each Justice handles about fifteen complaints a month. He usually passes them on to his law clerk, who prepares a memorandum on each, concluding with his own recommendation on whether the complaint should be dismissed. The memorandum, which the Justice discusses with the clerk, often forms the basis of the "mini-votum"—usually no more than five pages—that is taken up in committee. Needless to say, nearly ninety-five percent of all complaints are unanimously rejected by the committees.

THE DYNAMICS OF
THE JUDICIAL PROCESS

So far we have recounted the basic steps and procedures involved in arriving at decisions within the Constitutional Court. We have stressed mainly the role of the individual Justice in this process, reserving until now a consideration of judicial relationships. Any attempt to describe these interrelationships poses two major difficulties, however. First, the researcher has no opportunity to observe or to participate in the Court's processes. Nor is he able to lean on judicial biography or memoirs—so valuable in studies of the American Supreme Court—for these are almost nonexistent in Germany. He must depend almost entirely on interviews and what the Justices themselves say about these processes and each other. Second, the researcher is dealing here with living Justices, who expect and insist that matters of a highly personal nature, which obviously affect patterns of influence inside the Court, be kept confidential. Still, these problems should not deter the political scientist from trying to open the secrets of an institution of public life so long as confidentiality is honored and the task compatible with discretion and good sense.

Judicial Roles, Norms, and Influence

The social structure of the Federal Constitutional Court cannot be plotted with any sociometric precision. But the Justices do see each other on a relatively frequent basis, formally each Tuesday in conference and informally at other times during the working week. The frequency of these informal contacts depends, of course, largely upon the personalities and work habits of the individual Justices. Some Justices are almost always in their offices available for consultation with aides and fellow Justices, while others are seldom to be found on the Court's premises.

One way of ordering the myriad activities occurring within the Constitutional Court is to consider the role orientations of the Justices. These role orientations are based in part on the allocation and specialization of work inside the Court. We have already noted that each Justice is very much his own boss up to the point where he is ready to submit a votum to the judgment of his colleagues. Most judge-time is actually spent in the preparation of these vota. Justices estimate that the preparation of vota consumes between fifty and sixty percent of their time; twenty-five percent of their time is spent going over the vota of other justices, and the remaining time is devoted to conferences and three-judge committee work. Justices ordinarily prepare vota in their areas of competence, one effect of which is to fling them into leadership roles in given spheres of constitutional law.

These areas of specialization are rather loosely defined, however. A Justice may spend most of his time on constitutional cases arising mainly out of criminal, labor, or administrative law, or he may receive all or most cases failing under given articles of the Basic Law. Justice Böhmer, for instance, is concerned largely with Article 14 (property rights) cases; Justice Geiger has become, over the years, the Court's expert in civil servant law, and receives most civil servant cases falling under the jurisdiction of the Second Senate, no matter what article of the Basic Law is involved; Justice Haager is the First Senate's expert on tax law; Justice Kutscher was the Second Senate's reporter in most cases involving international law. Not all Justices are wholly pleased with their roles on the Court. One Justice expressed disappointment over his selection to the First instead of the Second Senate, since the latter dealt with matters in which he had greater interest.

The fact that particular Justices do influence the growth of law in their areas of specialization was acknowledged recently by West Germany's Federal President Gustav Heinemann. On December 8, 1971, at a formal gathering in honor of several retiring Justices, President Heinemann said of Justice Stein: "You should be singled out Herr Stein, for your work in clarifying the constitutional relationship between church and state. Also, as your colleagues have assured me, no other Justice has done more than you in defining the meaning of basic rights in cultural areas."[18] (Stein was Hesse's Minister of Culture prior to his appointment to the Constitutional Court in 1951 and indeed did have a life-long interest in church-state questions.) Germans generally, and apparently also the Justices, defer to such learning and expertise. Leibholz, on the other hand, has been absorbed with the subject of political parties and political representation since the early 1930s. Heinemann remarked: "You, too, Herr Leibholz, need to be mentioned, not only for your elucidation of the special significance and place of the Federal Constitutional Court within the framework of our state, but also for your great influence upon the development of the rights of political parties."[19] Years earlier, Justice Kutscher also had noted publicly that Leibholz was largely responsible for shaping the Court's views toward the principle of equality as applied to political parties and elections.[20]

How the Justices perceive their own roles on the Court was revealed in interviews. Some are judicial activists who consciously work toward the implementation of policy goals in certain areas of constitutional law. For example, one Justice is dedicated to ridding the penal code of provisions that punish behavior falling into what he regards as private morality. Another is personally committed to watching over the rights of women and illegitimate children; when the opportunity presents itself, he seeks to invalidate discriminatory provisions in the civil code against these groups. During his long tenure on the Court, Justice Leibholz gave his undivided attention to cases involving political parties and election law, as noted by President Heinemann, fields in which he holds strong and well-developed views. According to some of his colleagues, he never dissipated his energies by embroiling himself in a multitude of issues; nor did he "fight for small things."

Rather, he chose a single major target and chose to rivet his attention on those cases which offered him the best opportunity to further his policy objectives. This is not to say that his constitutional views on political parties and the electoral process always prevailed; they did not. Nevertheless, as Justice Kutscher suggested, Leibholz's workmanship is clearly evident in many of the Court's decisions interpreting Article 21 of the Basic Law.

The judicial activists also include Justices who perceive their role as one of protecting the political system as a whole. Justice Leibholz, ideologically committed to the *Parteienstaat*, clearly falls into this category. Some Justices perceive themselves as defenders of the federal system; others feel obligated to maintain a regime of individual liberty in West Germany. All these Justices see the Court as a powerful moving force in the society and are acutely aware of the Court's political role in the Federal Republic. Both liberal and conservative Justices are among those who bluntly subscribe to an extremely activist role for the Court. Said one Justice: "The Court's function is to direct the general trend of the political system." Said another: "The Court must always step in to maintain the continuance of the basic democratic order." Said a third: "When Parliament fails to meet its reponsibilities in certain areas of public life the Court must fill the gap."

Yet, while acknowledging the Court's important political role, the Justices do not concede that they are political decision-makers. They take pains to differentiate between the Court's decisions, which they regard as the product of objective constitutional interpretation, and the effects of those decisions, which are admittedly political. To their minds, the purpose of the Constitutional Court is to bring public law and the behavior of public officials into conformity with the Basic Law. The process of constitutional interpretation, in their view, is not a matter of translating personal values into constitutional law, although many do admit that an element of personal judgment is frequently involved in this process.

Other Justices, who might be described as judicial passivists or neutralists, do not appear to have strong policy views. At the same time, these Justices are extremely solicitous about arriving at the "right" decision. The neutralist is frequently a broker between contesting "blocs" on the Court. He wishes primarily to reach a decision which will command wide agreement among his colleagues and is willing to suppress his own personal views to achieve such a result. Yet this attempt to place the Justices in neat, mutually exclusive categories based on their responses to the writer's queries is not an adequate summary of their roles on the Court. The Justices themselves would regard any such classification as an oversimplification of the judicial process. Indeed, they themselves are aware that their roles or contributions to the total process of decision-making are varying and sometimes subtle. They are also aware that judicial roles change from issue to issue and even at different stages of the decisional process in which a single case is being decided. Finally, they are aware that institutional values and structural variables intrude to limit and circumscribe the roles of individual Justices.

In the group phase of the decisional process, it is of interest to note how often even some of the more policy-oriented Justices would speak of the necessity to produce the "right" decision. Many of them seem to think that unanimous decisions possess this character. Some Justices even suggested that if the Court is still seriously divided at the moment of final decision, something must be wrong somewhere. Moreover, a "right" decision is not to be understood as a paring down of intracourt divisions to the lowest common denominator of agreement. One senses a belief on the part of the Justices that the only solvent for disagreement is argumentation and dialogue, and that in the course of conference proceedings a "right" answer, satisfying the claims of both political prudence and legal logic, will emerge to win the consent of all but the most recalcitrant. At the group stage, the process of decision-making is one that inches along by discussion and consensus, without the intrusion of multiple dissents or dissensus-creating formal vote-taking. For this reason, "dissenting" Justices often minimize friction by yielding to the views of the majority in the interest of preserving the appearance, at least, of unanimity, a factor that many Justices, the neutralists above all, continue to regard as a major foundation of the Court's authority. On the other hand, the right to dissent is respected—and most Justices clearly favor it—but most also believe that its use should be restricted to matters about which a Justice feels most deeply.

In arriving at their decisions, the Justices are not bound by some of the norms that govern decision-making in the U.S. Supreme Court. For instance, the German Justices are not at all bound by the rule of *stare decisis*. Often they do follow their own precedents and cite previous cases in their decisions, but they would never adhere to a ruling merely because of an earlier decision. The rule of precedent is simply not compatible with the teleological approach to judicial decision-making that prevails in German courts. The job of constitutional interpretation is to clarify the broad purposes of the Basic Law, and this is done mainly by examining the literal language of the *code constitutional*. Thus, constitutional interpretation is a process that looks forward to discovery—of "truth" and the "right" decision—and not backward to previous cases. It is for this reason, too, that German Justices do not rely as much as American Justices on the framers' intent, despite the fact that the Basic Law is only twenty-five years old and the conditions of its historical origin wholly within the personal memory of all the Justices.

Let us turn now to some of the dimensions of personal influence on the Constitutional Court. Insight into this problem is afforded by the Justices' willingness to talk freely about the values and characteristics that they esteem in a Constitutional Court Justice. Five characteristics were most frequently mentioned. First, and most importantly, a Justice should be competent. He should be on top of his specialized areas of law. He should be able to write a well-researched, well-organized, well-argued votum. Second, a Justice should be forthright, clear, and firm in his views, and any Justice with character should be willing to fight for them. Justices obviously need time for thought and reflection, but the constant hedger is regarded as a person lacking self-confidence. Third, and at the same time, a Justice should be willing to listen to alternative points of view. He should be open to new ideas. In short, strong convictions should not be confused with stubbornness or an unwillingness to compromise. Fourth, a Justice should be reliable. He should do his homework and come to conference fully prepared to deliberate and, above all, to present and defend his own votum. Finally a justice should have a political sense. He should be able to appreciate the realities behind a case and the political effects that a decision is likely to generate.

As might be expected, there was disagreement over how much judicial experience a Justice should have prior to coming on the Court. One sitting Justice candidly remarked: "The qualifications of the members of this Court have dropped measurably when compared to the original appointees." This Justice spent most of his career in the judiciary and was obviously upset by what he regarded as the declining quality of the Court's decisions, which he attributed to an increasing tendency to recruit Justices from among civil servants and politicians outside the judiciary. A contrary view was expressed by another Justice, who observed: "The judicial technician is the last person we need on this Court. A justice must have broad knowledge, intellectual humility, and a feeling for political trends and questions." In the same vein, another Justice noted: "I am not impressed with great legal learning. It is better to decide cases on practical grounds." Still, we should not exaggerate the differences between the "judicial technician" and the "judicial statesman." Almost invariably, the statesmen are men who also appreciate the value of a good argument while the technicians are not unmindful of the political implications of judicial decisions. It is largely a matter of temperament and orientation. There is no reason for believing that the technician is any more influential than the statesman.

There is a wide range of individual styles or types found at the group level of the judicial process. These types are suggestive of the kind of structural role orientations which exist within the Court, and we might identify them by what the Justices themselves had to say about some of their colleagues:

Type A: "He is very able and businesslike. When he summarizes his votum, that is that. He doesn't get excited, he doesn't argue, and he accepts the results stoically, as a good Justice should."

Type B: "He is extremely able in debate, very logical, but very legalistic and a stickler on procedure."

Type C: "He is a fighter, has good juristic qualities, and is very precise."

Type D: "He always gives lengthy performances. He is extremely thorough and competent, but has a tendency to explore every aspect of a case."

Type E: "The only thing that interests him is getting a result and getting it as soon as possible."

Type F: "His style is baroque. He is the Court's most politically conscious Justice. He always keeps in the forefront of his mind the political background to a case."

Type G: "He started out not knowing what to do, but has developed himself, and now has a good sense of what is required."

Type H: "He is not a hard man and is very easy to get along with."

Whatever their impression of the workmanship of colleagues, the Justices manifested an interesting kind of subinstitutional loyalty toward their immediate working group. For instance, the Justices frequently drew distinctions between the First and Second Senates, making more favorable judgments about the unit to which they belonged. One member of the First Senate criticized the Second for its internal divisions, remarking with satisfaction that such cleavages had not occurred in the First. On the other hand, a Justice of the Second Senate felt that there was less dissensus among his colleagues than among the Justices of the First Senate. Another Justice of the First Senate ranked the quality of his unit's decisions higher than those of the Second. In short, the Justices were very conscious of their group identity.

In discussing the group context of judicial decisions, we should not lose sight of the leadership roles played by the presiding officers. We shall confine our remarks here to Höpker-Aschoff, Wintrich, and Katz, all of whom are deceased. We know virtually nothing, of course, about task leadership on the Federal Constitutional Court. Interviews with Justices who remember the workways—and influence —of these presiding officers are our only source of information about this elusive subject. Formally, as with the American Supreme Court, the "Chief Justice" or presiding officer of each senate is *primus inter pares*, but in actuality he is in a position to exercise decisive control over the outcome of cases. This process is extremely difficult to explain, for the influence of a presiding officer seems not to be achieved by dictation or even by maneuver, but by the force of character and personality. Doubtless, the conference role of the presiding officer is critical. Indeed, in a situation where the object is to produce, as far as possible, a group decision, his role is probably more critical than that of a Chief Justice presiding over a tribunal less concerned with unanimity.

Be that as it may, the Justices clearly value leadership on the part of the presiding officers. What is more, they themselves distinguish between strong leadership and weak leadership. And what is so helpful to this analysis is that the Justices, in recalling their experiences, were virtually unanimous in their assessment of the three "chiefs." Höpker-Aschoff and Katz were uniformly regarded as effective leaders, while Wintrich was uniformly considered to be ineffective. Yet, the styles and personalities of the three men were profoundly different.

According to many Justices, the main function of a presiding officer is to find that area of common agreement so necessary for an institutional decision. Höpker-Aschoff is said to have been a genius in forging such agreements. He took charge of conference discussions, yet did not force his views on anyone. Indeed, he is said to have respected opposition and to have given his opinion last. "He knew how to handle people," said a former Justice. Another Justice of the First Senate, who served with three presidents, said that Höpker-Aschoff was seldom overruled, in contrast to later presidents. He is not remembered as a great legal mind, but as a generous and reasonable person who treated his colleagues fairly. Several Justices spoke of his liberality. Yet he was reserved and very much an authority figure, for his life was a bridge that linked Germany's past, beginning with the monarchy, to the present. One Justice described him as "elegant," going on to remark that he was the only president graced with a dignity which prompted his colleagues to rise whenever he entered the conference room.

Katz, vice president from 1951 to 1961, was also an effective leader. A person of considerable warmth, he appears to have had a close personal relationship to many of the Justices on the Second Senate. At the same time he was an adroit tactician. He would make an effort, inside and outside conference, to round up a majority in the interest of the view that he represented. Yet, prior to decision, he would allow conference discussions to run their course, without too much interference from the chair. He held strong views on constitutional policy, but is said to have accepted defeat gracefully. One receives the impression that Katz had a tougher time reaching unanimity than

Höpker-Aschoff, which was probably owing not only to his policy interests, but also to the rugged independence of many of the men who served with him on the Second Senate.

Wintrich, on the other hand, was considered to be a weak president even by close friends who shared his views and others who admired his intellectual brilliance. Unlike Höpker-Aschoff and Katz, he was philosophical and reflective. Though a "disciple of the Jesuits," as one Justice referred to him, he appears to have changed his mind frequently, moving from one side of an issue to the other depending, as another Justice remarked, on whom he had spoken to last. He appears to have exasperated his colleagues by his lack of forcefulness in conference, for he was burdened by a scrupulous conscience and worried incessantly. He is said to have been frequently overruled in conference. But his leadership really collapsed at the point where it was most needed—namely, in those highly charged cases where the Court was internally divided and subject to outside political pressures. Wintrich seemed unable to cope with these divisions and pressures. The most notable example of such a case was the Adenauer government's petition for a ban on the Communist Party. The subsequent tale of Wintrich's woe possesses the elements of human tragedy. Wintrich was convinced that the government had erred politically in bringing the case in the first place. The case dragged on for nearly two years, not only because of the President's inability to extract a decision out of a divided senate, but also because of his own reluctance to decide, firmly, one way or another.

Wintrich himself is even reported to have personally pleaded with Adenauer to withdraw the case.[21] In addition, the outside pressure on the Court was tremendous. The First Senate was continually in the limelight, and Wintrich disliked the publicity attendant upon the Communist Party Case. Government spokesmen chided the Court for its procrastination. The First Senate, still regarded as a "red" body, was under particular pressure because of a proposal in Bonn to shift jurisdiction over all Article 21 cases (political parties) to the Second Senate, where the government expected less resistance. Pressure from Parliament and the Chancellor's refusal to withdraw the petition for a ban on the Communist Party simply prolonged Wintrich's suffering, which was now aggravated by failing health. The Court did finally ban the Communist Party in 1956, and shortly afterward Parliament also shifted Article 21 cases to the Second Senate. Two Justices who participated in the Communist Party Case remain firm in their personal opinion that the entire episode brought about the illness which culminated in Wintrich's death in 1958; one remarked that "the case almost killed him."

We have recorded the impressions of several Justices about three persons who served in formal positions of leadership on the Federal Constitutional Court. These impressions do not, of course, add up to a definition of leadership. Indeed, leadership means different things to different Justices. In their reference to presidents and vice presidents, many Justices seem to identify leadership with effective chairmanship. Katz and Höpker-Aschoff were obviously effective chairmen. Wintrich was not. A few Justices were also aware of a second and more important dimension of leadership—namely, the ability of a presiding Justice to marshall the group behind a policy favored by him or, alternatively, to produce decisions that represent genuine group consensus. Anyone familiar with small group behavior knows, of course, that leadership is not always to be identified with formal positions of power. Leadership is fundamentally a relation between individuals and, what is more, such relations change from issue to issue. We shall discuss some of these relationships in the next section.

Judicial Politics and Strategy

Inside the Court: In considering the dynamics of decision-making inside the Federal Constitutional Court, we might employ the approach used by Walter F. Murphy in his study of the U.S. Supreme Court. In *Elements of Judicial Strategy*, Murphy looked at the judicial process in terms of what the Justices would be *capable* of doing if they wanted to maximize their influence and incorporate their views on constitutional policy into Supreme Court decisions.[22] This is a useful approach so long as the imagination is securely reined and informed by a genuine sense of what is really possible. Murphy's diggings into the memoirs and papers of former Justices gave him an empirical basis for discussing individual strategies and tactics within the Supreme Court. Interview data and newspaper reportage provide a similar basis of discussion here.

Influence on the Federal Constitutional Court begins at the point of case distribution. We noted earlier that many cases are not divided randomly among the Justices, but are assigned to them by the presiding officer on the basis of their specializations. But, as we also noted, these specializations are loosely defined, the result being that Justices often work in overlapping areas. At the outset, the tactical advantage is with the president or vice president, for he has some leeway in deciding which Justices receive what cases. If he is personally interested in the outcome of a case, he might assign it to a Justice whose policy views correspond to his own, to a Justice whose judgment he is confident he can influence, or, as a last resort, he may assign the case to himself.

The assignment process is extremely important because of the role of the reporter. His influence over the outcome of a case is potentially very substantial. He is the Court's expert in the case, for he may have spent weeks or even months in preparing the votum. Only a limited amount of time is available to examine the vota of other Justices. Indeed, as one Justice remarked, many a Justice short on time has occasionally gone to conference having had little more than a cursory glance at a colleague's votum. Thus, there is a tendency to defer to the reporter's judgment and expertise. In this connection, it is noteworthy to observe that the reporter's recommendation is carried, according to the estimates of most Justices, in seventy to eighty percent of all cases, and in a large percentage of these the reporter receives unanimous backing.

Still, as these figures indicate, vota are not automatically accepted. There is strong feeling on the Court that a reporter must justify the support of his colleagues and *win* their consent. Vice President Seuffert remarked in an interview that "it is the responsibility of the individual Justice to find his own majority." Other Justices, too, in talking about the reporter's function, often spoke of his responsibility to "find" a broad basis of agreement. One of the best ways of doing this, the Justices insist, is to produce a votum that is well researched and one that convinces. Said a Justice simply: "A good votum influences, a bad one does not."

An example of such influence was Justice Kutscher's votum in the Alien Tax Case, discussed earlier in this chapter. The votum was dated April 10, 1968. The opinion of the Court, also written by Kutscher, was handed down on May 14, 1968.[23] The rapidity with which the official opinion followed the votum seems to have been a mark of the Court's confidence in Justice Kutscher. It is to be noted also that the substance and organization of the opinion did not deviate substantially from the votum. In brief, Justice Kutscher *won* the support of his colleagues, easily it seems, although a succinct note at the end of the opinion revealed that two Justices voted against the result.

Other Justices do not enjoy such confidence. According to several members of the Court, some reporters are very frequently reversed, and their vota almost never accepted as written. In these situations, judicial opinion writing can become a long drawn out process. Not all Justices are equally skilled in writing vota. Not all are equally deft in debate. Some may enter the conference room ill-prepared to defend a votum. "He never gets his work done," said one Justice about a colleague. For most Justices, the conference is the moment of truth. If a Justice lacks confidence in himself, is ill prepared, or is wanting in intellectual capacity, it will show in conference, the consequence being a likely loss of influence.

Yet ability alone does not dictate outcomes in small group decision-making. Personal characteristics such as likability and willingness to compromise are also extremely important. The Justice who initiates consultation with his brothers prior to conference is likely to have more success in getting his votum accepted than the Justice who does not. Justice Kutscher remarked that he had conferred with colleagues in preparing the votum on the Alien Tax Case; in so doing, he may have helped his case. By the same token, a Justice interested in a votum other than his own might himself initiate contact with the reporter for purposes of discussion and negotiation.

Once the votum is printed and distributed, the reporter often receives further feedback from interested Justices. This process of communication is wholly informal and very subtle, but it gives the reporter a good reading of his colleagues' views, and at this stage he may be prepared to entertain further suggestions about the contents of a case. The Justices were not very clear in describing the pre-conference phase of the judicial process, but it seems clear that Justices do have some opportunity at this stage to strike bargains and lobby for given policies.

A reporter does not necessarily lose his influence over a case should he find himself in the minority, for he still has the task of writing the Court's opinion. If he combines political sagacity with a deft literary hand, he is likely to leave his imprint on the finished opinion. He cannot, of course, change the result of a case, but he might find a way of bootlegging his policy views into the body of the opinion. At the same time, the reporter may be "pressured" into considering other minority views. A Justice in the minority whose views are ignored might threaten to write a "dissenting opinion" and circulate it privately among his colleagues, which was permissible prior to the formal adoption of dissenting opinions in 1970. But dissents were rarely written and used only as a last resort in cases involving deep personal convictions. One Justice of the Second Senate estimated that since 1958 no more than five or six such "dissents" had been written, underscoring again the importance attached to consensus decision-making.

The consensus approach often led to frustration, however. The Federal Constitutional Court is made up of personalities no less vibrant and independent than Justices of the U.S. Supreme Court, and it is difficult for many of the Justices to submerge themselves in an institutional opinion. A clear majority of the Justices whom the writer interviewed in 1968 were in favor of personalized dissenting opinions; many formerly had been opposed to published dissents, but had changed their minds as a result of their experience on the Constitutional Court. Nevertheless, the formal adoption of dissenting opinions was delayed until December 1970, mainly because President Müller was opposed to published dissents and because many Justices felt that the authority to dissent should come from the legislature.

Only twice since 1951 did cracks appear in the Court's blissful façade of internal unity, once in 1952 and then again in 1966. The first rupture occurred when Social Democratic legislators petitioned the Court for an advisory opinion on the constitutionality of the European Defense Community Treaty. Under law, only the Plenum could issue advisory opinions, but would such an opinion bind the senates? In a twenty to two decision, the first time any judicial vote had been recorded, the Plenum ruled that its advisory opinions are binding on the senates in any subsequent case that might involve identical or similar issues.[24] Justice Willi Geiger, to the dismay of his colleagues, made public his dissent, causing a jar within the German legal profession.[25] The second rupture occurred in the Spiegel Seizure Case, where the issue was freedom of the press versus the state's interest in military security. Here the Court was evenly divided (four to four). The effect of this decision was to uphold the government. But the official decision was the first in the Court's history to include the "minority" opinion, although the identity of the dissenting Justices was not disclosed.[26] The case reflected not only a deep ideological rift within the First Senate, but also mounting pressure from the Justices to publish dissenting along with majority opinions.

A few months after the Spiegel decision, the Second Senate began the practice of disclosing the vote in each case. Though dissenting Justices were still not identified, the vote disclosure uncovered a substantial measure of disagreement, at least among the Justices of the Second Senate. In the 147 cases in which the judicial vote was disclosed—stretching from May 2, 1967, to December 2, 1970—the Second Senate was divided in 45 of them. In many cases, however, these were partial dissents. In 3 cases, separate votes were taken on numerous points of law. Table 13 presents the alignments and their frequencies in the 42 remaining cases where dissents were either partial or total. Disclosure of alignment in these cases was a monumental departure from German tradition and also the cause of considerable disagreement within the Court, for the practice was not followed by the First Senate. Indeed, some First Senate Justices, including the president, doubted the legality of the Second Senate's disclosure of the judicial vote.

At any rate, the above figures contrast sharply with dissent patterns subsequent to the formal adoption, on December 13, 1970, of personalized dissenting opinions. From that date until November 27, 1973, the two senates decided exactly 200 cases with full opinion.[27] The Court was divided in only twenty (or ten percent) of them. But the

TABLE 13

VOTING ALIGNMENTS IN THE SECOND SENATE FROM
MAY 2, 1967 TO DECEMBER 12, 1970
(non-unanimous decisions)

Alignment	Number of Cases
7-1	6
6-1	4
6-2	13
5-3	9
5-2	4
4-3	5
4-2	1

SOURCE: *Entscheidungen des Bundesverfassungsgerichts* (Tübingen: J.C.B. Mohr
[Paul Siebeck]; 1967-1971), vols. 21-29.

pattern of cleavage is interesting, for the tendency to dissent was much
more pronounced in the Second than in the First Senate. Of the 200
cases, the Second Senate decided 108, with dissents in 17, while the
First Senate decided 88, with dissents in 3. In all, there were 25
dissenting opinions, 4 in the First Senate, 21 in the Second. Of the
First Senate's 3 dissenting opinions Justice v. Brünneck authored 2
lone dissents, Justice Stein a single lone dissent, while Justices v.
Brünneck and Simon joined in a dissent. The low incidence of dissent
in the First Senate has continued under the presidency of Ernst Benda.
Justices on the First Senate are obviously extremely judicious in their
choice of cases on which to dissent. Each of the 3 cases in which
dissents were written is enormously important. Two were free speech
cases (the Mephisto Case and the Film Censorship Case) while the
third involved an individual war claim arising out of Nazi
persecution.[28] In all three cases the dissenting opinions were in favor
of the individual.

The voting behavior of the Second Senate commands greater
attention because of the frequency of dissents there. From December
15, 1970, to November 15, 1971, prior to the departure of Leibholz
and Geller, the following patterns of Justices in dissent appeared in
the official records:

Geller-Rupp	Geiger-Rinck-Leibholz
Geller-Rupp	Leibholz-Rinck-Schlabrendorf
Geller-Rupp-Schlabrendorf	Leibholz-Rinck-Seuffert
Geller-Rupp-Wand	Geiger
Geller-Rupp-Wand	Seuffert
Geller-Wand	Seuffert
Wand-Rinck-Geiger	Seuffert
	Seuffert

The eleven cases in which these fifteen dissents were written are a mixed group; only four of the eleven deal with basic liberties and two of these were conflicts between states and the federal government over legal controls on radio and television stations. The remaining cases deal largely with unrelated subjects.[29] Hence, it is much too early to identify, by the use of judicial dissents, "ideological" divisions on the Second Senate. The identification of any such division would be difficult even with a larger sample of dissenting opinions. For one thing, unless a Justice writes a lone dissent there is no way of telling which Justice is the main author of a dissent. For another, the recorded vote in a case does not always correspond to the number of Justices joining in a dissenting opinion. For example, in the Religious Oath Case, the vote was five to two in favor of the individual's claim to religious liberty, but Justice Schlabrendorf dissented alone.[30] The First Senate, incidentally, continues, under President Benda, its previous practice of not revealing even the judicial vote; its published dissents are, therefore, even less representative of its internal divisions.

It is of interest to note that the Justices of the Second Senate have written fewer dissents since the departure of Leibholz and Geller, who, as we have seen, were replaced by Rottmann and Hirsch. From December 8, 1971—when Rottmann and Hirsch donned their red robes—through November 27, 1973, the Second Senate handed down full opinions in sixty-four cases; in only six, or eight percent, of the cases did Justices write dissenting opinions.[31] By contrast, there were dissenting opinions in twenty-seven percent of the cases decided by the Second Senate when Leibholz and Geller were present. Moreover, two of the six cases where dissents appeared were highly unusual, in that the issue was whether Justice Rottmann should be excluded from participation in the Intra-German Basic Treaty Case because of bias. In Exclusion Case I, which ruled in favor of the Justice, a dissenting opinion was written by Justice Wand.[32] In Exclusion Case II, which reversed the earlier decision and excluded the Justice, Seuffert, Rupp, and Hirsch—all Social Democrats— dissented.[33] (The Rottmann Exclusion Cases are discussed at length in Chapter 7.)

It is clear that the Justices are exercising their new freedom to dissent with considerable restraint. On the Second Senate, the published dissent is becoming increasingly the exception. A lingering bias against dissenting opinions is probably operating here to limit the range of judicial independence. The feeling is still predominant among the Justices that a judicial dissent is a serious matter to be undertaken only in serious situations.

We conclude this section with a few words about the interplay between the two senates. Although the senates are, for all practical purposes, independent tribunals there have been situations of conflict between them. Cases related to conscientious objection to military service are an illustration of how policy conflicts between the senates may occur. The First Senate's jurisdiction extends to all cases involving basic substantive liberties, including claims to conscientious objection. Most of these cases involve members of the Jehovah's Witnesses, who refuse to perform the substitute service required of all conscientious objectors. The First Senate has dealt harshly with these claimants. In 1965, the First Senate upheld the constitutionality of substitute service and, in 1968, it sustained a prison sentence against a person refusing to perform such service.[34] In a subsequent case, a three-judge committee of the First Senate dismissed a complaint by a person convicted several times for refusing alternative service. The dismissal became the initial point of conflict between the senates, for a multiple conviction case was also before the Second Senate. Here, however, a procedural right was being claimed, which is the province of the Second Senate. Could the Second Senate override a decision of a three-judge committee of the First Senate? Under the Constitutional Court Act, a senate wishing to depart from a ruling of the other must submit the matter to the Plenum for decision. The Second Senate did not do so. On March 7, 1968, just two days after the First Senate affirmed the prison sentence just mentioned, the Second Senate invalidated by a five to two vote multiple convictions in nine different cases. These convictions, said the Second Senate, violated Article 103, paragraph 3 of the Basic Law. The Court also ruled that its decision did not conflict with the jurisprudence of the First Senate, maintaining that the rule requiring an appeal to the Plenum in the event that one senate wishes to depart from a ruling of the other applies only to full senate decisions.[35]

In subsequent cases on conscientious objection, dissenting Justices in the Second Senate tried to employ a decision of the First Senate to force an issue into the Plenum as a strategy for achieving their policy goal. On May 26, 1970, the First Senate upheld successive punishments for repeated refusals of a soldier to perform military duties, holding that the penalties in question violated neither Article 103 nor the principle of *Rechtsstaat*.[36] The First Senate distinguished this case from the multiple conviction case of the Second Senate by noting that double jeopardy was not involved; here punishment was imposed not to atone for a crime, but rather to maintain military discipline. A year later, the Second Senate had a chance to modify this decision, at least insofar as certain procedural questions were concerned. Surprisingly, however, Justices Seuffert, Rupp, and Geller dissented in a case which they felt actually narrowed the rights of conscientious objectors even further. These Justices now claimed that the Second Senate was departing from a legal rule laid down by the First Senate—namely, that disciplinary measures may not be imposed on a soldier after his application for conscientious objection is approved, even though he is being disciplined for refusal to perform military service prior to such approval—and claimed that the issue should be settled by the Plenum. The majority, however, regarded this "rule" as *obiter dicta*, a strategy which did not call for submission of the case to the Plenum, which may have changed the result.[37]

Outside the Court: A Justice whose strategy inside the Court fails has a recourse other than the writing of a formal dissenting opinion. He may resort to an "outside strategy" by taking his case into another forum. He may not, of course, reveal anything about the nature of the

Court's deliberations; he most certainly would invite the wrath and censure of his colleagues were he ever to question the motives of the Court as a whole or publicly disclose his disagreement with a colleague, mentioning him by name. But no rule of propriety bars a Justice from giving vent to his views on constitutional questions in books, articles, or public lectures. The Justices do so frequently and some have done so even in pending cases.

The special role of law commentators in Germany, along with the German practice of not adhering to the rule of *stare decisis*, make the articulation of off-the-bench opinions a feasible strategy. A decision of the Federal Constitutional Court settles a constitutional dispute and has, in addition, the force of general law. But such a decision is not always regarded, in the legal academic community at least, as the most authoritative interpretation of the Basic Law. Constitutional exegesis in Germany is carried out in an open market of scholarly activity. The market is supplied mainly with the ideas and theories of textwriters, professors of public law, and other experts. Justices of course can get into the act by expressing their off-the-bench opinions. What needs to be underscored here is that Federal Constitutional Court decisions are but one source of opinions struggling for supremacy in the marketplace. The opinion that rules the market (*die herrschende Meinung*) may or may not accord with the Federal Constitutional Court opinion. Indeed a Justice's "dissenting" opinion expressed in an off-the-bench commentary may enjoy greater market value or authoritative regard than the Court's official view. Because of the importance of this market in the German system of constitutional interpretation, lawyers filing briefs with the Constitutional Court are as apt to cite the opinion of an expert authority as one of the Court's own prior decisions. Equally striking, especially for a positivistic legal culture, is the Constitutional Court's own willingness to use outside sources in arriving at decisions and often to treat them with the same respect it shows for its own decisions.

The point to be made here is that a Justice with an ax to grind may make a measurable contribution to this literature and thereby influence the market of ideas on constitutional issues. A bibliographical check of the Justices' off-the-bench work during and after their terms of office discloses a staggering amount of intellectual labor—approximately 382 speeches, articles, and monographs on West German constitutional matters.[38] Most of these speeches and publications were not, of course, occasioned by judicial defeats inside the Court. Indeed, many of them sought to correct misunderstandings or misinterpretations of the Court's decisions, which is simply a confirmation of the proposition that the Justices have a felt need to involve themselves in the ongoing competition of the market.

Strategy designed to influence the market in any event is necessarily long-range. It does not yield, as inside strategy may, an immediate payoff. Like inside dissents, off-the-bench opinions are calculated to influence public opinion and to generate support among critical elite groups. Such utterances are important because they furnish the basis for further inputs into the Court. In time, given a change in the climate of opinion or in the Court's personnel, "dissenting" views may win majority support inside the Constitutional Court.

But outside strategy involves risks. This was no more clearly illustrated than in the cases of Justices Leibholz and Rottmann, both of whom were excluded by their colleagues from participation in critical cases because of their off-the-bench remarks. Justice Leibholz was excluded from Party Subvention Case II (1966). Since the Rottmann case is discussed in another context in Chapter 7, we will confine our remarks here mainly to the predicament of Justice Leibholz.

Leibholz has long been known for his espousal of the doctrine of the *Parteienstaat*.[39] Political parties, in his view, are the only really legitimate agencies of representation in a democracy; hence, they must be nurtured, protected, and, if necessary, publicly supported by the state, a view that some of Leibholz's Second Senate colleagues, who perceive parties mainly as voluntary associations of private citizens, have never wholly accepted. In 1965, a federal statute providing for the financial support of political parties represented in the national parliament, but excluding extraparliamentary parties, was challenged by the Socialist state of Hesse, together with the far-right National Democratic Party (NPD), before the Constitutional Court's Second Senate. While the case was pending, amid rumors that the Senate was deadlocked, Leibholz delivered a lecture at the University of Würzburg where he reiterated his well-known views on the

Parteienstaat. He described the plaintiffs in the Party Subvention Case as an "unholy alliance of liberals and anti-democrats" working against the party state, the implication being that liberals, besieged by their traditional distrust of the state, were inadvertently assisting anti-democratic parties, notably the NPD, by undermining Bonn's democracy, much as they had "conspired" to destroy the Weimar Republic.[40]

The remark cost Leibholz further participation in the case. The NPD formally moved to have Leibholz removed from the case for bias. If, after a challenge for bias, a Justice declines voluntarily to remove himself, the full Senate, in a separate proceeding and in the absence of the challenged Justice, must decide whether he is to be excluded. Leibholz, as expected, refused to remove himself, whereupon he was then excluded by a vote of his colleagues in what several observers construed as a power play inside the Court to ensure a decision against the general financing of political parties.

The Justices on the Second Senate emphatically denied, however, that Leibholz's exclusion was a result of power politics on the Court. Other observers were of the opinion that Leibholz's removal was based on the Justices' personal conviction that he was indeed biased and therefore incapable of rendering an impartial decision. Whatever the motives of the Justices themselves, the Leibholz Exclusion Case is clear enough about the Legal standard applied in the removal of the Justice. There the principal question was whether the NPD had a substantial reason for believing that Leibholz would not render an impartial judgment. It was the challenger's state of mind, not that of Leibholz or of the Court, which ostensibly governed the decision to exclude the Justice.[41]

Leibholz's removal clearly generated new risks for any justice expressing certain views off the bench. The case prompted a warm debate in Germany about the propriety of off-the-bench commentary on constitutional questions likely to come before the Court. The debate focused mainly on the Court's professorial contingent. Were Justices to be challenged for scholarly views put forth in their capacity as professors of law? Is university teaching compatible with a judgeship on the Federal Constitutional Court? The argument did not close until 1971 when, in an apparent rebuff of the majority in the

Leibholz case, Parliament amended the Constitutional Court Act by providing that "the expression of a scientific opinion about a question of law relevant to a proceeding [before the Constitutional Court] shall not constitute a ground for excluding a justice from participation in a case."[42]

In spite of the Leibholz Exclusion Case, there seemed to have been no noticeable decline in off-the-bench speeches on constitutional matters, although the Justices were probably more cautious in addressing themselves to issues broadly related to pending cases before the Court. The Rottmann Exclusion Cases show that a Justice must exercise caution both about the groups before which he speaks and about the statements he makes even in private letters. Rottmann spoke to a Free Democratic Party gathering in Karlsruhe about Berlin's international status when Bavaria's case against the validity of the Intra-German Basic Treaty was pending before the senate on which he was a member. Bavaria's motion for the removal of the Justice on the basis of his public remarks failed.[43] Bavaria moved for Rottmann's exclusion a second time after the contents of a letter in which he defended Brandt's Eastern policy were made public. For this indiscretion he was excluded from the case.[44] Whether Rottmann's removal will prompt Justices to cease talking in public about politically sensitive issues likely to come before the Court remains to be seen.

NOTES

1. See David Easton, *A Systems Analysis of Political Life* (New York: John Wiley, 1965), p. 59.

2. See Ferdinand A. Hermens, *The Representative Republic* (Notre Dame: University of Notre Dame Press, 1958), pp. 358-360.

3. Letter from Prof. Dr. Ulrich Scheuner, July 28, 1968.

4. Decision of May 4, 1955 (First Senate), BVerfGE 4: 157-169 (1956).

5. See Decisions of February 26, 1954 (First Senate), BVerfGE 3: 357 (1954); July 20, 1955 (First Senate), BVerfGE 4: 214 (1956); June 4, 1957 (Second Senate), BVerfGE 7: 29 (1958); and May 28, 1963 (Second Senate), BVerfGE 16: 188 (1964).

6. Decision of November 29, 1967 (First Senate), BVerfGE 22: 373 (1968).

7. BVerfGG, Sec. 93a.

8. Ibid., Sec. 93a (4).

9. Geschäftsübersicht des Bundesverfassungsgerichts für das Kalenderjahr 1971 (mimeographed).

10. It should be noted, however, that because of variations in the kinds of complaints filed with the Court each year, the senates have not shared this work evenly. In 1971, for example, 992 constitutional complaints were deposited in the Second Senate's docket, while only 461 went to the First Senate. However, when the First Senate added its pending complaints to those newly filed, the total was 897 in contrast to 1,192 in the Second Senate.

11. Geschäftsübersicht des Zweiten Senats des Bundesverfassungsgerichts für das Kalenderjahr 1971 (mimeographed).

12. Three-Judge Decision of March 16, 1960 (Second Senate), 2 BvR 253/60.

13. Gerhard Leibholz and Reinhard Rupprecht, *Bundesverfassungsgerichtsgesetz* (Cologne-Marienburg: Verlag Dr. Otto Schmidt KG, 1968), pp. 306-307.

14. BVerfGG, secs. 18, 19, 27, 30, 32.

15. Ibid., sec. 30.

16. Justice Hans Kutscher was kind enough to allow the writer to inspect the votum which he prepared in the Alien Tax Case.

17. In constitutional complaints against statutes, where state and federal ministers are afforded the opportunity to file a reply, the Constitutional Court may itself refuse to permit oral arguments if, in its view, no further enlightenment would be forthcoming.

18. *Das Bundesverfassungsgericht 8. Dezember 1971: Festakt* (Karlsruhe: Verlag C.F. Müller, 1972), p. 10.

19. Ibid.

20. Hans Kutscher, "The Role of the Bundesverfassungsgericht in Insuring Equality Under Law," *Jahrbuch des Oeffentlichen Rechts,* 9: 198-199 (1960).

21. In interviews with the writer, several of the Justices mentioned Wintrich's attempt personally to persuade Adenauer to withdraw the KPD case.

22. Walter F. Murphy, *Elements of Judicial Strategy* (Chicago: University of Chicago Press, 1964).

23. Alien Tax Case, Decision of May 14, 1968 (Second Senate), BVerfGE 23: 288 (1968).

24. Advisory Opinion Case, Decision of December 8, 1952 (Plenum),

●

BVerfGE 2: 79 (1953).

25. See *Der Kampf um den Wehrbeitrag* (Munich: ISAR Verlag, 1953), II: 822-828.

26. Spiegel Seizure Case, Decision of August 5, 1966 (First Senate), BVerfGE 20: 162, 223-238 (1967).

27. These 200 cases include all of the decisions in volumes 30 through 33 of the official German reports, together with all decisions handed down by the Court from July 19, 1972, through November 27, 1973.

28. See Decisions of February 24, 1971 (First Senate), BVerfGE 30: 173, 200-227 (1971); October 20, 1971 (First Senate), BVerfGE 32:111, 129-144 (1972); and April 25, 1972 (First Senate), BVerfGE 33: 52, 78-90 (1973).

29. See Decisions of December 15, 1970 (Second Senate), BVerfGE 30: 1, 33-47; January 26, 1971 (Second Senate), BVerfGE 30: 149, 157-164; January 27, 1971 (Second Senate), BVerfGE 30: 165, 169-170; March 10, 1971 (Second Senate), BVerfGE 30: 272, 289-291 (1971); May 4, 1971 (Second Senate), BVerfGE 31: 94, 100; July 27, 1971 (Second Senate), BVerfGE 31: 314, 334-357; July 27, 1971 (Second Senate), BVerfGE 31: 388, 391-392 (1972); October 12, 1971 (Second Senate), BVerfGE 32: 157, 170-173; November 4, 1971 (Second Senate), BVerfGE 32: 173, 188-195; and November 15, 1971 (Second Senate), BVerfGE 32: 199, 227-249 (1972).

30. Religious Oath Case, Decision of April 11, 1972 (Second Senate), BVerfGE 33: 23, 35-42 (1973).

31. Ibid. See also Decisions of February 28, 1973 (Second Senate), BVerfGE 34: 325 (1973); May 8, 1973 (Second Senate), BVerfGE 35: 41 (1974); May 29, 1973 (Second Senate), BVerfGE 35: 171 (1974); June 16, 1973 (Second Senate), BVerfGE 35: 246 (1974); and November 27, 1973 (Second Senate), BVerfGE 36: 174, 192 (1974).

32. Rottmann Exclusion Case I, Decision of May 29, 1973 (Second Senate), BVerfGE 35: 171 (1974).

33. Rottmann Exclusion Case II, Decision of June 16, 1973 (Second Senate), BVerfGE 35: 246 (1974).

34. First Substitute Service Case, Decision of October 4, 1965 (First Senate), BVerfGE 19: 175 (1966) and Second Substitute Service Case, Decision of March 5, 1968 (First Senate), BVerfGE 23: 127 (1968).

35. Third Substitute Service Case, Decision of March 7, 1968 (Second Senate), BVerfGE 23: 191 (1968).

36. Soldier Refusal Case, Decision of May 26, 1970 (First Senate), BVerfGE 28: 264 (1970).

37. Military Arrest Case, Decision of October 12, 1971 (Second Senate), BVerfGE 32: 40 (1972).

38. Most of the speeches, articles, and books of the Justices are listed in Josef Mackert and Franz Schneider, *Bibliographie zur Verfassungsgerichtsbarkeit des Bundes und der Lander* (Tübingen: J.C.B. Mohr [Paul Siebeck], 1971).

39. See Gerhard Leibholz, "Parteien und Wahlrecht in der modernen Demokratie" in *Parteien, Wahlrecht, Demokratie* (Cologne and Opladen: Westdeutscher Verlag, 1967), pp. 40-60. An excellent analysis of Leibholz's position is contained in Konrad Ammermüller, *Das Proportionalwahlverfahren im modernen Parteienstaat* (Doctoral Dissertation, University of Cologne, 1966), pp. 10-38.

40. See *Die Oeffentliche Verwaltung* 18: 806-808 (1965).

41. Leibholz Exclusion Case, Decision of March 3, 1966 (Second Senate), BVerfGE 20: 9 (1967).

42. BVerfGG, sec. 18 (3) (2).

43. Rottmann Exclusion Case I, Decision of May 29, 1972 (Second Senate), BVerfGE 35: 171 (1974).

44. Rottmann Exclusion Case II., Decision of June 16, 1973 (Second Senate), BVerfGE 35: 246 (1974).

6

POLICY

The Basic Law of the Federal Republic of Germany includes 151 articles nearly half of which have been the subject of authoritative interpretation by the Federal Constitutional Court. The Court's 1,151 published decisions appear in thirty-three volumes of *Entscheidungen des Bundesverfassungsgerichts*, representing what Justice Leibholz openly calls "the political law of the Constitution."[1] Clearly, we cannot consider this political law in its totality or even the doctrinal value of most of the Court's decisions. Instead, we shall describe briefly the main principles of constitutional interpretation developed by the Court and identify the subject areas of judicial review which have most engaged the Court's attention. Then, in the main body of the chapter, we shall trace developments in selected areas of constitutional policy. One purpose in reviewing these developments is to show how the Court has used principles of constitutional interpretation to determine policy. But the main purpose is to examine the Court's policy-making roles in certain areas of constitutional law. To simplify this task, we have organized our material around certain roles played by the Court in the German system. These roles may be designated as *protector* of individual rights, *umpire* of the federal system, *custodian* of party democracy, and *equalizer* of socio-economic opportunity.

It is of some interest to note that the Justices themselves, when interviewed, mentioned these roles most frequently in their own personal assessment of the Constitutional Court's significance. By no means, however, do these roles exhaust the political influence of the Federal Constitutional Court. Nor do we suggest, in giving them special attention here, that only the Court plays these roles or that it is even the most important public agency performing them. Rather, our task is the modest one of showing that the Court matters as a policy-making institution in the Federal Republic and that its activity should be appreciated for a fuller understanding of German politics.

JUDICIAL REVIEW:
AN INTRODUCTION

Principles of Interpretation

The Constitutional Court is the main fount of constitutional doctrine in the German Federal Republic. Unlike other judicial tribunals, it decides constitutional disputes and the constitutionality of laws.[2] Politically, the adjudication of constitutional disputes is a most delicate and sensitive task, requiring modes of interpretation or judicial approaches which differ from the process of decision in regular German law courts. Regular German courts, for example— like tribunals in most civil law systems—are not bound by the rule of precedent. But the Constitutional Court cannot so easily ignore its own precedents, even though formal legal theory says otherwise. For one thing, Constitutional Court decisions, unlike ordinary court rulings, have the effect of general law and bind all public officials and branches of government. It is also one of the purposes of a constitutional tribunal to ensure the continuity of fundamental rules governing a political system. Any dramatic shift in doctrine by such a tribunal would by definition amount to a constitutional revolution.

But a constitutional court is not likely to survive as an institution by engineering revolutions. It is more apt to maintain its authority by limiting its policial roles. Such limitations are often expressed by procedural rules or self-denying ordinances which form the basis for the development of a constitutional tradition at the same time as they aid the Court in coping with political reality.

Soon after its creation in 1951, the Federal Constitutional Court moved quickly to establish its authority. In its first major decision—the Southwest Case (1951)—the Court set forth in a lengthy opinion several fundamental principles of constitutional interpretation and even proceeded to specify the main constitutional principles on which the Federal Republic is based. Comparable to the American cases of *Marbury* v. *Madison* and *McCulloch* v. *Maryland*, the decision stands among the Court's most important statements of constitutional policy.[3] Five fundamental propositions appear in Southwest. First, the Federal Constitutional Court is absolutely supreme in the interpretation of the Basic Law. Second, the Court's function is to examine the legality or validity, not the wisdom, of public policy; the legislature has wide discretion to make policy under the Basic Law, yet the extent of that discretion, said the Court, is a constitutional question on which it reserves finality of decision. Third, constitutional provisions are to be interpreted not as independent rules standing alone but within the context of the Basic Law as a whole. No constitutional right, duty, or power is absolute; it is to be measured instead by competing rights and responsibilities under the Basic Law. Fourth, there are certain fundamental principles—such as democracy, federalism, and the rule of law—which can be deduced from the Basic Law as a whole and to which all other constitutional provisions are subordinate. Finally, certain higher law principles constitute standards against which positive law and the actions of public officials are to be reviewed. It might be mentioned in this connection that the Southwest Case was decided by the Second Senate, which included several Catholic jurists and several Justices who fled Hitler's Germany. The appeal to higher law principles signaled in any event a complete juridical break with the recent historical past. It reflected a judicial need to stand up squarely in support of a free society.[4]

Over the years, the Court moderated some of these principles, broadened others, and invented still others. For instance, not since the Southwest Case has the Court made a general reference to natural or higher law as a standard by which to determine constitutionality. Yet the Court has formulated certain "unwritten constitutional principles" believed to have their source in the organizing ideas which inspired the founding fathers and informed the deliberations of the parliamentary council, but not expressly put down in any specific constitutional provision. One of these is the principle of "federal comity" (*Bundestreue*), which the Court derives from the federal nature of the political system. In essence, it requires federal and state governments not only to observe the prescribed rules of the Basic Law governing their relationship, but also to exercise restraint and to give due regard to each other's interests in the planning and execution of policy.[5] The doctrine of *Parteienstaat* (party state) is another unwritten principle of the Basic Law. The *Parteienstaat*, in the Court's view, constitutionally requires a competitive party system as well as political parties organized effectively to represent the popular will.[6] Finally, the Court has postulated the existence of constitutional principles so fundamental to the political order that even the various provisions of the Basic Law are subordinate to them. Thus, even a constitutional amendment is subject theoretically to review on constitutional grounds if it offends or abrogates one of these principles, giving rise to the possibility of an "unconstitutional constitutional norm."[7]

Two other principles developed by the Court deserve attention. The first is the principle of the "social state" (*Sozialstaatsprinzip*) which the Court derives from Article 20 of the Basic Law, declaring West Germany to be "a democratic and social federal state." Under this principle, the state is bound by a rule of social responsibility; it cannot constitutionally ignore the demands of social justice when making làw.[8] Thus, the Court has bracketed the concept of *Sozialstaat* with that of *Rechtsstaat*, regarding both as linchpins of democratic constitutionalism in the Federal Republic. The second is the principle of proportionality (*Verhältnismässigkeitsgrundsatz*), a close German equivalent of the Anglo-American notion of due process of law. Implicit in the idea of *Rechtsstaat*, proportionality is a concept that requires a rational connection between ends and means; the punishment must fit the crime, and methods of governance generally must be reasonably related or proportionate to the objectives sought.[9]

Certain principles of human dignity, to which the Court incessantly refers in its decisions, need also to be mentioned here. If there are preferred provisions of the Basic Law, they most certainly would be Article 1 ("The dignity of man shall be inviolable. To respect and protect it shall be the duty of all state authority.") and Article 2 ("Everyone shall have the right to the free development of his personality insofar as he does not violate the rights of others or offend against the constitutional order or the moral code."). These articles are more than rhetorical exhortations; they are operative principles of German constitutional law, for they have been used on numerous occasions to strike down federal and state legislation.

A final word needs to be said about general theories of constitutional interpretation developed by the Court over the years. We have already made reference to the contextual theory or systematic method, as it is sometimes called, by which the Court derives the meaning of a constitutional norm from its relationship to other parts of the Basic Law. A second approach is the literal method, where the Court tries to assay, frequently at the outset of an inquiry, the plain meaning of the words used in the Constitution. A third approach is the historical method. Here the Court seeks to locate the meaning of constitutional provisions in the intent of the founding fathers. But the divining of historical intent rarely settles a constitutional dispute with finality. Like the literal method, historical intent is used mainly to support a rationale already developed by the contextual or, what is more likely, by the "teleological method," as the Germans call it. By the latter method, the Court seeks to specify the "telos," purpose, or function of certain rules laid down in the Basic Law. To the extent that purpose or function is found in the framers' intent, the technique is not wholly distinguishable from the historical method. To the extent that it is found by looking at the Constitution as a whole it is not wholly distinguishable from the contextual method. More often the "telos" of the Constitution is determined by asking what is the *present* purpose or meaning of a rule, a rather circuitous way of saying that the Basic Law must be interpreted in light of changing social conditions.[10]

These broad methods of constitutional interpretation obviously leave much room for judicial maneuver. Like the unwritten constitutional principles, they can be used to enlarge the Court's freedom of action or to contract it. Few constitutional norms are the subject of invariant application through time. Already it is possible roughly to divide the Court's brief history into three periods on the basis of its approach to constitutional interpretation. During its early years, from 1951 to about 1957, the Court followed a policy of judicial restraint, dictated in part by political realities. The Court sought mainly to define and to consolidate its own authority rather than to challenge the authority of other branches of government. After 1957, the Court moved into a period of judicial activism and experimentation which lasted into the mid-1960s. Since about 1968, while certainly not reverting to the caution of its early years, the Court has been less innovative than in the middle years, manifesting a greater tendency than before to sustain governmental policy; moreover, during this time, the Court has been extremely pragmatic and interest-balancing in its approach to constitutional questions. It might be noted that some measure of empirical support for dividing the Court's history into these time periods is supplied by the data presented in Table 14. Still, we must bear in mind that these periods do not represent sharp divisions in time or clearly distinguishable styles of judicial behavior. The transition from one period to the next was gradual and never wholly discontinuous. Moreover, the Second Senate has always exercised its authority with less restraint than the First, an accidental result partly of its jurisdiction and partly of its personnel.

It is sometimes suggested that the Federal Constitutional Court, because it must confine itself to constitutional questions, has less freedom of action than the U.S. Supreme Court. The Constitutional Court is not, to be sure, an appellate tribunal in the ordinary sense. For example, it cannot avoid a constitutional question by settling a case on other grounds, for its judisdiction ceases upon the entry of nonconstitutional questions. According to Justice Hans Rupp, the Court is "never tempted to take a case only because it feels that it should be decided otherwise on its merits,"[11] which appears, in his view, to make the German Justices less result-oriented than American Justices. Still, these propositions ring faintly of mechanical jurisprudence and ignore that human "stream of tendency" which, according to Cardozo, "gives coherence and direction to thought and action."[12] What is a constitutional question must surely be a subject of disagreement among Justices who do not share common notions of what the Basic Law means. The boundary between constitutional and nonconstitutional disputes must pose difficulty for those who would try to locate it in complex situations. What is to prevent a result-oriented Justice from using the Basic Law to mask a decision on public policy? The rule limiting the Court to deciding only constitutional questions may very well exert a restraining influence on what the Justices feel they can—or should—decide. It certainly limits the form of the decision. Upon reflection, however, this limitation turns out to be a formidable power, for it allows—indeed, demands— that the Justices themselves transpose *all* questions they decide into constitutional issues. Thus, the German Justices do legislate; they make policy *whenever* they decide. How much policy they make would seem to depend, in the end, as it does with American judges, on their own sense of self-restraint.

Judicial Review in Operation

Which public acts and controversies have commanded most of the Court's time and energy? Cases arising under the Court's constitutional complaint and concrete judicial review procedure are most relevant because they have generated the overwhelming majority of the Court's published opinions. In the exercise of this jurisdiction, the Court has reviewed hundreds of statutes. On the whole, these statutes fall into three main categories. The first involves cases arising under various social welfare and regulatory statutes, notably federal laws on pensions, unemployment compensation, sales and income taxes, and fair trade practices. A large number of the state laws challenged in these cases deal with various restrictions on occupations and professions, including regulations pertaining to the training and licensing of artisans and tradesmen, and on the use and disposition of property. Many cases have also arisen under federal and state laws regulating the tenure, conditions of work, compensation, and retirement benefits of civil servants.

Federal laws compensating German citizens and others for injustices connected with National Socialism and World War II have occasioned a second major category of cases. Bewildering in their variety and complexity, these laws include countless provisions designed, *inter alia*, to rehabilitate the victims of Nazi persecution, to restore the legal rights and pensions of persons formerly employed in the civil service, to assist persons who fled Germany for political reasons and wish to return, to reimburse those persons who sustained personal injury and property damage arising out of Nazi war crimes, to indemnify German citizens for losses suffered as a result of their expulsion from certain territories after the war, and to compensate Germans detained by the Allies subsequent to the German surrender. These cases frequently turn on equal protection arguments under statutory definitions of what constitutes "material loss," "German citizenship," "repatriation," and the like. A large number of constitutional complaints have also been directed against the application of these statutes by courts and government agencies.

The third and by far largest category of cases arise under the general provisions of the civil and criminal codes, including federal highway traffic laws and the Code of Civil and Criminal Procedure. On the civil side, most constitutional cases involve challenges to specific provisions of contract, property, inheritance, or family law. Most criminal cases present questions arising out of the arrest and detention, pre-trial investigation, notification and hearing, legal representation, and trial procedure provisions of the criminal code. A large subcategory of the Court's opinions in the area of procedure, incidentally, deals with its intepretation of jurisdictional provisions of the Constitutional Court Organization Act of 1951.

The Constitutional Court has invalidated many statutory provisions. The frequency with which the Court has negated governmental rules is best illustrated by a consideration of concrete review cases where statutes, state or federal, may be challenged directly by court referral. Table 14 shows that some eighty-nine provisions of federal and state law have been declared unconstitutional. The time periods

TABLE 14

PROVISIONS OF LAW INVALIDATED IN CONCRETE
JUDICIAL REVIEW CASES 1951-1972

Period	Total Cases	Statutory Provisions Invalidated Federal	State
1951-1957	42	2	10
1958-1967	183	35	18
1968-1972	113	17	7
TOTAL:	338	54	35

SOURCE: *Entscheidungen des Bundesverfassungsgerichts,* Volumes 1-33, covering the period from 1951 to July 19, 1972.

correspond to the three eras that we were vaguely able to discern earlier in speaking about the Court's relationship to other branches of government. It is appropriate to point out, however, that only a very small percentage of the cases in Table 14 involved reversals of major legislative policies; most of the statutory provisions nullified by the Court were of minor significance. A total view of the Court's activity in reversing governmental policy would have to include the outcome of constitutional complaint cases, which constitute about fifty-five percent of all the Court's published decisions. But very few of these cases involve challenges to statutes. Scores of administrative regulations promulgated pursuant to laws have been struck down in constitutional complaints. But the large bulk of complaints, at least those which are the subject of the Court's opinions, are brought against court judgments, mainly in criminal cases.

PROTECTOR OF
INDIVIDUAL RIGHTS

The fundamental rights of Germans, enumerated in Articles 1 through 19 of the Basic Law, include social and economic rights such as the right to choose a trade or occupation (Article 12), the right of inheritance (Article 14), and the right to marry and raise a family (Article 6). Our concern here, however, is with the basic freedoms of religion, speech, press, association, movement, and citizenship. Where do these rights rank in the scale of West German constitutional values? The Basic Law itself pulls in two directions. On the one hand, Article 19 (paragraph 2) seems to attach a preferred status to fundamental rights by specifying that "the essential content of a basic right [may not be] encroached upon." However, under the terms of Article 79 only Article 1, proclaiming the inviolability of man's dignity, is beyond the amendatory power of Parliament. Indeed, the Constitutional Court itself, as mentioned previously, has repeatedly emphasized the primacy of Article 1, asserting that man's dignity is the "highest legal value" of the constitutional system.[13]

On the other hand, while obliging the state to respect human dignity and individual rights, the Basic Law predicates these rights upon the observance of certain principles of political obligation. Thus, everyone has the right to the free development of his or her personality so long as "he does not violate the rights of others or offend against the constitutional order or the moral code" (Article 2, paragraph 1); freedom of expression is "limited by the provisions of the general laws, provisions of law for the protection of youth, and by the right to inviolability of personal honor" (Article 5, paragraph 2); freedom to teach "does not absolve from loyalty to the Constitution" (Article 5, paragraph 3); all Germans have the right to associate, but activities "directed against the constitutional order or the concept of international understanding are prohibited" (Article 9). Moreover, freedoms of expression, press, teaching, assembly, and association may even be forfeited if used "to combat the free democratic basic order" (Article 18). (Owing to several 1968 constitutional amendments on national defense and emergency, fundamental rights were limited in still other ways, not to be considered here.)

In practice, West German courts have exercised a vigilant watch over fundamental rights. The prevailing judicial attitude on this question was well expressed by the Federal Supreme Court:

"The Basic Law views the fundamental rights as rights valid *per se*, pre-existent to and binding upon both the constitutional legislator and the ordinary legislator. Even though by virtue of provisions in its text it authorizes the ordinary legislator, in varying degrees, to derogate from the fundamental rights, it is an unacceptable interpretation, in law at any rate, that the legislator is entirely free, by virtue of these provisions, to tamper with the fundamental rights.''[14]

But it is the special province of the Federal Constitutional Court to convert these broad principles of interpretation, when confronted by official restrictions on personal freedom, into statements of constitutional policy.

Religion and Conscience

Religious toleration came late to German public life. From the Peace of Augsburg in 1555 to the Napoleonic conquest in 1806 religious life in Germany was governed by the principle *cuius regio, cuius religio*. Lessing's plea for religious liberty, set forth so powerfully in his *Nathan the Wise* (1779), was drowned out, along with other voices of the German Enlightenment, by tidewaters of religious intolerance that rushed, unabated, far into the nineteenth century until, with the cessation of Bismarck's *Kulturkampf* with the Catholic Church, they finally receded. During most of the century, and indeed until the Weimar Constitution of 1919, nearly all the German states, including Prussia, adopted Lutheranism as the state religion. Church and state were separated only with the coming of the Weimar Republic, although under the 1919 Constitution religious bodies were explicitly granted certain privileges enjoyed by other organizations incorporated under public law.

The Basic Law continues the Weimar principles of religious liberty. It prohibits the establishment of a state church, bars compulsory disclosure of religious convictions, bans compulsory participation in religious ceremonies, forbids religious oaths contrary to conscience, and makes the enjoyment of civil and political rights, including eligibility for public office, independent of religious creed.[15] For historical and cultural reasons, however, including the anti-religious ferocity of the Nazi regime, it does not erect an American-designed wall of separation between church and state. Religious education forms a part of the ordinary curriculum in state and municipal schools and is given in accordance with the tenets of the major denominations. The state is constitutionally obliged to protect Sundays and religious holidays and to accord religious bodies privileges similar to those enjoyed by other corporate groups. Collectively, these provisions recognize the important social role played by organized religious bodies in German public life. The West German theory of religious freedom does not imply, as it does in the United States, the state's total withdrawal from religion.

The Federal Constitutional Court was relatively silent in church-state matters until 1965. The Concordat Case (1957) was the only major decision affecting the relationship between church and state.[16] At issue in the case was whether Lower Saxony could lawfully construct a single system of public schools in apparent violation of the German-Vatican Concordat of 1933, obligating the nation to establish confessional schools in certain communities. But this was mainly a federal-state conflict and will be treated in greater detail later. We will simply note here that the state law did not disturb the place of religion in the public schools, that religious instruction continues to be a common feature of the public school curriculum in Germany, and that there has been no judicial disturbance of this policy on constitutional grounds. While religious practices in the public schools are a frequent occasion for heated conflict in the United States, there is no German equivalant of *McCollum* v. *Board of Education* (1948) or even of *Engel* v. *Vitale* (1962).[17] So far these issues have given Constitutional Court Justices little cause for concern.

The one religious issue which has given the Justices pause is the church tax, around which most controversy over church and state revolves. Every state in Germany has a church tax law (*Kirchensteuergesetz*).[18] A wage earner affiliated with one of the two major religious demoninations is subject to a church tax which takes the form of a compulsory surcharge (usually ten percent) on income tax. The surcharge, like the income tax, is withheld by the employer, collected by official agencies, and then turned over to religious bodies for their general support. Only persons who resign (or contract out of) their church membership or declare themselves unaffiliated with any religion are exempt from it. In some states, church bodies have themselves been authorized to levy additional taxes for given purposes.

The tax itself, which has brought immense prosperity to German churches, has never been subject to serious constitutional attack. But it was clear from the number of cases filed with the Constitutional Court from 1957 onward that the Justices (First Senate) were having difficulty in determining how far these tax laws should reach. Some of these cases remained undecided for as long as eight years. One can imagine a delay arising out of an internal "kulturkampf" between Catholic and Protestant Justices over the applicability of the 1933 Concordat to these cases. One can imagine also disagreement among the Justices over state laws conferring tax power on church bodies. Over and above such likely cleavages were other complex and sensitive constitutional issues. For example, how was the Court to reconcile the free exercise provisions of Article 4 with the privileges, including the power to levy taxes, granted to religious communities under articles of the Weimar Constitution incorporated into the Basic Law through Article 140.

On Decmeber 14, 1965, the Court handed down eight separate opinions which tried to resolve some of these issues. The Court held, *inter alia*,

(1) that a wage earner unaffiliated with a church cannot be compelled to pay church taxes merely because his wife is a church member,

(2) that this applies equally to a tax levied by a church on property for which both spouses in such a marriage are legally co-responsible, and,

(3) that it is invalid to impose a church surcharge on even half the income tax of a married couple, one of whom is a church member, if the income-producing spouse is not religiously affiliated.[19]

The principle which emerges from these cases seems clear: No person can be forced to pay a church tax based on his income or even part of his income for the support of a religion other than his own or for the support of any religious group if he belongs to no church.

What is interesting about the church tax cases is that the Court did not rest on the religious freedom clauses of Article 4, but rather on Article 2, paragraph 1, of the Basic Law, guaranteeing every person the right to the free development of his personality. Disagreement among the Justices on the applicability of the religious clauses is one possible explanation for the Court's use of Article 2. At the same time, Article 2 would seem to permit a more pragmatic approach to judicial policy-making in this area of church-state relations. At any rate, the church tax cases show that Article 2 is an extremely flexible provision of the Basic Law and one in which almost any other basic right can be incorporated, when convenience dictates.

What, then, of the religious clauses of Article 4? Where have they been applied in German constitutional law? It was not until the Prison Tobacco Case of 1960 that the Court had a chance to flesh out the meaning of Article 4. The case involved a fanatical Nazi and former storm trooper of militantly anti-Christian views jailed for attempted treason. While in prison, he sought fervently to persuade fellow inmates to drop their religious affiliations, with promises of tobacco to those who followed his advice. Viewing his proselytizing activities as evidence of his inability to live a law-abiding life on the outside, the Federal Supreme Court upheld a denial of his petition for parole. In reviewing his constitutional complaint, the Federal Constitutional Court (First Senate) made clear that the Basic Law protects all manner of belief—religious belief, nonreligious belief, and anti-religious belief. Freedom of faith and creed was interpreted to include also the right to quit one's church, to conceal one's faith, and, most importantly, the right to win adherents to one's belief and to convert those of other beliefs. Despite the cutting of this broad swath, the Court rejected the complaint in this instance because the petitioner had used "morally objectionable means" of persuasion.[20] The Court came astonishingly close to suggesting that the use of subrational appeals like the offer of a material reward (tobacco) to bring about a person's conversion is an offense against man's dignity.

In other cases involving freedom of conscience and religious exercise the Court held (1) that a divorce judgment could not validly find a wife guilty of a marital offense for having changed her religious affiliation against her husband's wishes, (2) that a husband could not be convicted for refusing to call a doctor and seek medical advice about a blood transfusion for his dying wife who, until the moment of her death, consciously chose, on religious grounds, not to receive medical attention, and (3) that a defendant could not validly be compelled to take an oath on the Bible when he personally believed that the Bible itself forbids such oaths.[21]

The Court has also decided two important cases involving the commercial activity of religious organizations. In the Watch Tower Bible and Tract Society Case (1965), the Court held that while freedom of conscience and belief extend to religious associations as well as to individuals, this right does not exempt such groups from paying a state turnover tax on the sale of food, drink, and other products not inherently religious.[22] One interesting sidelight was the Constitutional Court's attempt to distinguish this case from *Murdock* v. *Pennsylvania*, an American case which the complainant, a Pennsylvania group proselytizing in Germany, brought to the Court's attention.[23] Three years later, however, in the Rumpelkammer case, the Court voided a judicial order prohibiting a Catholic youth organization from having a scrap drive to raise money for poor people in underdeveloped countries publicized from the pulpit. The order was obtained by a scrap dealer whose business was on the verge of ruin owing to the group's activity. The concept of "religious practice" embraced not only acts of worship, said the Court, but also "manifestations of religious and philosophic life," including "expressions of active love for one's neighbors."[24]

The most troublesome cases arising under Article 4 have involved conscientious objectors. Between 1956 and 1970 around 65,000 German youths sought conscientious objector status.[25] The Basic Law confers the right to refuse military service on grounds of conscience, but substitute service may be required, as it is by the Military Service Act of 1956. In 1960, the Court held that freedom of conscience under Article 4 protected only those persons objecting to war as a matter of general principle, thus ruling out selective conscientious objection.[26] The most troublesome question to arise in these cases was the requirement of substitute service, even though such service was not connected with the armed forces.

In the First Substitute Service Case (1965), the Court sustained the alternative service requirement over the religious objections of a member of Jehovah's Witnesses.[27] The constitutional issue then shifted to the form and duration of punishment that could be inflicted on a person refusing alternative service. In the Second Substitute Service Case (1968), the First Senate affirmed a seven-month prison sentence imposed upon a member of the same sect over the objection that such a penalty was an unusually harsh price to pay for following one's conscience.[28] Whether longer stretches in jail would constitute an invalid intrusion on religious freedom was a question which the Court left unanswered. Later cases showed that the Court was more sympathetic to the claims of Jehovah's Witnesses who had been subjected to successive convictions arising out of repeated refusals to perform alternative service. The Court, now speaking through the Second Senate, declared such multiple convictions to be unconstitutional under Article 103, paragraph 3, which states that "no one may be punished for the same act more than once." In a liberal construction of the double jeopardy principle, the Court chose to regard these successive violations as "the same act" within the meaning of the Basic Law. The Justices took this position because no community interest could be found to override the fundamental right of conscience in the circumstances of these cases.[29]

But suppose a person applies for conscientious objector status *after* his induction into the armed services. May he be militarily disciplined on successive occasions for persisting in his refusal to submit to military training prior to a final judicial determination of his application? In the Soldier Refusal Case (1970), the Court declined to apply the double jeopardy clause since punishment was not imposed to atone for a crime but to maintain military discipline.[30] One year later, the Second Senate, over the dissent of three Justices, sustained a conviction for disobedience of military orders where punishment was imposed after the soldier in question was legally recognized as a conscientious objector.[31] But the disobedient act occurred prior to the time that the religious sincerity of the applicant had been determined. Cases of this vintage continue to receive the attention of the Court as it seeks, in looking carefully at the special circumstances of each case, to balance the individual's right to conscience against the state's interest in maintaining a military establishment.

Speech and Press

Freedom of expression in Germany has not had a happy history. The spirit of Schiller has been snuffed out too often and too frightfully by that of Fichte. Speech suppressed and other restrictions on personal freedom have been associated with a political and legal tradition that largely subsumed the citizen into an order of liberty, morality, and reality regarded as qualitatively superior to the individual—namely, the state. True, the Weimar Constitution incorporated guarantees of basic rights, but these remained unenforceable by judicial means. Political extremism resulted in their gradual erosion; national socialism, in their total negation.

The Basic Law lays down the legal basis for the creation of a regime of free expression. The creation itself, however, and the specification of the regime's boundaries is one of the functions of the Federal Constitutional Court. In defining these boundaries, the Court has spun an intricate web of free speech theory, although there are knots in the weave and the interlacing threads do not yield a consistent pattern. Unfortunately, we do not have space to restate here all the rules laid down by the Court with respect to all modes of expression or communication. We propose merely to take the Court's leading decisions and extract from them the main strands of German free speech policy.

Before discussing these cases, we need to note the ringing declaration of free expression that appears in Article 5, paragraph 1, of the Basic Law. It says: "Everyone shall have the right freely to express and freely to inform himself from generally accessible sources. Freedom of the press and freedom of reporting by means of broadcasts and films are guaranteed. There shall be no censorship." But paragraph 2 asserts: "These rights are limited by the provisions of the general laws." The upshot of the "general law" limitation is that community rights defined by public law and even private rights secured by the civil code severely limit the boundaries of free expression. Whether speech and press take precedence over competing public interests depends on the circumstances of each case. Speech and press do not even enjoy preferred status among competing values found in the Basic Law. We noted earlier the primacy of Article 1, which proclaims man's dignity, as well as the importance of Article 2, which speaks of the free development of personality. Speech and press are clearly limited by those standards which the Court finds implicit in the nation of human dignity. Again the Court's approach is to balance the individual's right to expression against the social interest protected by the restriction on speech. Actually the Court seems to have elevated the balancing test into a fixed rule of constitutional interpretation.[32]

The cases break down roughly into three categories: Those dealing with internal security laws, those dealing with personal honor and reputation, and those dealing with speech intended to injure persons economically. The Court has made it very clear that laws relating to internal security, military defense, and public order, under which the most troublesome constitutional questions have arisen, are "general laws" which validly limit speech and press. Here we may note the high incidence of journalistic treason cases, the most noted and controversial of which is the Spiegel Seizure Case.

In 1962, West German federal and state police mounted a coordinated night raid on the premises of the popular weekly newsmagazine *Der Spiegel*. Before morning, mountains of papers and documents belonging to *Der Spiegel* had been carted away in vans to police headquarters and several editors and publishers had been arrested. All this followed the magazine's cover story about a NATO exercise intended to unmask West Germany's military weakness.[33] There was no proof that any military secret as such had been divulged. But it was possible at the time to commit treason in Germany by taking fragments of legitimate information found in widely scattered places, previously published sources included, and piecing them together in such a way as to offer a coherent picture of military strategy or policy useful to the enemy and dangerous to the existence of the Federal Republic. The "mosaic" theory of treason was left undisturbed in the Spiegel case. In upholding the constitutionality of the police seizure of *Der Spiegel's* editorial offices, the Court barely distinguished the situation in this case, which raised profound questions of editorial freedom in Germany, from an ordinary felony.[34]

Any mention of the Spiegel Seizure Case or the hundreds of other cases before German courts where charges of treason have been countered by claims of free speech, must include the observation that these proceedings were partly the result of the Cold War between East and West Germany and a pervasive anti-communism whose virulence was especially apparent during the Adenauer years. The Constitutional Court itself contributed to the mood of the times by ruling the Communist Party unconstitutional in 1956, noting that West Germany is a "fighting democracy" which offers no protection to political parties putting forth totalitarian ideas subversive of the liberal democracy ordained by the Basic Law.[35] After this decision, Communists and Communist propaganda were prime targets for every prosecutor's office in West Germany.

We may note also in this connection that postal and customs officials have confiscated, pursuant to federal law, hundreds of thousands of brochures, newspapers, magazines, and printed circulars containing subversive propaganda, nearly all of it from East Germany. In three cases decided in 1969, the Court left no doubt about the legitimacy of such laws, although it seems to be taking a close look at their administration to make sure that legitimate speech with genuine informational value to the citizen, particularly if the latter personally solicits the information or receives it from personal friends abroad, is not swept up along with speech found dangerous to the security of the state.[36]

In the second group of cases involving reputation, German free speech policy offers an interesting contrast to American theory. For example, the German press does not enjoy the protection *New York Times* v. *Sullivan* affords to the American press.[37] In Germany false statements about persons, *especially* public officials, are punishable under libel and slander laws. In Germany's civic culture there is a tendency to treat public officials as somehow above the din of politics and neutral executors of the people's will, an attitude which seems to be a spillover from the dignified objectivity that the public mind once associated with the Kaiser's *Beamtenstaat*. Lawsuits by politicians and other public officials against newspapers for statements deemed to be false or in derogation of their character are a common occurrence in Germany. Occasionally such lawsuits produce odd results, as the example of the Schmid-Spiegel Case shows. There the president of a high state court unleashed a savage verbal assault on *Der Spiegel* because of misleading statements the magazine had made, strongly

intimating, among other things, that he was a communist sympa-
thizer. The judge was found guilty of slandering *Der Spiegel*.
Reversing, the Constitutional Court noted that the magazine's
misleading comments warranted in this case an equally misleading
reply. No less than the quality of public opinion was at stake, said the
Court, for the controversy dealt with public policies relating to
judicial appointments, a matter concerning which citizens need valid
information.[38] Although here the Court used Article 5 to overrule a
technical charge of libel, the case's real meaning is to be found in the
First Senate's interesting justification of untruth in the interest of
truth.

The Mephisto Case of 1971 is a notable example—and the best
contrast to American constitutional policy—of the limits which the
notion of human dignity imposes on free speech. The case involved
the publication of a new edition of Klaus Mann's *Mephisto*, a satirical
novel about a German actor who attained fame and fortune during the
Nazi period. Mann based his story on the life of a famous Faustian
actor who attained Hitler's favor. The fictional character, wholly
immoral and corrupt, admittedly was a pale image of the real actor
who, incidentally, had died in 1963, as had Mann himself several years
earlier. But in 1968 the actor's adopted son secured a judicial ban on
the book, the lower courts taking the view that it defamed the honor
and memory of his stepfather. The Constitutional Court rejected the
constitutional complaint of the publisher. Because *Mephisto* was a
caricature of the actor, the First Senate found freedom of expression
to have been abused, for the novel infringed the right to personal
honor secured to all persons by Article 2, entitling every person to the
free development of his personality.[39] (Apparently the constitutional protection afforded here extends to persons dead as well as
living.)

The third group of cases deals with speech intended to affect
economic opportunities. Illustrations are the Luth-Harlan Case (1968)
and the Blinkfuer Case (1969). In the first, Hamburg's Public Press
Superintendent Luth called upon film distributors and theater owners
to boycott at a German film festival a film by Harlan, a former Nazi
film director. In the 1930s, the latter had produced notoriously
anti-semitic films. Harlan procured a cease and desist order against

Luth since calling the boycott was, under the civil code, contrary to public morals. In reversing the lower court decision, the Constitutional Court did not, however, invalidate the law prohibiting boycotts. What is interesting about the case is the attention the First Senate paid, not to the words spoken by the claimant, but to his motives for speaking. The Court held that speech must prevail in this instance since Luth's motives were, as the Senate noted, "pure"; Luth sought not to further his own economic interests but to protect the moral and cultural interests of the community.[40]

But the Court failed to apply the Luth reasoning to the Blinkfuer Case, where a large newspaper concentration—the Alex Springer Publishing House—threatened to cut off delivery of its papers to newsdealers selling a left-wing magazine which advertised radio and television programs from East Germany. The magazine in question sought damages in a civil court and lost. The Federal Supreme Court affirmed the judgment on the ground that a decision for the magazine would violate Springer's right to free speech. Again, the Constitutional Court reversed, holding in this case that economic pressure could not be used to spread one's views. The critical distinction between Luth and Blinkfuer seemed to be the degree of the pressure applied. The Court was impressed with the fact that in Luth the distributors were left with a free choice to show or not to show Harlan's films, but in Blinkfuer the magazine in dispute had no alternative but to sustain a substantial loss of business.[41]

From the point of view of technical soundness and logic, these decisions are extremely untidy. The Court seems to be deciding them on an ad hoc basis and apparently pursuant to difficult negotiation inside the Court. We might also note that like the religious freedom cases, the free speech decisions were handed down by the First Senate. Measured in terms of the number of times free speech claims were upheld, the record of this body is conservative. Only in the Spiegel Seizure Case (1966) did the judicial vote appear close, and three of the four Justices presumed to have dissented there are now gone. Two of them—Stein and Rupp v. Brünneck dissented in Mephisto (1971). Free speech seems not to be an issue neatly separating Social from Christian Democrats, Protestants from Catholics, or even Justices who once suffered for their political views from those who did not.

Free speech liberalism or conservatism appears to transcend most classifications based on judicial background characteristics.

But would the result have been different if the above cases had been decided by the Second Senate? Probably not, if its decisions in areas related to free speech are any guide. The Second Senate's most notable decision touching on freedom of expression is the Federal Television Case of 1961, which was fundamentally a federal-state conflict. More relevant are the Soldiers' Free Speech Cases (1970).[42] The principal case involved a noncommissioned officer who was punished by a military court for telling his men while on duty that there was no freedom of opinion in West Germany and those who protest the government's policies are put down by force. He was punished under a federal law that imposes a duty on military officers to express their opinions with restraint so as to maintain the respect of their subordinates. The constitutional complaint was dismissed by a six to two vote. In the course of the opinion, after noting the one-sided nature of the soldier's remark, the Court said: "The Federal Republic of Germany is a democracy whose Constitution expects from its citizens a defense of the liberal democratic order and will not put up with any misuse of a basic right for the purpose of fighting against this order."[43] The decision does not make indisputably clear whether this principle is to be limited to the military domain. In any case, the Second Senate's views on fundamental freedoms are not markedly at variance with those of the First.

While speech and press are protected in Germany, one familiar with Germany's civic culture would not expect free speech boundaries to be as wide as they are in American constitutional law. Moreover, the Justices do not seem eager to move in the American direction. Justice Rupp-v. Brunneck cited with approval *New York Times* v. *Sullivan* in her dissenting opinion in the Mephisto Case,[44] but it had no impact on the rest of the Court. Personal honor and truth in public discussion are values that the Justices wish very much to preserve even if it means—so it would seem—risking a less robust regime of free expression.

Association and Travel

The rights of association and travel are subject to all the limitations governing the rights of speech and press. Article 8 of the Basic Law also grants a separate right of assembly, but the Federal Constitutional Court has decided no case squarely on the basis of this provision. From a literal reading of the Basic Law, it might appear that these rights do not apply as broadly as the rights to speech and press. While the Basic Law secures to "everyone" the right to free speech, it confers on "all Germans" the right to assemble peaceably (Article 8), to form associations and societies (Article 9), and to freedom of movement (Article 11). At the same time the makers of Bonn's Constitution wanted to make indisputably clear that these rights, particularly the right to freedom of movement, extended to all Germans resident in the Soviet Zone of Occupation as well as to the Soviet sector of Berlin.

The Court's decisions in the areas of association and travel reflect a policy of judicial restraint. The Court has narrowly construed its own jurisdiction under Article 9, paragraph 2, which prohibits associations whose purposes are directed against the constitutional order or the concept of international understanding or which are in conflict with criminal law. There is ample ground for holding cases arising under this provision to be within the exclusive jurisdiction of the Constitutional Court. In a 1961 decision, however, the First Senate held that such cases fall within the jurisdiction of ordinary courts. Thus, political associations can be suppressed in the ordinary course of criminal litigation.[45] An earlier decision by the Second Senate ruled in addition that political parties are not "associations" within the meaning of Article 9.[46] The most important cases dealing with the right of association are the political party cases, but these are the subject of Article 21, a *lex specialis* of the Basic Law to be taken up later.

The associational rights which the Court has protected under Article 9 are, for the most part, economic in nature. May a business firm be compelled to join a chamber of commerce? May a doctor be forced into membership in a physician's pension fund? May certain industries by grouped together by the state for special tax purposes?

May electrical and mining companies in a given area be forced into a water conservation union endowed with independent authority to control water usage by the member industries? In each of these cases, the Constitutional Court has ruled against the individual claim, holding that Article 9 does not prohibit the inclusion of such persons (individual or corporate) into associations organized under public law, to perform public functions in the public interest.[47]

The right of labor to organize for economic reasons is constitutionally secured. But the Court has had no opportunity to decide what rights workers themselves may assert against their own unions. The few labor cases which have come before the Constitutional Court arose initially under collective bargaining statutes and involved decisions which excluded certain categories of people from engaging in collective bargaining. In one of these decisions, the First Senate overruled a judgment of the Federal Labor Court which construed the term "union" so narrowly as to exclude certain associations which do not as a matter of policy engage in strikes for better wages and working conditions.[48] In effect, said the Constitutional Court, this ruling violated the right of certain trades or occupations to form an association—any association—to improve their working conditions, a right expressly protected under Article 9, paragraph 3, of the Basic Law.

With regard to freedom of movement, the Court has said that every German has the right to travel unhindered or settle anywhere within the boundaries of the Federal Republic. But this right is clearly limited, according to the Court, by the state's interest in allocating housing and in accounting for the location of its citizens. Thus, state laws may require persons to register with and obtain the approval of local housing officials prior to the acquisition of living quarters.[49]

Whatever rights freedom of movement under Article 11 may confer upon Germans, these do not include the right to travel abroad. The right to leave the country is regarded as a fundamental right; but, like so many freedoms (and limitations on freedom) already cited in this chapter, it is found to inhere in Article 2, guaranteeing the free development of personality. The Court has actually inferred from the personality guarantee a corollary right to "general freedom of action" (*Handlungsfreiheit*) from which the right to travel is derivative, a doctrine set forth in the 1957 Passport Case. It is relevant to interject that in the Passport Case the First Senate, which one year earlier banned the Communist Party as unconstitutional, upheld the denial of a passport to a citizen wanting to attend a conference for world peace on the ground that the person in question would endanger the security and substantial interests of the Federal Republic.[50] The case is relevant here because the Court did not closely examine or succeed in specifying the interests which the state presumably was protecting in denying the passport. The individual involved was not even a member of an unconstitutional political party; he was a Christian Democratic member of a state legislature, but he was a leading spokesman in opposition to the government's policy on rearmament and German reunification. The decision in this case cannot really be separated from the general political context in which it was decided—one of virulent anti-communism.

Defendants' Rights

The field of defendants' rights offers an excellent opportunity to illustrate further the uses the Constitutional Court has made of the personality guarantee of Article 2 of the Basic Law. It might be noted parenthetically that a solid half of all constitutional complaints resulting in full opinions by the Court involve questions of due process of law, mainly in criminal proceedings. That the complaint is sustained in one out of every three such opinions is one sign of the Court's vigilant role in watching out for the rights of defendants. Most defendants' rights cases arise under paragraph 1 of Article 103, which says, "In the courts everyone shall be entitled to a hearing in accordance with law." In several cases, however, the Court has chosen to base its argument on the personality guarantee.

Arrest and detention cases offer one illustration of the use of the personality clause. Article 104 of the Basic Law provides, *inter alia*, that the liberty of the individual may be restricted only by a formal law and that only judges may decide on the admissibility or continuation of any deprivation of liberty. Armed with this provision and the all-purpose weapon of Article 2 (personal inviolability), the

Constitutional Court struck down a federal traffic ordinance imposing a two-week jail sentence on drunken drivers, held that a guardian may not legally commit his incapacitated ward to a closed institution even with judicial authorization, and ordered an accused person held on suspicion of having committed a serious crime of violence out of solitary confinement.[51] In the first case, the Court asserted that an ordinance may not deprive a person of liberty under a statute that does not expressly provide for such deprivation; in the second, that the confinement of a person to an institution is a public function that no court can transfer to a private citizen; in the third, that total deprivation of personal liberty, especially with regard to a person held in custody, is evil and unreasonable.

The personality and human dignity clauses have also been applied in cases where evidence of criminal activity is procured by means of physical intrusions upon the body. In the Neurosurgical Case, the Court voided a judicial order requiring a person accused of embezzlement to submit to a sanity test through an occipital puncture; the operation, said the Court, basing its decision on an expert opinion solicited from a leading German neurosurgeon, is both painful and dangerous and hence incompatible with the dignity of man under Article 2.[52] In the Encephalography Case, the Court voided a judicial order which would have required surgical penetration of the vertebral canal.[53] It is noteworthy that the Constitutional Court declined to decide whether these physical intrusions violated due process standards under Article 103. Similar cases decided by the U.S. Supreme Court have been treated as due process questions.[54] The broad concept of human dignity incorporated into the meaning of Article 2 apparently imposes greater restrictions on criminal administration in Germany than any limitation of due process of law that might be derived from Article 103 or, for that matter, from the principle of *Rechtsstaatlichkeit*.

UMPIRE OF THE
FEDERAL SYSTEM

The area of federal-state relations, besides providing us with another illustration of the Constitutional Court's policy-making role, offers further examples of how the Court has applied the unwritten constitutional principles discussed at the start of this chapter. Federal-state conflicts, of course, may be either direct or indirect. Direct conflicts occur when both levels of government confront each other in their corporate capacities before the Constitutional Court. Indirect conflicts between state and federal governments may occur under various jurisdictional categories. An example of an indirect conflict is the Federal Wiretapping Case (1971) where, incidentally, the Court was also asked to declare a constitutional amendment unconstitutional. Article 10 of the Basic Law, which secured the secrecy of mail and telecommunications, was amended in 1968 to permit official interference with these communications in times of emergency and without recourse to the courts. In an abstract judicial review proceeding, Hesse challenged both the amendment and legislation enacted pursuant to it on constitutional grounds. Hesse's case included the argument that failure to provide judicial recourse under the amendment violated two basic principles of the Basic Law— namely, the dignity of man (Article 1) and the rule of law (Article 20). The federal government, Bundesrat, and Bundestag, as interested parties, all filed briefs in support of the amendment and related legislation, whose constitutionality the Court (Second Senate) upheld by a narrow four to three vote.[55] So, while the federal government as such was not a direct party to the suit, it would have sustained a serious defeat had the vote gone the other way.

In the remainder of this section, we confine ourselves to direct federal-state conflicts. No one could have predicted what role the Court would play in resolving such conflicts; the Court's eventual role was largely the product of unplanned development, dictated by accident. One of these circumstances was the Allied decision to convert the old territories of Baden and Württemberg into three new states, over strong German objections. An attempt in 1951 to redress this artificial splitting of traditional geographic boundaries furnished the Court with an opportunity to address itself to the nature of the federal-state relationship. The issue raised in this case—the Southwest Case—was whether the federal government had the authority under the Basic Law to suspend elections and extend the term of a state legislature pending the outcome of a popular referendum merging the state in question with another state.[56] The Southwest Case was the Court's first major decision and, in the absence of any binding constitutional law or the constraint of unwritten constitutional practice, it had enormous scope at this early time to create doctrine on the question of the nature of German federalism and on its own role in mediating federal-state disputes.

Taking a firm stand on both questions, the Court set forth in unambiguous language the conditions that limit the federation's power over the organization of new states. Clearly signifying its intention to guard the autonomy of the states, the Court struck down as violative of the federal principle the above-mentioned law extending the life of a state legislature. As Justice Leibholz wrote, "The Court established that, under the Basic Law, the German Federal Republic is a true federation and that the individual states are endowed with sovereign powers—a power of their own which is not derived from, but acknowledged by, the federation."[57]

The powers of the German states under the Basic Law are not comparable to the authority reserved to the states in other federal systems such as Canada, Australia, or even the United States. This is one reason, perhaps, why the Constitutional Court may have chosen to secure so vigilantly what little autonomy the states do have against federal encroachment. In seven of nine direct federal-state conflict cases, the federal government emerged as the losing party. In three cases of jurisdictional disputes where both state and federal governments had concurrent legislative authority, the Court sustained the state. In the first case, the Court upheld a North Rhine-Westfalia statute providing higher salary scales for civil servants than those applicable to civil servants subject to federal law. The Court did not consider the state law to be in violation of Article 75 which grants to the federation power to enact general rules or "framework" legislation (*Rahmenvorschriften*) with regard to the legal status of state civil servants.[58] In the other two cases, the Court upheld state claims that the federation had unconstitutionally intruded upon state jurisdiction over the administration of federal law.[59]

Two federal-state cases are of vital importance in the history of German constitutional law. The first is the well-known Concordat Case, the German equivalent of *Missouri* v. *Holland*.[60] At issue was the validity of the German-Vatican Concordat of July 20, 1933, which accorded to Catholics certain rights and privileges in education. The case arose out of Lower Saxony's Public Education Act of 1954, which set up a single system of public schools. Establishing these schools on a Christian basis and providing for religious instruction within them along denominational lines, the act nevertheless appeared to curtail the church's rights under the Concordat. Lower Saxony denied this allegation. The federation, largely in response to protestations from the Papal Nuncio, brought action against the state in the Constitutional Court. Hamburg and Hesse filed briefs in support of Lower Saxony, arguing that the Concordat itself was invalid *ab initio*, because it was concluded by an unlawful government and also because it had never been enforced. In one of its longest and most ambivalent opinions, the Constitutional Court upheld the treaty as a binding commitment upon the federal government in international law, but then turned around and ruled that the treaty could not validly be enforced in the states since the Basic Law reserves to them exlusive control over education.[61] The case effectively represented a victory for the states, quite at variance with the outcome in the *Holland* case, where a federal treaty took precedence over a reserved power of the American states.

The second decision of historical significance is the Federal Television Case (1961). The Adenauer government created a private television corporation, in which the federation would hold controlling stock, to compete with public television corporations organized under state law. The federal government sought to base its authority on Article 74, conferring exclusive power on the central government over postal and telecommunication service. The states objected mightily, asserting that any federal television station would violate not only the reserved right of the state under Article 30 to govern its own cultural affairs, but also Article 5 (freedom of expression) since any such instrument would interfere with the free flow of public opinion within the states. The Court seemed to accept both arguments, but rested mainly on the principle of "federal comity" (*Bundestreue*).[62] Under this unwritten constitutional principle, said the Court, the federal government is obligated to consider the interests of the states as a whole, which it did not do here. The principle emerging from this and other cases is that even lawful power may be limited in its exercise if found to abuse the rightful interests of constituent units of the federal system.[63]

It was squarely on the basis of this principle that the federal government attained one of its few notable victories over the states. This occurred when the Constitutional Court invalidated the decision of certain municipalities in Hesse to hold referenda on the Adenauer government's plan to arm German troops with atomic weapons. The Constitutional Court held, pursuant to Adenauer's application to have the referenda invalidated, that because of the federal government's primacy in foreign and military affairs the principle of comity requires that neither a state nor one of its units may hold a referendum which would undermine national policy.[64]

It needs to be observed in conclusion that federal-state conflicts were not usually the product merely of disagreements among levels of government. Most federalism cases mask the real controversy, which is between Social Democrats and Christian Democrats. The typical case is where a state controlled by one party sues the national government controlled by the other. Thus, federal-state cases are often partisan disputes dressed up in constitutional raiment. At bottom, the Concordat Case was a policy dispute between political parties. So were the Atomic Referenda Case and the Federal Television Case. It is of some interest to note too that several pending federalism cases were withdrawn from the Court's docket after Social and Christian Democrats united in the Grand Coalition of 1966.

CUSTODIAN OF PARTY DEMOCRACY

Few of the world's constitutional tribunals have said as much about the relationship between political parties and representative government as the Federal Constitutional Court. Few courts, including the U.S. Supreme Court, have imposed as many ground rules on participation in the electoral process. Because the Court's opinions on parties and suffrage are numerous and complex we must content ourselves here with a rapid survey of its main policies. We shall also note how these policies relate to the views of Justice Gerhard Leibholz.[65]

Articles 21 and 38 of the Basic Law are most relevant to this discussion. They deserve to be quoted in full:

Article 21

(1) The political parties shall participate in the forming of the political will of the people. They may be freely established. Their internal organization must conform to democratic principles. They must publicly account for the sources of their funds.

(2) Parties which, by reason of their aims or the behavior of their adherents, seek to impair or abolish the free democratic basic order or to endanger the existence of the Federal Republic of Germany, shall be unconstitutional. The Federal Constitutional Court shall decide on the question of unconstitutionality.

Article 38

(1) The deputies to the German Bundestag shall be elected in general, direct, free, equal, and secret elections. They shall be representative of the whole people, not bound by orders and instructions, and shall be subject only to their conscience.

Perhaps the best way of handling the material in this section is to indicate briefly how the Court has applied these constitutional provisions and then to articulate the general theory (competing theories, really) of party and representation upon which the Court's decisions are based.

Under the jurisdiction conferred by paragraph 2 of Article 21, the Court has banned the neo-Nazi Socialist Reich Party (SRP) in 1952 and the Communist Party of Germany (KPD) in 1956.[66] These decisions are of obvious relevance to the rights of speech and association in Germany. The Court does not apply a "clear and present danger" test in cases arising under paragraph 2 of Article 21. If a political party is committed to totalitarian values, as measured by its program, official declarations, ideological literature, and the structure of its leadership, it is *ipso facto* unconstitutional. In the Communist Party Case the Court declared, "No action in the sense of the criminal code is needed for a party to be unconstitutional. What is necessary is this: The political struggle of a party must be fixed by a purpose and it must be directed; furthermore, it must show a constant proclivity toward the struggle against the established constitutional system. This must find expression in political action according to a definite plan."[67] Thus, it is the *plan* of action as measured by speech and association, not the action itself, that is prohibited. The Court's policy, which clearly is supportive of the regime's policy, flows logically from the major articulate premise of the Communist Party Case: That West Germany is a "fighting democracy" (*streitbare Demokratie*) which cannot maintain a posture of neutrality toward parties which reject the principles of liberal democracy. These principles, the Court has made clear, are absolute values that the state is obligated to defend against any attack.

No area of German constitutional law, apart from the party prohibition cases, offers a better example of the Court's intrusion into the political process than in the field of elections and representation. But here the Court has followed a liberal policy of expanding the rights of voters and furthering equality of opportunity among competing political parties. It might be remarked that nearly every major provision of federal and state election laws has been reviewed by the Constitutional Court; in most cases, the electoral policy was validated. For instance, the mixed system of proportional representation and single-member districts has been sustained. (In federal elections, each voter receives two ballots; on one he votes for a district or constituency representative; on the other he votes for a party list drawn up by state party organizations. State legislative bodies are chosen mainly by proportional representation.) The formula by which legislators are chosen under proportional representation has been sustained, and so has the rule denying political parties representation in the Bundestag if they fail to acquire five percent of all votes cast in a national election.[68]

On the other hand, the Court has nullified statutes which exceed the five percent rule, and it has also established as a matter of constitutional policy the one man-one vote rule in single-member districts. Moreover, it has limited the discretion of political parties in choosing representatives under proportional representation. For instance, candidates elected from party lists must be chosen, the Court insists, in the order of their appearance on the ballot; a party, though legally responsible for submitting a nomination list, is not free to designate which members on the list are to be elected, for this would violate the principle of "direct elections."[69]

With regard to political parties as such, the Court has struck down several federal statutes. In 1958, the Second Senate voided a federal law permitting individuals and corporations to deduct contributions to the political parties (up to ten and five percent, respectively) from their taxable income.[70] Since the law favored parties supported by wealthy interests, said the Court, it violated the principle of equal opportunity for political parties. In 1966, the Second Senate struck down a federal law providing for the general financing of political parties. The law was voided for several reasons, one being that it discriminated against minor parties not represented in the Bundestag. But the Second Senate stopped short of totally prohibiting party financing; reimbursement of campaign expenses, said the Court, is permissible.[71]

In several other decisions, the Court has exercised close survelliance over state and local laws governing the admission of new parties to the ballot. The net effect of these decisions has been an enlargement of opportunity for minor parties in the states. At the municipal level, although the Court has ruled that "local parties" (*Rathausparteien*) or groups of voters do not qualify as political parties within the meaning of Article 21, they do have a constitutional right to put up candidates in their communities.[72] Another significant decision was the Equal Time Broadcasting Case, where the Court ruled that it is unconstitutional for a publicly owned radio station to deny minor parties participating in a state election access to broadcasting time for campaign purposes.[73] But the Court has not imposed an equal time policy; in a later decision, the Second Senate held that the length of broadcasting time allocated to the parties may be proportionate to their relative strengths in the community.[74]

Many of the above decisions are based on a theory of political representation that can be traced to the published writings and public views of Justice Gerhard Leibholz, who began writing on this subject when a young law professor in the 1930s at Göttingen University.[75] According to prevailing constitutional doctrine, the Basic Law consciously creates a state in which political parties are the principal agents of democratic representation. Under Article 21, political parties "participate in forming the political will of the people." This language has been used virtually to enthrone the theory of party responsibility in German constitutional law. The Constitutional Court has even elevated political parties to the rank of "constitutional institutions," the practical effect of which is to confer on parties the privilege of asseting their corporate rights in an *Organstreit* proceeding before the Federal Constitutional Court. Juridically, the Court is saying that parties are as integral to German *democracy* as are the representative organs of government. The function of political parties in Germany's "parliamentary political party mass democracy" —Leibholz's words—is to marshall the electorate for the purpose of securing an expression of the popular will. But there is language in the Court's jurisprudence to suggest that fully equal and just representation requires some form of proportional representation. The Court is aware of the values of majority voting, namely to promote political integration and governmental stability. But majority voting, emphasizing, as it does, personalities, compromise, and winning, dilutes the quality of political parties as effective agencies of policy determination. But then, would parties with vague and cloudy mandates be consistent with the notion of *Parteienstaat*? The Court's answer is unclear. What is clear is the Court's determination to protect the equal rights of minority parties, lest substantial clusters of opinion worthy of representation go unheeded in state and federal legislatures.

Concern for the integrity of parties as agencies of representation is expressed in the Court's antipathy toward interest groups. In a previous chapter, we noted the alarm with which some of the Justices viewed the prominence of interest groups in the law-making process. The Corporate Tax Case (1958), disallowing tax deductions to corporations for their contributions to political parties, was based partially on the Court's fear of interest group intrusion into the legislative process. It might be noted, incidentally, that Justice Leibholz, the reporter in the Corporate Tax Case and other cases involving political parties, is probably West Germany's leading intellectual adversary of an interest group theory of politics. On or off the bench, he is one of Germany's most outspoken protagonists of the *Parteienstaat* and what he regards as its necessary adjunct, namely proportional representation.

Is the theory of the *Parteienstaat* constitutionally broad enough to support state financing of political parties? During the 1960s this was a point of cleavage between Leibholz and most of his colleagues on the Second Senate. Leibholz believed that it is a permissible state function, perhaps even a constitutional duty, to support political parties with public funds if state financing of parties is required to maintain them as constitutional organs entrusted with forming the will of the people and to keep them free of interest group influence. In the Corporate Tax Case of 1958, the Court itself noted in dicta that public financing of parties was an alternative and, by implication, legitimate route to travel in reaching the aims specified in Article 21 of the Basic Law. The Bundestag responded to the cue almost immediately and, with the support of all parliamentary parties, enacted direct across-the-board financing for the general support of political parties, except that parties not represented in the Bundestag were excluded from public support.[76]

The Party Finance Act of 1959, along with subsequent legislation enlarging the subsidies to the parliamentary parties, was attacked almost immediately on constitutional grounds. Several minor parties excluded from the subsidies challenged the statutes in their capacity as "constitutional organs" of the state. The leading case, however, was Party Subvention Case I (1966), a product of an abstract judicial review proceeding initiated by the Hesse state government and one of the most far-reaching decisions in the history of the Federal Republic. We may recall that Leibholz's off-the-bench remarks about the Subvention Case resulted in his exclusion from participation in the decision.[77] In any event, the Second Senate—less Justice Leibholz— declared the general financing statute unconstitutional. But the Court did not ban public financing of parties altogether. Since political parties are constitutional organs of the state for the purpose of securing a popular input into the process of government, the state may reimburse them for "necessary expenses" incurred *during the course* of an election campaign; to finance parties between campaigns or to provide for their general support would, said the Court, involve an unconstitutional interference with the freedom of the political process. Parties are fundamentally social organizations, ran the argument, and are entitled to no greater claim to state support than other politically oriented voluntary associations.[78]

Clearly, Party Subvention Case I seems rooted in an old and still prevailing German view which draws a sharp distinction between state and society, a view that Leibholz rejects as a liberal myth wholly out of tune with political reality and with the needs of a modern democratic state. Still, Leibholz would most certainly have joined the Court in its view that any state reimbursement of allowable campaign expenses must be extended to all parties manifesting electoral support and not just to those already represented in Parliament. In response, the Bundestag enacted a law conditioning the reimbursement of parties for their campaign expenses on their achieving a minimum of two and one-half percent of the popular vote. But the Court's determination to continue its vigilant policy of protecting minority parties was again demonstrated in the Party Subvention Case II (1968), where the Second Senate—Leibholz this time participating— struck down the two and one-half percent rule. Even that minimal requirement, said the Court, after rehashing competing theories of the *Parteienstaat*, violates the principle of equality.[79]

We may note finally that many of the decisions concerning party and representation are marked by yet another ambivalence resulting in part from the tension between Articles 21 and 38. If parties are the primary agencies of political representation under Article 21, then how can members of Parliament be regarded as "representatives of the whole people, not bound by orders and instructions" under Article 38? Even Article 20 includes language arguably incompatible with the "party delegate" theory of representation found in some of the Court's decisions. It reads: "All state authority . . . shall be exercised by the people by means of elections and voting and by specific legislative, executive, and judicial organs." The article contains no language with respect to the intermediary role of political parties. But Article 28 of the Basic Law, which grants electoral autonomy to states and municipalities, seems also to undermine the theory of *Parteienstaat* read into Article 21. It was partly on the basis of Article 28 and the requirement of "direct" elections that the Court voided a state law prohibiting organizations other than political parties from competing in local elections.[80] So the tension between these constitutional provisions remains. Still, on the whole, the Constitutional Court's decisions reflect a judicial determination to establish and maintain an open system of electoral competition.

EQUALIZER OF SOCIO-ECONOMIC OPPORTUNITY

This section on socioeconomic opportunity might be prefaced by a few remarks about economic rights generally, especially the right to property, which is highly valued in West Germany. According to the Constitutional Court, "[property rights are] critically important to a social state based on law."[81] The Constitutional Court, like German courts generally, has been extremely vigilant in safeguarding the right to property. Yet, the Constitutional Court has come very near to adopting the U.S. Supreme Court's position, beginning with *Nebbia* v. *New York*,[82] of eschewing judicial review of the substance of statutes regulating property or other private economic interests. This is particularly true of tax policy impinging on property rights. In the widely known Investment Assistance Case (1954), which sustained a federal tax on manufacturing concerns to help certain basic industries operating under financial hardships, the Court even noted that the Basic Law is "economically neutral" as between a market-oriented or socially directed economy.[83] Thus, it is hardly surprising that the Court's policy so far has been one mainly of ratifying the political economy engineered by German political leaders as well as the system of private property on which it rests.

Within the framework of the existing political economy, however, the Federal Constitutional Court has used the equality provisions of the Basic Law to expand individual social and economic rights. The expansion of these rights depends mainly on the Court's use of the equality principle of Article 3, which states: "All persons shall be equal before the law," and adds, "Men and women shall have equal rights." Article 6 also guarantees equal rights to illegitimate children, while Article 12 grants all Germans the right freely to choose a trade or occupation. Germans incessantly invoke these provisions in constitutional complaints alleging unequal treatment or unfair discrimination at the hands of the state. In reviewing legislation alleged to incorporate unfair socioeconomic classifications, the Court adheres to a rule of self-restraint; it will not substitute its judgment for that of political decision-makers; and, usually, a classification must be manifestly arbitrary to offend the principle of equality. Yet the Constitutional Court has invalidated scores of statutory provisions on equal protection grounds, cutting a fearless swath through federal and state legislation that makes the U.S. Supreme Court look timid by comparison. This record of judicial activism may be related to the Justices' equalitarian social values, which were noted in an earlier chapter.

Illustrative of the Constitutional Court's use of the quality principle to protect and expand these social rights are several cases relating to women, children, and students. In the Parental Responsibility Case (1959), for example, the First Senate voided, contrary to an age-old German tradition of male dominance in family affairs, a provision of the Civil Code which vested the father with finality of decision in the upbringing of children in the event of parental discord. Parental responsibility for children, said the Court, is indivisible, and unresolvable conflicts between parents over the welfare of their children must be settled in family courts.[84] The Constitutional Court has expunged still other discriminations based on sex from the statute books. These include a federal law conferring on male heirs exclusive right of succession to farm land and a state civil service law providing pensions less in amount for widowers of female civil servants than for widows of male civil servants.[85]

The Court has also chipped away at legal distinctions which treat illegitimate children differently from orphans and other children in matters like inheritance and maintenance support. In the Orphans

Assistance Case (1969), the most sweeping decision in this field, the Court actually ordered the federal partliament to reform all provisions of the Civil Code relating to illegitimate children so as to place them on an equal footing with legitimate children.[86] In the Numerus Clausus Case (1972) the Court extended the protection of the equality principle to secondary school graduates seeking admission to German universities. Owing to critical shortages of space and facilities at most German institutions of higher learning, several states adopted a policy of limited admissions to professional schools. This case arose out of limitations on medical school admissions imposed by the Universities of Munich and Hamburg. The Court ruled that an absolute numerical limitation upon university admissions, in the absence of explicit standards by which applicants are ranked and selected, would violate the principle of equality. Reading the equal protection clause in tandem with Article 12, guaranteeing all Germans the right to choose a trade, the Court actually hinted that any restricted admission policy which would keep a qualified person from pursuing a career of his choice, would approach the borderline of unconstitutionality.[87]

The Court is particularly watchful over rules which limit competition and restrict membership in a trade. Thus, the Court has voided laws (1) restricting milk sellers to persons capable to selling a minimum quantity of the product, (2) putting a lid on the private taxicab trade, (3) allowing business residences, like flower shops, to operate automatic vending machines around the clock while restricting operators of independent machines to regular shop hours, (4) requiring evidence of specialized knowledge before a person could be licensed to enter the retail general merchandise trade, and (5) excluding certain doctors' participation in a state medical insurance plan.[88] On the other hand, the Court has sustained laws (1) compelling members of a profession to participate in pension insurance plans, (2) restricting the sale of certain products to pharmacies, (3) imposing age limitations on entry into certain professions, (4) denying laymen the right to act as counsel in courts of law, (5) prohibiting bakers from plying their trade at night, and (6) preventing the expansion of flour mills if the needs of the population in a given area are already adequately met.[89]

Presumption of constitutionality is the working principle governing the Constitutional Court's approach to legislation involving socio-economic classifications. Still, the scope for discretion in determining socioeconomic policy under the principle of equal protection seems less broad in Germany than in the United States. For example, the Constitutional Court has dealt harshly with certain state and local tax policies on business concerns; its decisions include nullifications of a municipal fire-fighting tax, a business tax on joint stock companies, a retail branch establishment tax, and a branch bank establishment tax.[90] By no American standard could any of these measures be regarded as invidious discrimination or an abuse of legislative discretion.

CONCLUSION

It is clear that the Federal Constitutional Court has been extremely active as a policy-making institution in the Federal Republic of Germany. Its policies have touched vital areas of German public life, from the taxing power of state governments to the federation's concern for internal security. In most instances, the Court's role has been one of validating governmental policy. But the Court has also nullified policy and occasionally has even sought to reshape it. The Court has watched over the administration of criminal justice and has defined with considerable particularity the boundaries of personal liberty in the domains of speech, press, association, and religious freedom. Even the sensitive area of federal-state relations has been subject to judicial definition. Lastly, the Court has sought to preserve an open system of elections and political competition.

This chapter has not sought critically to examine judicial policy in any substantive field of German constitutional law. Such a treatment, though fully warranted, would be the subject of another book. Suffice it to remark that the judicial policies considered here leave much to be desired as statements of constitutional doctrine. Many cases bear the stigma of crumpled logic and tell us very little about the doctrinal evolution likely to follow in their wake. But perhaps this is the place to remind ourselves once more that a technically sound decision may not be a politically feasible one. Yet political feasibility, as we shall see in the next chapter, is likely to characterize the decisions of a constitutional tribunal bent on the preservation of its own authority.

NOTES

1. Gerhard Leibholz, *Politics and Law* (Leiden: A.W. Sijthoff, 1965), p. 273.

2. The role of constitutional interpretation in West Germany is not the exclusive preserve of the Federal Constitutional Court. Any German court may refuse to give effect to a law passed prior to May 23, 1949—the effective date of the Basic Law—on the ground that it violates the Basic Law. Courts generally are also permitted to strike down administrative orders and regulations if they conflict with the Basic Law. The constitutional jurisprudence of German courts, the high federal courts especially, built on cases challenging such rules and regulations is very substantial. What these courts may not do is to strike down state and federal *statutes*. Yet, in upholding statutes against constitutional objections, the courts may, and often do, address themselves to constitutional issues, frequently without reference to the rulings of the Constitutional Court, and occasionally in opposition to them.

Major studies of federal court constitutional jurisprudence are Martin Baring, "Rechtspechung des Bundesverwaltungsgerichts zum Grundgesetz für die Bundesrepublik Deutschland," JOR 9 (1960): 93-150; Walter Bogs, Die Rechtsprechung des Bundessozialgerichts zum Grundgesetz," JOR 9 (1960): 151-178; Willi Geiger, "Die Rechtsprechung des Bundesgerichshofs zum Grundgesetz," JOR 11 (1962): 121-172; Hans Joachim Becker, "Rechtsprechung des Bundesverwaltungsgerichts zum Grundgesetz," JOR 15 (1966): 263-320; Gerhard Schnorr, "Die Rechtsprechung des Bundesarbeitsgerichts zum Grundgesetz," JOR 16 (1967): 163-182; and Hans Hoachim Faller, "Die Rechtsprechung des Bundesgerichtshofes zum Grundgesetz," JOR 17 (1968): 407-436. A good representation of the constitutional decisions of German high courts is included in Claus-Dieter Shumann, *Verfassungsrecht* (Berlin and Frankfurt a.M.: Verlag Franz Vahlen GMBH, 1968).

3. *Marbury* v. *Madison*, 1 Cranch 137 (1803); *McCulloch* v. *Maryland*, 4

Wheat. 316 (1819); and Southwest Case, Decision of October 23, 1951 (Second Senate), BVerfGE 1:14 (1952).

4. See Southwest Case, ibid., pp. 32-40.

5. The doctrine of federal comity was first enunciated in the Interstate Financial Adjustment Case, Decision of February 20, 1952 (First Senate), BVerfGE 1: 131 (1952). A notable application of this principle is Federal Television Case, Decision of February 28, 1961 (Second Senate), BVerfGE 12: 205, 254-259 (1962).

6. One of the first cases to set forth this doctrine was South Schleswig Voters Association Case, Decision of April 5, 1952 (Second Senate), BVerfGE 1: 208, 223-230 (1952). For a discussion of the role of this doctrine in German constitutional law, see Donald P. Kommers, "Politics and Jurisprudence in West Germany: State Financing of Political Parties," *American Journal of Jurisprudence* 16: 215 (1971).

7. See Civil Servant Case, Decision of October 5, 1955 (First Senate), BVerfGE 4: 294, 296 (1956).

8. Youth Welfare Case, Decision of July 18, 1967 (Second Senate), BVerfGE 22: 180, 204 (1967).

9. See Water Association Case, Decision of July 29, 1959 (First Senate), BVerfGE 10: 89, 117 (1960).

10. For a general discussion of these methods of constitutional interpretation see G. Leibholz and J.J. Rinck, *Grundgesetz für die Bundesrepublik Deutschland: Kommentar an Hand der Rechtsprechung des Bundesverfassungsgerichts*, 4th Ed. (Cologne-Marienburg: Verlag Dr. Otto Schmidt KG, 1971), pp. 3-16.

11. Hans Rupp, "Judicial Review in the Federal Republic of Germany," *American Journal of Comparative Law* 9 (1959): 33.

12. Benjamin N. Cardozo, *The Nature of the Judicial Process* (New Haven: Yale University Press, 1921), p. 12.

13. See, for example, Conscientious Objector Case, Decision of December 20, 1960, (First Senate), BVerfGE 12: 45, 53 (1962).

14. Decision of January 25, 1953, BGHZ 11 (Appendix).

15. Article 136, Weimar Constitution of August 11, 1919. This and other provisions of the Weimar Constitution related to church and state (Articles 136 to 139 and Article 141) have been carried over into Bonn's Constitution and appear there as an appendix to the Basic Law.

16. Concordat Case, Decision of March 26, 1957 (Second Senate) BVerfGE 6: 309 (1957).

17. See 333 U.S. 203 (1948) and 370 U.S. 421 (1962).

18. These laws trace their origin to certain nineteenth-century state

constitutions where, as in Hamburg, the tax officers of church and state were virtually indistinguishable. The modern basis of these laws is Article 140 of the Basic Law which incorporates certain church-state articles of the Weimar Constitution; one of these provisions is Article 137, paragraph 6 (Weimar Constitution). It states: "Religious bodies that are corporate bodies under public law shall be entitled to levy taxes in accordance with Land law on the basis of civil taxation lists."

19. Württemberg Church Tax Case, Decision of December 14, 1965 (First Senate), BVerfGE 19: 226 (1966); Baden Local Church Tax Case, December 14, 1965 (First Senate), BVerfGE 19: 242 (1966); and Mixed Marriage (Church Tax) Case, Decision of December 14 (First Senate), BVerfGE 19: 268 (1966).

20. Prison Tabacco Case, Decision of November 8, 1960 (First Senate), BVerfGE 12: 1 (1962).

21. Religious Defection Case, Decision of April 7, 1964 (First Senate), BVerfGE 17: 302 (1965); Blood Transfusion Case, Decision of October 9, 1971 (First Senate), BVerfGE 32: 98 (1972); and Religious Oath Case, Decision of April 11, 1972 (Second Senate), BVerfGE 33: 23 (1973). It is worth noting that in the Concordat Case (1957) the Court was also of the opinion that freedom of conscience did not require the state to create public schools that would accommodate all religious and philosophical minorities. See Concordat Case, op. cit., p. 309.

22. Watch Tower Bible and Tract Society Case, Decision of October 4, 1965 (First Senate), BVerfGE 19: 129 (1966).

23. 319 U.S. 105 (1943).

24. Rumpelkammer Case, Decision of October 16, 1968 (First Senate), BVerfGE 24: 236, 249-252 (1969).

25. *Weisbuch 1970 zur Sicherheit der Bundesrepublik Deutschland und zur Lage der Bundeswehr* (Bonn: Presse-und Informationsamt der Bundesregierung, 1970), p. 82.

26. See Conscientious Objector Case, op. cit., p. 45.

27. First Substitute Service Case, Decision of October 4, 1965 (First Senate) BVerfGE 19: 135 (1966).

28. Second Substitute Service Case, Decision of March 5, 1968 (First Senate), BVerfGE 23: 127 (1968).

29. Third Substitute Service Case, Decision of March 7, 1968 (Second Senate), BVerfGE 23: 191, 206-208 (1968).

30. Soldier Refusal Case, Decision of May 26, 1970 (First Senate), BVerfGE 28: 264 (1970). On the same day, the First Senate ruled also that a soldier may validly be punished for breach of duty by refusing to follow a military order while his application for conscientious objector status is

pending. See Military Discipline Case, Decision on May 26, 1970 (First Senate), BVerfGE 28: 243 (1970).

31. Military Arrest Case, Decision of October 12, 1971 (Second Senate), BVerfGE 32: 40 (1972).

32. Freedom of Information Case, Decision of October 14, 1969 (First Senate), BVerfGE 27: 104, 109 (1970).

33. Spiegel Seizure Case, Decision of August 5, 1966 (First Senate), BVerfGE 20: 162 (1967). For an account of the Spiegel affair, see Donald P. Kommers, "The Spiegel Affair: A Case Study in Judicial Politics" in Theodore L. Becker (ed.), *Political Trials* (Indianapolis and New York: Bobbs-Merrill, 1971), pp. 5-33.

34. Spiegel Seizure Case, ibid.

35. Communist Party Case, Decision of August 17, 1956 (First Senate), BVerfGE 5: 85 (1956).

36. Subversive Literature Case, Decision of October 3, 1969 (First Senate), BVerfGE 27: 71 (1970); Post Office Censor Case, Decision of October 14, 1969 (First Senate), BVerfGE 27: 88 (1970); and Freedom of Information Case, op. cit.

37. 376 U.S. 255.

38. Schmid-Spiegel Case, Decision of January 25, 1961 (First Senate), BVerfGE 12: 113, 124-132 (1962).

39. Mephisto Case, Decision of February 24, 1971 (First Senate), BVerfGE 30: 173.

40. Luth-Harlan Case, Decision of January 15, 1958 (First Senate), BVerfGE 7: 198 (1958).

41. Blinkfuer Case, Decision of February 26, 1969 (First Senate), BVerfGE 25: 256 (1969).

42. Military Free Speech Case, Decisions of February 18, 1970 (Second Senate), BVerfGE 28: 36, 51, and 55 (1970).

43. Ibid., pp. 48-49.

44. Mephisto Case, op. cit., p. 225.

45. Democratic Women's Association Case, Decision of October 18, 1961 (First Senate), BVerfGE 13: 174 (1963).

46. Society for German-Soviet Friendship Case, Decision of March 21, 1961 (Second Senate), BVerfGE 12: 296, 300 (1962).

47. See Chamber of Commerce Case, Decision of December 19, 1962 (First Senate), BVerfGE 15: 235 (1964); Bavarian Doctors Case, Decision of Febuary 25, 1960 (First Senate), BVerfGE 10: 354 (1960); Investment Assistance Case, Decision of July 20, 1954 (First Senate), BVerfGE 4: 7 (1956); and Joint Stock Corporation Case, Decision of July 29, 1959 (First

Senate), BVerfGE 10: 89 (1960).

48. Catholic Domestic Association Case, Decision of May 6, 1964 (First Senate), BVerfGE 18: 18 (1965).

49. Housing Application Case, Decision of July 23, 1958 (First Senate), BVerfGE 8: 95 (1959).

50. Passport Case, Decision of January 16, 1957 (First Senate), BVerfGE 6: 32 (1957).

51. See, respectively, Drunk Driving Case, Decision of July 3, 1962 (Second Senate), BVerfGE 14: 174 (1963); Special Detention Case, op. cit.; and Institutional Commitment Case, February 10, 1960 (First Senate), BVerfGE 10: 302 (1960).

52. Neurosurgical Case, Decision of June 10, 1963 (First Senate), BVerfGE 16: 194, 196-198 (1964).

53. Encephalography Case, Decision of July 25, 1963 (First Senate), BVerfGE 17: 108 (1965).

54. See *Rochin* v. *California*, 342 U.S. 165 (1952) and *Breithaupt* v. *Abram*, 352 U.S. 432 (1957).

55. Federal Wiretapping Case, Decision of July 7, 1970 (Second Senate), BVerfGE 30: 1 (1971).

56. Southwest Case, op. cit.

57. See Gerhard Leibholz, "The Federal Constitutional Court in Germany and the 'Southwest Case,'" *American Political Science Review* 46: 726 (1952).

58. Competitive Salary Scale Case, Decision of December 1, 1954 (Second Senate), BVerfGE 4: 118 (1956).

59. Under Article 83 of the Basic Law, the states "execute Federal laws as matters of their own concern insofar as this Basic Law does not otherwise provide or permit." See State Steam Boiler Case, Decision of March 15, 1960 (Second Senate), BVerfGE 11: 6 (1961) and River Transportation Case, Decision of April 11, 1967 (Second Senate), BVerfGE 21: 312 (1967).

60. 252 U.S. 416 (1920).

61. Concordat Case, op. cit.

62. Federal Television Case, op. cit.

63. Ibid., pp. 255-259.

64. Atomic Referenda Case, Decision of July 30, 1958 (Second Senate), BVerfGE 8: 122 (1959). In an abstract review proceeding, the Second Senate struck down on the same day, but for different reasons, Bremen and Hamberg laws providing for statewide referenda on atomic rearmament. See Bremen and Hamburg Referendum Cases, Decision of July 30, 1958 (Second Senate), BVerfGE 8: 104 (1959).

65. These views are more completely discussed in Kommers, "Politics and Jurisprudence in West Germany," op. cit., pp. 223-228.

66. Socialist Reichs Party Case, Decision of October 23, 1952 (First Senate), BVerfGE 2:1 (1953) and Communist Party Case, op. cit.

67. Communist Party Case, ibid., p. 144.

68. The combined system of elections was sustained in South Schleswig Voters Association Case, op. cit.; the list system of elections in Proportional Representation Case, Decision of July 3, 1957 (Second Senate), BVerfGE 7: 63, 69 (1958); the five percent rule in Bavarian Party Case, Decision of January 23, 1957 (Second Senate), BVerfGE 6: 84 (1957); and the one man/one vote rule in Equal Representation Case, Decision of May 22, 1963 (Second Senate), BVerfGE 16: 130 (1964).

69. See Bundestag Election Case, Decision of August 26, 1961 (Second Senate), BVerfGE 13: 127 (1962). On the question of whether local political associations are entitled to run as political parties, see Municipal Representation Case, Decision of November 11, 1953 (Second Senate) BVerfGE 3: 45 (1954). On whether party leaders may substitute names on party lists at will, see Party List Case, Decision of July 9, 1957 (Second Senate), BVerfGE 7: 77 (1958).

70. Corporate Tax Case, Decision of June 24, 1958 (Second Senate), BVerfGE 8: 51 (1959).

71. Party Subvention Case I, Decision of July 19, 1966 (Second Senate), BVerfGE 20: 56 (1967).

72. German Center Party Case, Decision of May 7, 1957 (Second Senate), BVerfGE 6: 367 (1957).

73. Equal Time Broadcasting Case, Decision of September 3, 1957 (Second Senate), BVerfGE 7: 99 (1958).

74. Free Democratic Party Case, Decision of May 30, 1962 (Second Senate), BVerfGE 14:121 (1963).

75. A selection of Leibholz's earlier work on parties and representation is included in Gerhard Leibholz, *Strukturproblem der Modernen Demokratie* (Karlsruhe: Verlag C.F. Müller, 1967).

76. See, for example, Law on Party Finance, March 18, 1965, BGBl. II, p. 193 (1965).

77. Leibholz Exclusion Case, Decision of March 3, 1966 (Second Senate), BVerfGE 20: 9 (1967).

78. Party Subvention Case I, op. cit.

79. Party Subvention Case II, op. cit.

80. Community Election Case, Decision of July 9, 1957 (Second Senate), BVerfGE 7: 77 (1958).

81. Finance Company Case, Decision of August 7, 1962 (First Senate), BVerfGE 14: 263, 277 (1963).

82. 291 U.S. 502 (1934).

83. Investment Assistance Case, op. cit., p. 18.

84. Parental Responsibility Case, Decision of July 29, 1959 (First Senate), BVerfGE 10: 59 (1960).

85. Male Inheritance Case, Decision of March 20, 1963 (First Senate), BVerfGE 15: 337 (1964) and Hamburg Widow Case, Decision of April 11, 1967 (Second Senate), BVerfGE 21: 329 (1967).

86. Orphans Assistance Case, Decision of January 29, 1969 (First Senate), BVerfGE 25: 167, 187-188 (1969).

87. Numerus Clausus Case, Decision of July 18, 1972 (First Senate), BVerfGE 33: 303 (1973).

88. See Small Milk Dealer Case, Decision of December 17, 1958 (First Senate), BVerfGE 9: 39 (1959); Taxicab Case, Decision of June 8, 1960 (First Senate), BVerfGE 11: 68 (1961); Automatic Vendor Case, Decision of February 21, 1962 (First Senate), BVerfGE 14: 19 (1963); Retail Licensing Case, Decision of December 14, 1965 (First Senate), BVerfGE 19: 330 (1966); Medical Insurance Case, Decision of March 23, 1960 (First Senate), BVerfGE 11: 30 (1961).

89. See Bavarian Doctors Case, op. cit.; Drug Regulation Case, Decision of January 7, 1959 (First Senate), BVerfGE 9:73 (1959); Midwife Case, Decision of June 15, 1959 (First Senate), BVerfGE 9: 338 (1959); Legal Consultant Case, Decision of November 17, 1959 (First Senate), BVerfGE 10: 185 (1960); Baker's Case, Decision of January 23, 1968 (First Senate), BVerfGE 23: 50 (1968); and Flour Mill Case, Decision of December 18, 1968 (First Senate), BVerfGE 25:1 (1969).

90. See, respectively, Municipal Fire-Fighting Case, Decision of May 20, 1959 (First Senate), BVerfGE 9: 291 (1959); Business Tax Case, January 24, 1962 (First Senate), BVerfGE 13: 331 (1962); Branch Establishment Tax Case, Decision of July 13, 1965 (First Senate), BVerfGE 19: 101 (1966); and Bank Establishment Tax Case, Decision of February 14, 1967 (First Senate), BVerfGE 21: 160 (1967).

7

IMPACT

This chapter turns to an examination of the Constitutional Court's impact on the West German political system. It must be added at the beginning, however, that precisely to determine the effects of any judicial tribunal is risky. We can plot the sequence of political events and show that certain results followed judicial decisions, but it is hazardous to equate sequential with cause-and-effect relationships. Perhaps the best we can do with the limited investigative resources and techniques at our disposal is to treat judicial decisions and the behavior of judicial officers in association with other political events in the modest hope of making sensible and guarded statements about the Constitutional Court's influence upon the public mind and in the political system.

The term "impact" is extremely broad and includes a variety of responses to judicial decisions and consequences of judicial policy. Judicial decisions may affect government agencies, public opinion, organized groups, the legitimacy of public policy, the public at large, or the political system as a whole. They may also generate reactions which are fed back into the Court, affecting its future decisions, modes of operation, and personnel.[1] Not all these dimensions of impact can be examined in this chapter. Some impacts would in any case be extemely difficult to monitor; for example, the long-range social consequences or outcomes of judicial policy or even the effect of Constitutional Court decisions on private parties bringing constitutional complaints. Unless an individual person comes forward publicly to announce that he or she has filed a constitutional complaint, there is no easy way of establishing a complainant's identity, for compainants' names are not revealed in judicial decisions.

This exploratory study of the Federal Constitutional Court's political impact relies on data that are readily accessible to a single investigator. The data have been organized around the notions of awareness, support, compliance, and durability. Although lacking the elegance of conceptual refinement, these terms furnish us with a convenient frame of reference for assessing the relative impact of the Federal Constitutional Court. *Awareness* is defined as the level of information about the Constitutional Court available to the public and special elite groups. A principal object of our investigation here is to examine the means used to communicate information about the Constitutional Court and the extent to which its activities and decisions are publicized. *Support* refers to the approval which the Court and its policies enjoy in the Federal Republic. In Eastonian terms, support may be diffuse or specific—we shall examine both dimensions. *Compliance* means acquiescence in Constitutional Court decisions. Here we deal mainly with the Court's relation to other branches of government. Finally, *durability* refers to the Court's capacity to survive as an authoritative institution over time. Durability, although it frequently directs attention back to the Court itself as well as to its role in the policy-making process, is treated here as an important dimension of political impact. How the Court's involvement in certain policy areas affects its own institutional status and capacity to influence events will be the subject of our inquiry.

AWARENESS

Communication of Judicial Decisions

How are Federal Constitutional Court decisions transmitted to the outside world? Who are the carriers of judicial messages and who is on the receiving end of these communications? How much attention is given to these messages? These queries are an important dimension of any analysis of judicial impact; indeed, the manner by which judicial messages are publicized and consumed seems sure to affect awareness, support, and implementation of judicial decisions.

We might begin with the channels of communication. Decisions of the Constitutional Court appear originally in mineographed form. As the decisions are handed down, copies are produced for distribution among the Justices, their clerks, and an extremely limited group of people outside the Court. Important or lengthy opinions usually contain headnotes (*Leitsätze*) prepared by the Justices themselves. The mailing list of recipients outside the Court includes the president and Chancellor of the Federal Republic, selected members of Parliament, the presidents of state and federal courts, certain cabinet officers and senior civil servants, some legal scholars, journalists and newscasters specializing in constitutional law, and other persons with a special interest in receiving the full text of the decisions immediately. (The list must be approved by the president of the Court.) The decisions are assembled quarterly and printed in an advanced edition—entitled *Entscheidungen des Bundesverfassungsgerichts*—much like the advanced sheets of the *United States Supreme Court Reports*—except that in Germany they are published exclusively by a private firm (J.C.B. Mohr [Paul Siebeck]) in Tübingen, a leading publisher of German legal materials. The bound volumes, comprising an average of thirty-five cases, appear about a year later. Serving a highly specialized audience, they are sent to university and state libraries, government agencies, and any other group or person with funds to purchase them.

Constitutional Court decisions reach an even wider audience of specialists through several notable journals, the most important of which is *Neue Juristische Wochenschrift*. Others include *Juristenzeitung*, *Die Oeffentliche Verwaltung*, *Deutsches Verwaltungsblatt*, and *Monatschrift für Deutsches Recht*, not to mention more specialized legal journals such as *Recht der Arbeit*, *Deutscher Steuerrecht*, and *Zeitschrift für das gesamte Familienrecht*. All are national publications with a large circulation and readership among lawyers, judges, civil servants, and law professors. Ordinarily these journals carry the full or partial text of selected Constitutional Court decisions. Ranging across the whole field of private and public law, these periodicals are major conduits of information on what is happening in German courts. Their role, incidentally, is somewhat analogous to American law reviews, although the German periodicals are produced and edited not by students but by distinguished practicing lawyers, judges, and law professors.

Equally important to the spread of knowledge about the Constitutional Court are certain quarterly and yearly publications whose readership includes not only academicians and lawyers, but all serious students of public affairs almost everywhere in Germany. The best known and most widely read is *Archiv des Oeffentlichen Rechts*, which devotes nearly half its space to analytical commentary on Constitutional Court decisions. The other periodicals include *Deutsche Richterzeitung*, *Jahrbuch des Oeffentlichen Rechts*, *Die Dritte Gewalt*, and *Zeitschrift für Rechtspolitik* as well as notable political science journals such as *Verfassung und Verfassungswirklichkeit*, *Der Staat*, *Politische Vierteljahresschrift*, *Die Politische Meinung*, and *Jahrbuch für Sozial Wissenschaft*. There seems little doubt that such journals have contributed measurably to awareness of the Federal Constitutional Court among legal and academic elites.

Interest group elites, through their own specialized publications, are also kept in touch with Constitutional Court decisions especially relevant to them. For example, decisions affecting civil servants are invariably discussed in the pages of *Der Deutsche Beamte*, *Bayerische Beamtenzeitung*, and *Der Beamtenbund*, among others. In addition, large numbers of German university students—elites to-be—are learning about their political system through the eyes of the Federal Constitutional Court. Leading textbooks used in the disciplines of law and political science contain more and more references to Constitutional Court decisions. A good example is Konrad Hesse's widely read primer on the Federal Republic's system of government; each successive edition is more heavily grounded in Constitutional Court decisions.[2]

Public officials learn of Constitutional Court decisions like ordinary citizens, through the public media. There is also an official transmission belt known as the Federal Law Gazette (*Bundesgesetzblatt*). Federal law requires that all rulings (not full opinions) declaring statutes to be compatible or incompatible with the Basic Law or other federal law or those which invalidate law altogether are to be published along with federal statutes in the Gazette, which is directly available to all legislators (state and federal) and civil servants entrusted with the enforcement of federal law. The actual publication of these rulings is the personal responsibility of the Federal Minister of Justice.[3]

We have noted how Constitutional Court decisions are communicated to specialized audiences,[4] but how are they communicated to the general public? Here we need to consider the quality and frequency of the messages sent out from the Court and the modes of their delivery. Before doing so, however, we need to say something about the larger context of the German communications system.

If newspaper and magazine circulation is any measure of a people's appetite for news, the Germans are surely among the most information-hungry in the world. In 1971, there were over 500 newspapers in Germany with a circulation of nearly 22 million copies. Periodicals and popular magazines are read with even greater attention. Those which deal with political matters alone number over 1,200 (just short of 11 million circulation). When added to several thousand other periodicals in the spheres of economics, culture, and general social interest, total circulation per printing exceeds 250 million, almost 4 for every resident German citizen. Germans are also tuned into around 16.2 million television sets (71 out of every 100 households), with 15 to 25% of viewing time devoted to political events and public affairs. Nearly every household has a radio. The ordinary citizen probably receives his day-to-day political fare from radio, television, and local newspapers. Political and institutional elites together with the educated middle classes are likely to receive their fare from "high-brow" daily and weekly national subscription newspapers such as *Frankfurter Allgemeine Zeitung* (circulation 255,000), *Die Welt* (235,000), *Süddeutsche Zeitung* (261,000), *Die Zeit* (261,000), and *Christ und Welt* (147,000). The weekly news magazine most read by both high and middle brows is, of course, the well-known—and pugnacious—*Der Spiegel* (1 million).[5]

The transmission of judicial messages to the general public through these media begins at the Constitutional Court itself, where the director prepares a press release (*Verlautbarung*) on each decision as it is handed down. These announcements are routinely distributed to the wire services, individual newspapers, and magazine reporters, and representatives of the broadcast media. Few of these releases, however, are newsworthy, and most of the Court's decisions go unreported in the media. But wide coverage is accorded to the "big" cases. The best news coverage of the Court appears in the "high-brow" publications, several of which are staffed by reporters and editors with expertise in legal affairs; a few have academic backgrounds in law or political science. Here it is possible to mention Hans Schueler and Theo Sommer (*Die Zeit*), Rolf Lamprecht (*Der Spiegel*), and Hans Schuster (*Süddeutsche Zeitung*); looming over them all is Friederick Karl Fromme (*Frankfurter Allgemeine Zeitung*), whose frequent articles on the Constitutional Court are on a par with the best coverage of the U.S. Supreme Court by reporters the calibre of Anthony Lewis (*New York Times*).

The Constitutional Court seems able to draw attention to itself in the media generally by a very careful spacing in time of important decisions, although this appears to be the fortuitous result of its internal mode of operation. It avoids bunching landmark cases at the end of a term, as so often happens with the U.S. Supreme Court, thus limiting the confusion and dilution of its communications. Nor are decisions handed down on any particular day of the week; rather they trickle down on a day-to-day basis in accordance with the convenience or design of the Justices. And because the Court rarely holds public sessions, it can usually guarantee a large press turnout on those occasions when it does decide to hear oral argument in a case; that oral argument is held at all usually signals a case of major public importance. On such occasions, too, the Court may choose to announce the decision in public session, with the presiding Justice reading the text in the glare of klieg lights and before a battery of reporters.

The Court is always in the news, of course, when Justices are being recruited, when they are engulfed in public controversy, or when a case of high political senstivity is before one of the senates. At such times, the Court and Justices are often the subject of television decumentaries and cover stories in influential magazines such as *Der Spiegel*. Recently, for instance, the Court received publicity owing to Bavaria's decision to challenge the validity of the Federal Republic's Basic Treaty with East Germany. The spotlight fell on Justice Joachim Rottmann, whose participation in the case was challenged following a public address in which he discussed the international legal status of Berlin. The entire episode provided grist for publication mills as well as an occasion for one of those menacing *Der Spiegel* interviews, for which the magazine is so popular, with President Ernst Benda. Going far beyond a discussion of the treaty itself, the interview included questions about the political background and personal views of the Justices and the general role of the Constitutional Court in German politics.[6]

The Court also manages to create news about its non-judicial activities. The retirement of distinguished or the swearing in of new Justices is ordinarily covered by the media. Such functions are usually attended by the president of the Federal Republic. In 1972, for example, there were two half-hour documentary programs about the Constitutional Court on prime-time television, one of them coincident with the swearing in of a new president and several new Justices. In addition, the press office frequently prepares press releases on the reception of foreign dignitaries inside the Court, on awards and honors received by Justices outside the Court, and on the anniversaries of the deaths of previous presidents and vice presidents.

Range of Visibility and Knowledge

As the burgeoning clipping files in the archives of the Federal

Constitutional Court will attest, the volume of reportage on the Court and its activities is substantial. Still this does not tell us who or how many Germans are receiving messages about the Court, however intuitively reasonable it is to assume that these numbers must also be substantial. Nor do we know how clearly these messages are getting through, but one would surmise from all we know about West Germany's political culture that they are being consumed with an appreciable knowledge of their content. Certainly we would expect political and institutional elites to score highly on awareness and knowledge of the Court. Fortunately, some empirical support is available to substantiate these impressions.

In the spring of 1968, a questionnaire was mailed to seven elite groups in West Germany whose attitudes toward the Court were presumed to be of critical importance. These groups consisted of federal judges, state judges, high civil servants, professors of public law, party leaders, interest group leaders, together with journalists and television commentators who write and report on law and judicial matters.[7] The questionnaire sought to solicit respondents' reactions to fourteen major Constitutional Court decisions. In only one instance did the "don't knows" and "no opinions" exceed positive and negative reactions. (We shall return to the specific results of this study in the next section.)

We would expect awareness to be strongest among elite groups, especially those associated with government. In 1968, Mannheim University's Social Science Research Institute conducted a systematic survey of elite attitudes, in part to determine what importance respondents attached to the influence of various institutions (public and private), including the Constitutional Court, upon West German politics.[8] (Respondents were asked to reply without regard to their personal feelings as to how much influence *should* be accorded to any institution.) Table 15 reveals the Court's impact upon the consciousness of critical elite groups. Greater significance was attached to the influence of the Federal Cabinet, Bundesrat, federal bureaucracy, federal bank, and private industry; nevertheless, consciousness of the Court in the minds of these elites is substantial when it is considered that most of these other institutions have far higher public profiles than the Constitutional Court.

TABLE 15

ELITE ASSESSMENT OF THE FEDERAL CONSTITUTIONAL COURT'S
INFLUENCE UPON THE WEST GERMAN FEDERAL REPUBLIC

Elite Groups (Respondents = 400)	Very Important	Important	Not Very Important
Top party functionaries	14%	41%	45%
Federal Legislative Leaders	37	42	21
State Legislative Leaders	10	66	24
Top civil servants (federal)	24	35	41
Top civil servants (state)	7	63	30
Publishers	31	44	25
Editors	24	48	28
Labor Leaders	23	40	33
Industrial Leaders	18	52	23
Professors	27	31	42

SOURCE: Rudolf Wildenmann, *Eliten in der Bundesrepublik: eine sozialwissenschaftliche Untersuchung über Einstellungen führender Posittionsträger zur Politik und Demokratie* (Mannheim University, August 1968), pp. 61-66.

The Mannheim Institute also found the general public measurably aware of the Constitutional Court, as Table 16 shows. The following question was included in a December 1967 survey of a random sample of West Germans: "Do you by chance know what the functions of the Federal Constitutional Court in Karlsruhe are?" A substantial number of Germans were able to iden ify these functions, indicating an awareness rivaling the visibility of the Supreme Court among Americans.[9]

Popular awareness of major judicial decisions is also quite substantial. For instance, one month after the Court's decision in the Federal Television Case (1961) was handed down, the Noelle-Neumann Allensbach Institute found that eighty-five percent of the population had heard about the case.[10] Years earlier, in 1954, when the European Defense Community Treaty was before the Court, fifteen percent of Allensbach respondents reported having discussed the case in detail with fellow citizens.[11] These data are consistent

TABLE 16

PUBLIC AWARENESS OF THE FEDERAL CONSTITUTIONAL COURT

Awareness	N = 2016	Percent
A. General		
1. No answer or knowledge		58
2. Aware		42
B. Functions mentioned by those aware		
1. Protects Basic Law		17
2. Decides constitutional complaints		8
3. Serves as general court of last resort		5
4. Tries cases involving espionage, treason, and other offenses against state security		3
5. Reviews legislation and acts of parliament, government, and the police		1
6. Safeguards the democratic order		1
7. Other		7

SOURCE: A random sample survey of the West German population conducted by the Social Science Research Institute of Mannheim University. The author is indebted to Professor Rudolf Wildemann and Dr. Max Kaase for their generosity in supplying these figures.

with Almond and Verba's finding that Germans follow accounts of political affairs as much as Americans, a curiosity which seems partly related to the Federal Republic's impressive system of communication.

SUPPORT

Elites and the General Public

Awareness alone is no measure of public support for the Constitutional Court, although it is surely one of its conditions. It is customary to distinguish between two kinds of support: diffuse and specific. Support is diffuse when an institution is sustained by generalized feelings of loyalty and affection; it is specific when the political community approves of its particular policies or decisions. In a phrase, support is related to public confidence in an institution and particularly to the legitimacy of its authority. We cannot chart here the total configuration of the Court's support. The available evidence allows us, at best, to sketch out the rough contours of *current* support for the Constitutional Court among Germans.

Easton regards ideology as an important source of legitimacy. If we take ideology to mean a system of beliefs or body of norms surrounding an institution there is reason to believe the Federal Constitutional Court enjoys "a reservoir of freely available [diffuse] support."[12] This may not have been so in the beginning when judicial review was very much in controversy among lawyers, academicians, and judges. Yet it is not adventurous to suggest that a majority of the informed public as well as critical elites now regard the Constitutional Court, if not always with affection, at least as an important component of West Germany's system of government. Increasingly the Court seems to be associated in the public mind with such values as constitutionalism, rule of law, liberal democracy, and protection of individual rights, expressive perhaps of the hopes, beliefs, and aspirations of the Basic Law itself. Nor is it unreasonable to suppose that the moral predisposition of Germans to accept their system of government and authoritative decisions made within it is another source of diffuse support for the Constitutional Court.[13]

Some empirical data are available to confirm the existence of diffuse support. One such measure is the acceptance of judicial review by critical elite groups. Here we may return to this writer's previously mentioned study of elite attitudes in Germany. When asked whether in their opinion judicial review was necessary for the stability and continuity of German democracy, forty-four percent of respondents replied "absolutely necessary," forty-nine percent "somewhat necessary," three percent "not very necessary," and one percent "unnecessary." When asked to appraise the Court's record during its first seventeen years of activity, twelve percent responded "very good," fifty-six percent "good," twenty-seven percent "satisfactory," and three percent "unsatisfactory." A slight difference in the responses of Social and Christian Democrats was discernible, however. Higher ratings were scored by Social Democrats, with seventy-seven percent recording "very good" or "good" compared with sixty-three percent of Christian Democrats; thirty-five percent of Christian Democrats scored "satisfactory" compared with twenty percent of Social Democrats, a result possibly related to Social Democratic success over the years in challenging Christian Democratic policies before the Constitutional Court.[14]

The Mannheim study once again tends to confirm these results. Table 17 is a disclosure of elite feeling on whether the Constitutional Court *should* have more or less influence on West German politics. We seem justified in presuming from these data considerable elite satisfaction with the Constitutional Court's role in the Federal Republic.

The Court also enjoys considerable specific support among elite groups. Table 18, based on this writer's survey, lists fourteen major decisions which occasioned much public comment and controversy; most were discussed in the previous chapter. However, the pattern of support in some cases varied considerably by party identification, as Table 19 shows. With respect to the remaining cases, the pattern of

TABLE 17

ELITE ASSESSMENT OF INFLUENCE CONSTITUTIONAL COURT
OUGHT TO HAVE IN FEDERAL REPUBLIC

Group (N = 400)	More	Less
Top Party Functionaries	20	10
Federal Legislative Leaders	14	14
State Legislative Leaders	10	6
Top Civil Servants (federal)	6	0
Top Civil Servants (state)	8	12
Publishers	20	0
Editors	38	0
Labor Leaders	20	0
Industrial Leaders	10	0
Professors	20	6
Total	14	14

SOURCE: *Eliten in der Bundesrepublik*, pp. 73 and 75.

TABLE 18

SUPPORT FOR CONSTITUTIONAL COURT DECISIONS*

Decision	(Respondents = 164) Agree	Disagree	No Opinion	No Knowledge
Communist Party Case (1956)	51%	31%	—	—
Passport Case (1957)	26	10	10%	17%
Homosexuality Case (1957)	29	27	10	17
Concordat Case (1957)	47	22	9	7
Income Tax Case (1957)	65	4	5	10
Luth Case (1958)	54	6	10	15
Party Subvention Case I (1958)	48	27	7	2
Atomic Weapons Case (1958)	52	17	8	8
Federal T.V. Case (1961)	53	21	5	6
Apothecary Case (1958)	63	15	2	5
Equal Time Case (1958)	57	8	7	11
Church Tax Case (1965)	62	4	3	11
Spiegel Case (1966)	48	26	4	—
Party Subvention Case II (1966)	48	31	4	2

*The percentages do not total 100 because of respondents' refusal to react to some cases or attempts by them to qualify their answers. Refusals and doctored responses do not appear in the table.

TABLE 19

SUPPORT FOR CONSTITUTIONAL COURT DECISIONS
BY PARTY IDENTIFICATION

Case	CDU/CSU (N = 60) A*	D	SPD (N = 56) A	D	FDP (N = 24) A	D
Communist party	67%	12%	41%	50%	42%	50%
Concordat	47	17	46	29	54	25
Homosexuality	33	8	25	41	21	46
Party Subvention I	22	40	70	14	50	37
Atomic Weapons	60	3	48	32	46	17
Television	25	43	82	5	79	4
Spiegel	42	23	52	34	58	33
Party Subvention II	30	43	66	21	42	46

*A: agree; D: disagree.

disagreement was rather uniform. On only the Federal Television Case, as noted in Table 20, is there empirical evidence of specific support on the part of the general public. The result here approximates the reaction of party elites in this writer's findings. Thus the Court seems able to count on substantial support from elites which may be considered crucial to the acceptance of judicial review in Germany.

TABLE 20

SUPPORT FOR FEDERAL TELEVISION
CASE BY WEST GERMAN POPULATION

	Good	Response to Decision		No Opinion
		Not Good	Undecided	
Total population	50%	8%	18%	24%
CDU/CSU supporters	46	13	20	21
SPD supporters	64	6	15	15
FDP/DVP supporters	63	12	8	17

SOURCE: Elisabeth Noelle and Erich Peter Neumann, *Jahrbuch der Offentlichen Meinung 1958-1964* (Allensbach and Bonn: Verlag fur Demoskopie, 1965), p. 115.

The Judiciary

A special word needs to be said about German judges generally and their support of the Constitutional Court. Lower court judges are extremely critical of the functioning of judicial review in Germany. First, lower courts feed cases into the Constitutional Court, allowing it to exercise its full authority; most statutes coming before the Court are there only because lower courts have *chosen* to petition the Court to review laws of doubtful constitutionality. Second, the Constitutional Court requires the support of other courts if its decisions are to have any impact at all on the administration of law. The constitutional complaints of ordinary citizens would probably keep the Court busy and sustain it as an institution, but a docket limited to such complaints would seriously affect the content of the Court's output and the character of its support as well. There was some fear in the beginning that judges, the large majority of who were recruited to the bench prior to 1945 and committed to a positivist jurisprudence, would impede the development of judicial review—and, hence, of constitutional law—by refusing to challenge the authority of the legislature on the basis of the higher values of the Basic Law.

After noting that the judiciary as a whole—composed of some 1,200 courts—submits fewer than sixty petitions (in concrete judicial review proceedings) yearly to the Constitutional Court, it is tempting to conclude that German judges lack enthusiasm for the Court as an institution and judicial review as a constitutional principle.[15] But this needs to be set off against the fact that the Constitutional Court itself has stiffened the rules gover ning the admissibility of such cases and that concrete review cases nevertheless occupy much of the Court's time and are a source of many important decisions. The tribunals which have petitioned the Constitutional Court least are the high federal courts of appeal. The presidents of these courts have even publicly vented their spleens against the Constitutional Court for decisions regarded by them as encroachments upon their own authority. (More on this in the next section.) Still, there is reason to believe that high federal judges are no less supportive of the Constitutional Court than other judges. Indeed, some evidence points to very positive support. Only a small minority of the seventeen federal court judges who responded to this writer's elite survey recorded negative attitudes toward the Constitutional Court. Though failing to answer the questionnaire, five high federal judges responded by letter to express their general approval of the Court. For instance, a senate president of the Federal Social Court wrote: "I am extremely satisfied with the jurisprudence of the Federal Constitutional Court. It has contributed significantly to the development in Germany of a free liberal state based on law." Commented a senate president of the Federal Administrative Court: "On the whole, I believe judicial review has been an advance for the Federal Republic of Germany and that the Federal Constitutional Court in Karlsruhe has managed to perform its assigned task quite successfully." Declining to reply, a senate president of the Federal Supreme Court noted: "My respect for the Federal Constitutional Court is simply too high, if I may say so, to dispose of its decisions with a checkmark indicating my approval or disapproval.''[16]

With respect to the judiciary generally, recent research by the Mannheim Institute has yielded some significant results. Interviews with 1,032 judges (from all ranks of the judiciary) revealed not only positive judicial attitudes toward the Federal Republic as a democratic system of government, but also toward the Constitutional Court. The judges were asked to rank twelve institutions (on a six-point scale) in terms of their actual and desired significance in the political system. The rankings presented in Table 21 seem to suggest that German judges prefer that political power be monopolized by the formal institutions of government. Whatever else may be suggested by these findings, it seems reasonable to conclude that the status of the Constitutional Court as an *authoritative* decision-maker is an important source of diffuse support, at least among judges.

TABLE 21

RANKINGS OF FEDERAL CONSTITUTIONAL COURT
BY GERMAN JUDGES (N = 1032)

Actual Significance		Desired Significance
Rank	Institution	Rank
1	Federal Chancellor	2
2	Federal Parliament	1
3	Federal Government	3
4	Political Parties	5
5	Mass Media	10
6	Federal Constitutional Court	4
7	Labor Unions	9
8	Ministerial Bureaucracy	11
9	Bundesrat	6
10	Big Business	12
11	Federal Bank	7
12	Federal President	8

SOURCE: Manfred Riegel, "Political Attitudes Towards and Perceptions of the Political System by Judges in West Germany" (Paper delivered at the Ninth World Congress of the International Political Science Association, Montreal, August 20-25), p. 5a.

It is appropriate to remark, finally, that the strongest support for the Constitutional Court within the judicial branch has come from the Court's own members. The Justices have in fact been the most ardent defenders of the Court in Germany. This is not surprising, but the off-the-bench activity of the Justices in their own defense, particularly during the Court's infancy, seems to have generated support—a kind of self-impact—for the Court in the wider political community. The first six years of the Court's existence found the Second Senate, because of accidental circumstances, with almost nothing to do. We may recall that the Second Senate was composed of some of the Court's most talented, prolific, and outspoken Justices: Katz Leibholz, Federer, Rupp, Geiger, Friesenhahn, and Schunk come to mind. All were heavily engaged at the time in off-the-bench activities—writing, lecturing, debating, and attending conferences. Five continued to teach law at German universities. Geiger had time to write an authoritative commentary on the Federal Constitutional Court Act while Leibholz and Schunck were preparing authoritative commentaries on the Basic Law itself. All were flooding law periodicals with articles about the Court and its role in the Federal Republic. All were true believers in the Court's appointed trust, as they scolded the Court's enemies and corrected the erring ways of its milder critics. They drummed away at the notion that the Court and they, the Justices, were the ultimate guardians of German liberty and democracy. They unceasingly reminded their countrymen, the bar, fellow judges, and Bonn politicians that the Court was not only the nation's highest tribunal but also a constitutional organ coequal in status with the Bundestag, Bundesrat, the federal president, and the federal government, and was supreme in constitutional matters.

All told it was a stellar performance, almost as if the Second Senate had been commissioned to defend and praise the work of the First. That the Court in these critical years was also able to decide several cases of momentous political importance without diminishing its authority or tarnishing its image as a mecca of the *Rechtsstaat* may be attributed largely to the cohesion, restraint, and sagacity of the Court as a whole under the strong yet facile leadership of Höpker-Aschoff. As every student of the American Supreme Court knows, this is a very subtle game to play, involving the use of symbols, myths, and the right combination of power and reason to establish a species of authority capable of generating public respect and influencing the public mind.

COMPLIANCE

As Joel B. Grossman and Richard S. Wells have noted, "The terms compliance and impact have different meanings." They caution that compliance "may occur because of other pressures or forces within the system." Yet they treat compliance as a form of impact, as we do here, so long as it is not forgotten that "widespread evasion or defiance or other unintended consequences may also follow from a Supreme Court decision."[17] This section considers the response of Parliament, the federal government, the states, and the high federal courts to selected decisions of the Federal Constitutional Court. The cases selected are mainly those where compliance was a problem or where resistance to judicial mandates might have been expected given the nature of the controversy or the form in which the judicial decision was cast. Only the responses of major branches of government are considered here. It would, of course, be interesting and relevant to monitor the behavioral responses of public officials (e.g., policemen, prosecutors, civil servants, lower court judges, etc.) ultimately responsible for carrying out the Court's directives. But any empirical study of patterns of compliance (or defiance) at this level of government—much like the study of the broad social consequences of judicial decisions—would require a research effort beyond the means of a single investigator.

Federal Parliament

One of the Federal Constitutional Court's functions is to review the constitutionality of parliamentary statutes. Whether the Court obtains a parliamentary reaction to a decision which nullifies a statute or provision of law depends on the nature of the case and the specificity of the court's instructions. A distinctive feature of German judicial review, it will be remembered, is that any decision which holds legislation unconstitutional has the force of general law and is binding on all public officials.[18] A proper—and compliant—response to such a decision would be an amendment expressly repealing the voided provisions. For example, just a few months after the Constitutional Court had invalidated a section of a 1952 tax law, Parliament amended the statute to conform to its ruling.[19] (The Court held that a provision of the Act which required husbands and wives to file joint tax returns was an unconstituional burden on marriage and the family in violation of Article 6 of the Basic Law.)

Parliament does not always respond so swiftly, however, as the Illegitimate Children's Case of 1958 shows. There the Court reminded Parliament of its duty to repeal all discriminatory provisions in the Civil Code against illegitimate children.[20] A decade later, perhaps because the Court's message appeared advisory in nature, these provisions were still in the Code. Impatient with legislative inaction, the Court directed Parliament in the Orphans Assistance Case of 1969 to enact reform legislation before the end of the legislative term. In an unusual exercise of judicial authority, the Constitutional Court warned that, in the event of Parliament's failure to act, the Court itself would instruct lower courts to implement Article 6, Section 5, of the Basic Law in appropriate cases coming before it. Moreover, the Court stated that it would not regard such decisions by courts of law as violative of the doctrine of separation of powers, since "judicial rulings evolving out of the inactivity of the legislature are of a subsidiary nature" (that is, not on the same level with statutes).[21] The Court's unambiguous language prompted an immediate parliamentary response; corrective legislation was enacted shorty thereafter.[22]

The Orphans Assistance Case, incidentally, is a recent and rather extreme example of the so-called "admonitory decision" (*Appellentscheidung*), a strategy which the Constitutional Court has begun to employ as a means of generating compliant parliamentary responses to its rulings. While the uncustomarily forthright language of the Orphans Assistance Case might well have precipitated a negative parliamentary reaction, the intent of the admonitory decision is to avoid head-on collisions between Court and Parliament. The

Court's intent is momentarily to withhold the full exercise of its authority and "appeal" to Parliament for legislative action.

Admonitory decisions have appeared in two forms. In one, the Court effectively says to Parliament: "We regard this statute as unconstitutional, but for the time being we shall refrain from formally declaring it so; however, in due course we expect that you will correct the situation by amendatory legislation." Two well-known cases exemplify this approach. The first is the Apportionment Case. By 1963, owing mainly to immigration from East Germany, gross population disparities had developed among parliamentary constituencies established by the Election Law of 1949. Rather than declare the 1949 statute unconstitutional, which would have rendered the Bundestag elected in 1961 illegal, the Court allowed it to stand, taking into consideration that the Act, when passed, had been constitutional, and strongly advised Parliament to bring the act into conformity with the Basic Law's principle of equality.[23] The Bundestag complied, in time for the 1966 national election. Another example is the Sales Tax Case (1966), which involved legislation discriminating against certain firms. To declare the statute in question unconstitutional would have created havoc in the entire tax structure. Acknowledging the harm that a declaration of invalidity would do to the tax system, the Court dismissed the constitutional complaint against the tax, but admonished the legislature to enact corrective legislation "without unnecessary delay."[24] Within six months, Parliament complied.[25]

The other variant of the admonitory decision is for the Court to hold a statute unconstitutional without declaring it null and void, a legal distinction reserved for situations where the law unintentionally neglects to confer rights or benefits on certain persons or groups who should be entitled to them on the grounds of equal protection. Here the Court will allow the statute and the scheme of benefits provided by it to stand, pending a legislative solution, concerning which the Court almost always tenders advice. The Court effectively threatens to declare the statute unconstitutional *and void* in the event of further parliamentary default. In most cases of this type, Parliament responds compliantly, choosing to adopt one of the various alternative solutions ordinarily proposed by the Court.[26]

The majority of decisions, however, are nonadmonitory in nature.

Such cases, which often involve constitutional complaints against judicial decrees, may not incorporate any clear message to Parliament, even though a constitutionally suspect statute may have determined the contested judgment. Here Parliament may be less quick to react, as the Guardianship Case of February 2, 1960, shows. The ruling there—that guardians may not commit persons under their care to a closed institution unless authorized to do so by a court of law—was not incorporated into the Family Code until nearly two years after the case was decided.[27] But by then Parliament may not have been responding to the Court; the lapse of time may have allowed the intervention of nonjudicial factors as primary determinants of legislative action.

Parliamentary compliance with Constitutional Court decisions has been most conspicuous in cases of high political sensitivity, arising out of abstract judicial review proceedings. Compliance in these situations is not hard to understand. The Basic Law sets forth the procedures by which government is to be conducted and restrained. These "rules of the game" include constitutional challenges to legislative action by constituent groups within Parliament itself as well as by other branches of government. Further, the Court is widely regarded as a legitimate forum in which to resolve such disputes, which tends to enhance parliamentary acceptance of even highly controversial and unpopular constitutional decisions.

Thus Parliament reacted almost instantly to Party Subvention Case I (1966), nullifying a comprehensive scheme of federal subsidies for political parties. One consequence of this decision was the introduction of an omnibus bill covering all aspects of party organization and procedure. The final outcome was the Political Parties Act of 1967, which brought party financing into line with the Subvention Case.[28] But the ink on the Parties Act was barely dry when the Court struck down one of its provisions—the clause requiring a party to achieve 2.5% of the national votes before qualifying for reimbursement of campaign expenses—in a case brought by a minor party excluded from the Act's benefits. The Court ruled that the 2.5% provision violated the principle of equality by imposing a special hardship on minor parties, and even boldly went on to suggest that 0.5% would probably clear the threshold of constitutionality. On July 22, 1969,

Parliament incorporated the Court's figure of 0.5% into existing law.[29]

We could easily multiply these illustrations. The political party cases are underlined here because the Court struck down provisions of law overwhelmingly approved by Parliament. Despite the grumbling of party leaders, the Bundestag moved swiftly to comply with the rulings. But the Political Parties Act as a whole, we might pause to note, was long in coming. For years, the Court had been admonishing Parliament to implement by appropriate legislation provisions of Article 21 of the Basic Law which asserts that parties must be organized on democratic principles and publicly account for the sources of their funds. Bills to carry out the provisions of Article 21 had been hanging fire for at least a decade. But the Court's impact on the regime's policy toward political parties seems clear, for the Parties Act codifies virtually all the rules and principles of party democracy and political representation that the Court had set forth in a number of cases stretching back to 1952.

Federal and State Governments

The Constitutional Court's impact upon federal and state governments has been substantial in certain areas of the political process. Here are some illustrations:

(1) The Concordat Case of 1957 did help to preserve state autonomy in education, for the federal government made no subsequent effort to prevent the states from establishing schools of their own choice; under the decision the states even retained the reserved power to negotiate concordats directly with the Vatican.[30]

(2) The Federal Television Case of 1961 effectively ended the federal government's attempt to establish and operate a national television station.

(3) The Atomic Referenda Cases did terminate state efforts to use the ballot for the purpose of influencing national defense policy.

(4) In 1952, the Court invalidated a Schleswig-Holstein law which excluded the Danish minority in that state from parliamentary representation. Not only did Schleswig-Holstein comply by lowering

the percentage of votes required for representation from 7.5 to 5%, but later exempted the Danish minority from the 5% clause altogether.[31]

(5) On May 29, 1973, in the University Governance Case, the Court ruled that professors at German universities must be accorded, pursuant to their constitutional right to freedom of teaching and research (Article 5, Section 3), at least 50% of all votes in university bodies which decide upon questions of research and teaching appointments.[32]

Federal Education Minister Klaus von Dohnanyi greeted the decision as "significant" while the government proceeded to incorporate the ruling into the proposed Federal University Guidelines Act, still pending in early 1974.[33] It would be tedious to multiply these examples of compliance. It is sufficient to note that overt and determined refusals by national and state governments to comply with the Court's decisions have been extremely rare.

Compliance has become a problem, however, in cases where the Court has issued mandates which are difficult to carry out. The best example of this is the Numerus Clausus Case of 1972. University applicants are as helpless today as they were before the decision. Up to now the cultural ministers in the various states have done little if anything to change university rules so that all qualified students may study at German universities. Implementation of the Court's ruling would require an enormous expansion of university facilities, which is financially beyond the capacity of most states. And there is no way, politically or legally, that the Court can force national or state governments to spend more money on education.

High Federal Courts

The relationship between the Federal Constitutional Court and other high federal courts has often been marked by rivalry. The latter tribunals may address themselves, it will be recalled, to constitutional questions when they have occasion to *sustain* laws against constitutional objections; and although they may not invalidate statutes, they may strike down administrative regulations on constitutional grounds;

when the constitutionality of a statute is involved, the high federal court in question may certify the case, along with its own advisory opinion, to the Constitutional Court. It is only natural, however, that federal judges would strenuously defend their constitutional "rulings." Federal judges rank high in the German judicial structure, and they take a dim view of any judicial body which would undermine their opinions on constitutional questions related to their specialized jurisdictions. Thus the Federal Finance Court has been considerably aggravated by the Constitutional Court's overrulings of its constitutional opinions in the area of tax legislation.[34] The Federal Supreme Court, the final court of review in civil law matters, has frequently contested the Constitutional Court's interpretation of the property right under Article 14 of the Basic Law. In the 1950s, both tribunals handed down conflicting opinions in this area, with the more conservative Federal Supreme Court taking the more expansive view of the right of property.[35]

The most notable example of high federal court resistance to the Constitutional Court occurred in litigation over the Civil Servants Act of 1951, which restored pension rights to civil servants who lost their jobs at the end of the war, but excluded former Nazis from its benefits. In 1953, the Federal Supreme Court challenged the statute in a concrete review proceeding and asked the Constitutional Court to invalidate the law as violative of a constitutionally secured property right.[36] The Constitutional Court did not settle the issue until 1957, when the First Senate—at that time still considered "red" in political tincture—dismissed the constitutional doubts of the Federal Supreme Court, holding that the right to employment in the civil service is not a property right protected by Article 14.[37] This and other disputes over constitutional matters furnished the occasion for a public attack on the Constitutional Court by the presidents of all five high federal courts. Believing that their authority had been encroached upon, the presidents asserted *inter alia* that "the Federal Constitutional Court is not the apex into which all jurisdiction flows."[38]

Since the Civil Servant Case of 1957, the high federal courts have rarely referred cases on concrete review to the Constitutional Court. Conflicts between the Constitutional Court and the high federal courts now usually arise out of constitutional complaints against high federal court decisions. Yet the public record discloses no case where, upon *remand* by the Constitutional Court, a high federal tribunal has refused to implement a specific ruling. Compliance is a more severe problem for administrators and legislators in those instances where conflicting judicial interpretations of constitutionality remain unresolved, either because a federal court does feel obligated to follow the Constitutional Court's lead in analogous cases or because the Constitutional Court has not directly settled a conflict between itself and a high federal court.

In concluding this all too brief consideration of compliance, it is worth repeating the mild caveat with which we started: Compliance may be a product of forces other than the judicial decision itself; this is more likely to be the case as the temporal distance between the decision and compliance increases. In some of the illustrations presented above, the Federal Constitutional Court decision was indeed one of several factors influencing the eventual outcome. For example, social reform legislation following the Orphans Assistance Case (1969) had been pending in Parliament for several years; moreover, Social Democrats, then in power, had long been committed to the passage of such legislation; the Political Parties Act had also germinated in Parliament long before the Subvention Case (1966); Schleswig-Holstein's decision to exempt the Danish minority from the five percent clause of its electoral law probably had as much to do with efforts of the federal government to establish and maintain friendly relations with Denmark as with the Schleswig-Holstein Election Case.

Once in a great while, a Constitutional Court decision, owing to the climate of the times, unleashes gathering forces poised to strike at all levels of government. Appropos is the Communist Party Case of 1956 which, as we saw in an earlier chapter, was to some extent a result of federal government pressure on the Court. The decision was greeted enthusiastically by most official centers of power and became the instrument for a massive clamping down on subversive activity throughout Germany. Federal and state governments amended their criminal and electoral laws to ban Communist Party activities; public prosecutors pursued tens of thousands of persons suspected of seditious activity against the state; court dockets bulged with cases against individuals and organizations accused of conduct in violation of the Communist Party ban; the incidence of convictions for subversion shot up in the nation's courts; and Communist party representatives lost their seats in state legislative bodies pursuant to court orders. The feedback into the Constitutional Court was also substantial, as the Court was petitioned any number of times to consider the validity of legislative and judicial applications of the Communist Party Case.[39] Eventually, the upheaval created by the case subsided, but not by any further decision of the Court. Rather, the ideological climate changed: Social Democrats came to power; the Cold War receded; detente was on the horizon; Konrad Adenauer and his counterpart in East Germany, Walter Ulbricht, had passed on. In the early 1970s, the Communist Party surfaced again under a different name, but until January 1, 1975, the federal government had made no serious move to petition the Court for another ban. Even if it did, there is no certainty, this time, that the Court, more sure of its power and less susceptible to executive pressure, would respond as it did in 1956.

DURABILITY

Another way of assaying the political impact of the Federal Constitutional Court is to consider its *durability*. Hence, we have adopted the commonsense perspective of R. Taylor Cole, who recently suggested that a constitutional tribunal's durability might be measured by its behavior under crisis conditions. He states: "On the assumption that the most crucial, final and decisive measure of impact would be determined under such conditions, we might look at selected governmental crisis periods to appraise the continuing role of the court under such conditions."[40] In effect, we are led to query what happens to a consitutional tribunal when suddenly set adrift on a stormy sea of clashing political currents. How does it preserve its prestige and authority in a time of stress?

We shall examine this question within the context of the Constitutional Court's involvement in two highly controversial and politically sensitive foreign policy decisions. The two instances of decision-making occurred in crisis (or near-crisis) periods for both the Court and the Federal Republic of Germany. The events recounted below certainly involved West Germany's two most far-reaching foreign policy decisions: the European Defense Community Treaty of 1951, and the Basic Intra-German Treaty of 1973. Litigation over these treaties was a severe test of the Constitutional Court's resiliency. One of the cases represented a major milestone in the Court's struggle for independence. The dates of the two treaties—1951 and 1973—span the life of the Constitutional Court, also presenting us with an opportunity to discern within the framework of a single policy area how the aspects of compliance, support, and awareness have changed over time.

Introduction: The Court and Foreign Policy

In its twenty-three-year history, the Federal Constitutional Court has been concerned only marginally with foreign policy. The shaping of foreign policy is primarily the responsibility of the Chancellor, but the federal president also has a role to play by virtue of his constitutional authority to "represent the Federation in its international relations" and to "conclude treaties with foreign states on behalf of the Federation."[41] The Constitutional Court's role has been one mainly of interpreting the constitutionality of treaties but also, and more importantly, one of settling jurisdictional disputes between the federal government and Parliament over treaty ratification. Under Article 59, clause 2 of the Basic Law, only treaties which "regulate the political relations of the Federation" need parliamentary approval. The definition of a "political treaty" within the meaning of Article 59 was bound to cause conflict in Bonn and, ultimately, in Karlsruhe.

The Court was very active in deciding treaty cases during the first two years of its existence. Adenauer, perhaps mindful of his razor-thin election as Chancellor in 1949, refused to submit a number of international agreements to Parliament. Some of these had enormous political and economic consequences for Germany, and precipitated a fight with the Social Democrats over the treaty-making process. Among these agreements were the Petersberg Agreement of 1949, which set Germany on the track to national independence, and the German-French Commercial Treaty of 1950. The Social Democrats claimed before the Federal Constitutional Court that Adenauer had acted unconstitutionally by not seeking parliamentary approval. The government's victory in both cases fed rumors that the Second ("black") Senate was controlled by a pro-Adenauer majority. In any event, the effect of these and other decisions was a judicial underwriting of overwhelming executive predominance in the making of foreign policy.[42]

Although the Court has clearly indicated that it does have the authority to review the constitutionality of treaties, this authority has been exercised with considerable restraint. Any nullification of a treaty by the Court could invite retributive actions against it by the political branches of government. Yet the Court has not been without influence in determining certain questions of both substance and form in foreign policy. For instance, the Concordat Case ruled that a federal treaty may not invade a reserved right of the states.[43] On the other hand, the Court has denied states the right to use referenda as a means of influencing national foreign policy decisions,[44] a severe curtailment not only of the process by which the states might influence foreign policy, but also of the right of citizens to express themselves politically.[45]

The Court and E.D.C.

The E.D.C. Treaty provided for German membership in a proposed West European military alliance at a time when most Germans were at best lukewarm toward the prospect of rearmament. The opposition of Social Democrats, who believed that rearmament would kill all chances of German reunification, was passionate. But Adenauer persisted in his determination to rearm Germany within the framework of the Western alliance. Such was the setting of the battle into which all three units of the Constitutional Court—First Senate, Second Senate, and Plenum—were ultimately drawn.

While the treaty was pending, Social Democrats petitioned the First ("red") Senate to enjoin the Bundestag from ratifying it on the ground that the Basic Law contained no provision expressly authorizing rearmament. Soon afterward, Dr. Theodore Heuss, the federal president, asked the Court for an advisory opinion on the treaty's constitutionality, advisory opinions at that time being within the competence of the Plenum (the two senates meeting together). The president's petition created an extremely delicate situation within the Court as a whole. The Court acquired some breathing space on July 30, 1952, when the First Senate dismissed the SPD petition on jurisdictional grounds; since the treaty was not yet ratified, said the Court, it was not a formal law and therefore not yet subject to judicial review—a perfect escape machanism.[46] Still, the petition of the president alarmed Adenauer supporters. For example, *Rheinischer Merkür*, a backer of the treaty, was constrained to say: "Adding to the absurdities of our Constitution is the fact that elementary decisions of foreign policy are subject to judicial review."[47] Most government spokesmen agreed.

Meanwhile, back at the Court, the problem of E.D.C.'s validity momentarily receded as the Plenum struggled with the question of whether an advisory opinion on the merits of any controversy would bind the two senates. This was an extremely important matter because the SPD had every intention of challenging E.D.C. once again in the First ("red") Senate immediately after ratification. But then, on December 6, 1952, the day after E.D.C.'s ratification, the federal government petitioned the Second ("black") Senate—on a procedural question within its exclusive jurisdiction to enjoin the SPD from contesting (in the First Senate) ratification by majority vote in the Bundestag. The SPD maintained in its suit before the First Senate that a constitutional amendment, which required a two-thirds vote in the Bundestag, would be necessary to authorize rearmament. Clearly, the federal government anticipated a favorable decision in the Second Senate while the SPD had reason for confidence in the outcome of a First Senate decision. On the horizon loomed the very real possibility of the senates deciding differently on E.D.C.

Two days later, however, on December 8, 1952, the Plenum resolved, by a vote of twenty to two, that an advisory opinion would bind the senates.[48] Outrage is the only word to describe the government's reaction; Adenauer's forces clearly expected defeat on the merits of E.D.C. in the Plenum. By this time it was also clear to the Justices that the Court was being used and manipulated by politicians on both sides of the rearmament question. This manipulation and the possibility of conflicting decisions within the Court, more than anything else, threatened the tribunal's institutional integrity. The vote in the Plenum showed that the Justices were willing to bury their known personal disagreement over E.D.C. to safeguard the Court's independence. The second show of solidarity inside the Court was when the Second Senate, on March 7, 1953, rejected the government's petition on procedural grounds.[49] Earlier, incidentally, President Heuss had taken the heat off the Plenum by withdrawing his petition for an advisory opinion on the merits of E.D.C. But the SPD petition still lay before the First Senate.

To complete our story, we must return to the interplay between the Court and the government following the Plenum's decision of December 8, 1952. It may be recalled that this decision so fired the temper of Justice Geiger—one of the two Justices voting against the resolution—that he published a dissenting opinion for which he was roundly criticized by bench and bar.[50] At any rate, the decision occasioned a heavy exchange between the Court and Bonn politicians. Government representatives in the Bundestag greeted the decision with howls of scorn while the federal government refused to accept it as binding, with the most defiant response coming from Minister of Justice Thomas Dehler (FDP), a close friend of Justice Geiger. In the most strident anti-Court speech ever delivered in the Bundestag, Dehler called the Plenum's decision a "nullity" and strongly intimated that neither the government nor the Bundestag would be bound by any anti-government decision on E.D.C. in the First Senate of the Constitutional Court.[51] Dehler's remarks and the general attitude of the federal government were viewed with utmost gravity in Karlsruhe. On March 14, 1953, Höpker-Aschoff, then president of the Constitutional Court, made a nationwide radio address to defend the Court publicly against Dehler's assault.

While welcoming professional criticism of judicial decisions, Höpker-Aschoff condemned verbal assaults which in his view impugned the Court's honor and undermined its independence.

Seeking to build public support for the Court, he lectured the government sternly on its sworn duty to uphold the law and the Constitution, and even spoke of the impropriety of public criticism by government officials having a special interest in pending litigation. Aiming directly at his old friend Dehler, he said: "The Justice Minister is also obliged to heed the decisions of this Court and to submit to those decisions even when he regards them as wrong. Under no circumstances may a Federal Minister of Justice describe a decision of the Federal Constitutional Court as a 'nullity,' for he is not above the law." Höpker-Aschoff ended his speech by reminding his audience that the Justices were also subject to the law of the Constitution; that they would not be faithful to their own oath of office if they incorporated their political views into their decisions; that their task, which they approached with awe and trepidation, was to interpret the Constitution; and that their decisions were the supreme law of the land.[52]

The president's counterattack recalled a public speech at Bonn University a few weeks earlier by Justice Friesenhahn (Second Senate), a distinguished professor of public law and highly respected in Bonn's governing circles. He defended the Court's competence to decide the constitutionality of E.D.C. and rebuked the Court's critics, especially Dehler. He asserted that the Justices would refuse to allow themselves to be influenced by the impact of their decisions in the political realm. As a model of how public officials should respond to a judicial decision of the "highest political significance," he pointed to the forthright and compliant behavior of President Truman in the recent Steel Seizure Case decided by the U.S. Supreme Court. Friesenhahn's message was simple: "We [Germans] have two alternatives: Either we shall be governed by a state based on law or we shall be ruled by the sovereign dictatorship of Parliament."[53]

Clearly, the Justices were brandishing their swords in an almost "its them or us" spirit. But they chose their turf carefully for maximum impact. It was easy to defend the Court's power in the absence of its actual exercise. The Justices were winning the battle of words; rumors were even afloat of Dehler's impending resignation as Minister of Justice. Back at the Court, however, there was little action. There was no decision from the First Senate on the SPD petition. The Court, choosing for the time being not to decide, preferred to wait out the results of the 1953 federal election, which settled the issue. In a smashing victory, the Adenauer-led coalition captured over two-thirds of the seats in the Bundestag, actually depriving the Social Democrats of the strength sufficient to initiate further court proceedings over E.D.C. In any case, the Bundestag proceeded forthwith to amend the Basic Law expressly permitting a German armed establishment.[54] But, ironically, E.D.C. died a few months later with its rejection by the French National Assembly, opening the way for West Germany's entry into the North Atlantic Treaty Organization.

The E.D.C. controversy is significant mainly for its impact upon the Court itself. For one thing, it gave a fledgling tribunal in need of public attention considerable visibility. For another, it brought about modifications in the Court's jurisdiction, recommended by the Justices themselves. In 1956, in the first overhaul of the Constitutional Court Act, Parliament withdrew the Plenum's authority to deliver advisory opinions and made other adjustments designed to ward off the possibility of jurisdictional conflicts between the senates. Hopefully, too, this would put an end to political attempts to play one senate off against the other.

In some respects, the outcome of E.D.C. begs comparison with the circumstances surrounding *Marbury* v. *Madison*. Both American and German courts were young and untried. Both situations involved confrontations between judicial and executive authority. Both judicial performances were brilliant feats of self-control, for neither American nor German officials were forced to knuckle under—nor were they handed the opportunity to resist the Court's authority. Finally, both tribunals gathered strength from their behavior, with power emerging, paradoxically, out of a conscious display of powerlessness.

The Court and the Intra-German Treaty

Twenty years later—1973—Germans found themselves embroiled in yet another historic foreign policy quarrel. But this time the political tables had been turned. Social Democrats were at the helm in Bonn with Christian Democrats in fervent opposition to Chancellor

Brandt's *Ostpolitik*, which included several treaties designed to achieve detente in Europe. One of these was the Intra-German Basic Treaty, which the Bundastag ratified on May 11; it sought to normalize relations between the Federal Republic and the German Democratic Republic, with each government committing itself, *inter alia*, to respect the territorial borders of the other. Christian Democrats in the Bundestag, under the leadership of Rainer Barzel, maintained that the treaty violated the Basic Law's provisions (Preamble) looking toward reunification. But in preferring a political solution, they made it known that they would not contest the treaty in Karlsruhe. Bavaria, controlled by the Christian Democratic Party's conservative wing, the Christian Social Union (CSU), was not so sanguine about accepting a decision in the political arena. After the Bundesrat approved the treaty on May 25, the Bavarian government—the only state to vote against the treaty—immediately petitioned the Constitutional Court for a temporary staying order to prevent Federal President Gustav Heinemann from signing it into law. The litigation lasted for two months. It was a stormy period, inside and outside the Court; and when it was all over, the Court had handed down—from May 29 to July 31—six decisions relating to the treaty.

This time it was clear from the first that the Court was not about to back away from the dispute. The Second Senate left no doubt in anyone's mind that Bavaria's action was wholly admissible and justiciable. And although the Court's initial maneuvering was enough to dishearten any treaty advocate, the federal government remained calm and approached the matter, in the words of Brandt's press secretary, "with the self-understood respect due to the Constitutional Court."[55] The media, however, were less restrained. As in the E.D.C. controversy, the pro-government press was extremely critical of the Court. Even less partisan reporters were appalled by the possibility of an anti-government decision in Karlsruhe. Still, it seemed unrealistic actually to expect a decision against the government. What worried the press most was the fact that the Justices appeared ready to postpone the implementation of the treaty pending a decision on the merits. This prompted several distinguished Court watchers to question the very propriety of any judicial resolution of the controversy.

From the point of view of many Germans and government officials, any delay in the treaty's implementation would severely embarrass the federal government. East Germany was momentarily expected to ratify the treaty, which would take effect in late June after an exchange of notes between governments. Applications for the entry of both East and West Germany were also before the United Nations, and officials feared that any delay in the treaty's ratification would cause serious problems for West Germany in the Security Council. Yet "the monarchs in Karlsruhe," wrote Hans Schueler, "feel no obligation to hasten their proceedings."[56]

Schueler's remark was occasioned by a strange series of events. On May 29, 1973, in the first of six decisions, the Second Senate rejected Bavaria's motion to exclude Justice Rottmann from participation in any decision on the main petition on the ground of bias. The motion was based on a newspaper report of a speech the Justice gave on the legal status of Germany under the Brandt treaties before a group of Free Democrats in Karlsruhe. The Court denied the motion because, the Second Senate ruled, under all the circumstances of the situation, not the least of which was the fact that Rottmann did not comment on the treaty's constitutionality, Bavaria did not have a justifiable reason for believing that the Justice was in fact biased.[57] The second event was a press report of a sudden visit by Justice Seuffert, president of the Second Senate, to the official residence of the federal president in Bonn, as the unsigned treaty lay on the latter's desk. It was reported that Seuffert was there as an emissary of the Second Senate to persuade Heinemann to withhold his signature from the treaty until the Court's decision on the merits. Apparently the Court did not wish to issue a temporary staying order against the president. Heinemann, determined not to hold up the promulgation of the treaty and precipitate a conflict of his own with the federal government, allegedly refused.[58] The Court then wasted no time in making the first move. On June 4, in a split decision (4 to 4), the Second Senate denied Bavaria's motion for an injunction against the president.[59]

Bavaria immediately returned to the Court—on June 13—with a petition to enjoin the treaty's implementation. The Second Senate scheduled a full hearing on the petition for June 16. But on June 15 Bavaria filed a second motion against Rottmann's participation in the case, this time because of the contents of a private letter in which the Justice sought to correct misinformation about his original lecture as reported by a German newspaper. The letter, which was made available to the Bavarian government, contained statements strongly supportive of the Eastern treaties. The very next day, in a surprising reversal of its May 29 decision, the Second Senate, by a vote of four to three, excluded Rottmann from further participation in the case.[60] Later that day, before the remaining seven Justices, and behind closed doors, Egon Bahr, the principal architect of Brandt's *Ostpolitik*, appeared before the Second Senate to argue the government's case against Bavaria. The government was almost obsequious in its approach to the Court. Spokesmen earlier announced that the government would regard the Court's decision as binding. In his opening remarks before the Senate, Bahr is reported to have addressed the Justices as follows: "Your honors, if only one of you regards the Basic Treaty with the DDR (East Germany) as unconsitutional you should allow the temporary injunction."[16] In what was described as a brilliant and convincing performance, Bahr assured the Justices that any delay in the treaty's implementation would have "grave and serious consequences." Two days later, on June 18, and on the basis of this assurance, the Senate unanimously rejected the Bavarian petition for a temporary injunction.[62] At the same time, the Court announced that it would hand down its decision on the constitutionality of the Basic Treaty by July 31.

The First Senate came into the act on June 19, when it rejected a constitutional complaint by a West German citizen, a former refugee from East Germany, who claimed, *inter alia*, that the treaty would violate his right to property and other rights once lost in the East. The petition was rejected in a two-page opinion by the unanimous senate.[63] There was, incidentally, some press speculation that the First Senate was disturbed over the Second Senate's procrastination and internal quibbling. A long-time observer of the Court, after noting that the Second Senate's record in the dispute manifests the Court's "incompetence to deal with a political question such as this," said bluntly: "the First Senate would have decided the issue in three hours."[64]

In view of the Second Senate's dismissal of Bavaria's application for a staying order, there was little surprise when on July 31 the Court, finally and unanimously, upheld the constitutionality of the Basic Treaty.[65] In one respect, the decision was a wise exercise in judicial self-restraint. But in another respect it represented a bold assertion of judicial power. Going far beyond the question of the treaty itself, the Second Senate formulated numerous guidelines for the future determination of all foreign policy decisions affecting the question of German unity. Among the Senate's declarations were the following propositions: That the German Reich did not end with military defeat in 1945, and continues to exist in international law; that no constitutional organ of the Federal Republic may constitutionally abandon the goal of German unity or embark on any policy which would obstruct reunification; that all Germans in both sectors of the nation are citizens of the Federal Republic; and that Germans who enter the territory of the Federal Republic are entitled to the protection of the courts and the basic rights of the Constitution. The Second Senate even went out of its way to say that the Basic Treaty itself is currently being violated by the presence of the Berlin Wall and border installations between East and West Germany, and admonished the federal government to do everything in its power, pursuant to the treaty, to eliminate these conditions. And, for good measure, the Justices warned the federal government never to doubt the ultimate power of the Constitutional Court to enforce the Basic Law's provisions on German unity.

The reaction to the decision in West Germany was one mainly of support. But the strongest words of support came from Chancellor Brandt, who alluded to the impact of the decision even in East Germany. In an address before the Bundestag on January 24, 1974 he remarked:

"The Federal Constitutional Court in its decision confirmed the constitutionality of the Basic Treaty. I had never any doubts about it. The applicant's opposite view was dismissed. Circles that were behind these applications are now trying occasionally to qualify the Court's verdict by attempting, for instance, to isolate passages or sentences from the Court's grounds and present them as political guidelines in their own right.

"The Federal Government regards such attempts as incompatible with the Court's status and functions. The Federal Constitutional Court interprets the Basic Law but does not engage in politics. Both Government and Court are in no doubt about this. However, anyone sowing doubts of this kind and trying to attribute to the Court a role which the Court itself refuses to accept, is doing our constitutional order a disservice.

"Respect for the Court and its important mission in connection with our Constitution commands the Government not to take part in such arguments. For the same reason it keeps out of the critical discussion that has arisen in juridical quarters over guiding principles and responses given in the judgment. We repudiate the biased and often quite absurd criticism of the Constitutional Court coming from eastern quarters."[66]

It seems clear that Brandt and the government would interpret the decision their way. But the decision also cleared the way for the full implementation of the Basic Treaty and of the Chancellor's Eastern policy in general. This was one consequence of the decision. The Court also created the broad framework within which any future discussion, debate, and strategy regarding the relationship between East and West Germany is likely to take place. This may very well turn out to be the decision's most significant political consequence. Moreover, the Court itself appeared to have gained from the decision by bolstering its prestige, authority, and support within the political community. The Chancellor's reverential nod toward Karlsruhe in the above remarks was probably good political strategy to maximize support for the Basic Treaty; but it was also an indication of how far the Court itself had come in the public mind since E.D.C. and Adenauer.

Conclusion

The political impact of the Federal Constitutional Court has been considered here under the aspects of awareness, support, compliance, and durability. Clearly these variables are limited in what they can tell us about the political impact of the Federal Constitutional Court. But they do suggest that the Constitutional Court's influence in the West German system of government is a continuing one. At the same time, care should be taken to avoid an inflated conception of the Court's significance in the German system. While the Constitutional Court has helped to shape the broad contours of West German politics, we have still a long way to go in determining more precisely its total impact.

The Court itself is well aware of the limits of its own power. It speaks grandly of its authority, but knows when not to use it. The Basic Treaty Case is a classic manifestation of such prudential wisdom. From a purely strategic point of view, the Court had good reason to welcome Bavaria's action. It furnished the Court with the rare opportunity of asserting its authority while everyone in Germany was watching. Here, as on other occasions, the Court was able to draw attention to itself as the highest and most authoritative interpreter of the Basic Law. The Court did indeed assert its authority by addressing itself to the merits of the constitutional controversy, but did so without directly setting itself in opposition to the government. In the end, the Court seems not only to have helped legitimize *Ostpolitik*, but to have enhanced its own institutional status as well.

NOTES

1. Existing research dealing with certain aspects of impact are ably analyzed in Stephen L. Wasby, *The Impact of the United States Supreme Court: Some Perspectives* (Homewood, Illinois: Dorsey, 1970).

2. See *Grundzuge des Verfassungsrechts der Bundesrepublik Deutschland,* 5th ed. (Karlsruhe: Verlag C.F. Müller, 1972).

3. BVerfGG, Sec. 31. It may be of interest to note here that the Federal Constitutional Court itself assumes the responsibility of communicating with those individuals whose constitutional complaints are denied. If the complainant has not been helped by counsel, notification takes the form of a short letter informing him of the dismissal. If the complainant was assisted by

counsel, the Court takes pains to indicate reasons for the dismissal. The Court does not believe that it can politically afford to leave lawyers in the dark relative to the merits of the claims they file on behalf of clients. This practice of responding, sometimes at length, to such complaints probably enhances the reputation of the Court, storing up good will among hundreds of ordinary lawyers.

4. The Federal Constitutional Court has consciously sought to heighten awareness of its own doings by undertaking to organize all existing knowledge about itself and by making this knwledge available to the public. It has done so through the systematic collection and cataloguing of all books, doctoral dissertations (of which there are hundreds), articles, commentaries, newspaper stories, and even unpublished manuscripts and letters dealing with the Court and its work. A bibliography of these materials containing thousands of titles was recently published under the editorship of the Court's two top librarians. Its significance as a measure of the Court's impact and as a spur to further awareness of the Court in the public consciousness was not overlooked by President Gebhard Müller. In a foreword to the bibliography, he praised the library staff for its extensive documentation of the "public response to the administration of German constitutional justice," which he interpreted as an "expression of public trust in the Federal Constitutional Court." See Josef Mackert and Franz Schneider (eds.), *Bibliographie zur Verfassungsgerichtsbarkeit des Bundes und der Länder* (Tübingen: J.C.B. Mohr [Paul Siebeck], 1971).

5. These data were derived from *Statistischen Jahrbuch für die Bundesrepublik Deutschland 1972* (Stuttgart and Mainz: Verlag W. Kohlhammer GMBH, 1972), pp. 91-92 and *Public Opinion* (Bonn: Press and Information Office of the Government of the Federal Republic of Germany, 1971). Circulation figures have been rounded off to the nearest thousandth.

6. *Der Spiegel*, June 25, 1973 (No. 26), pp. 32-38.

7. The sample included 480 respondents; members of some groups were selected by position, members of other groups at random. Questionnaires were sent to all presidents and senate presidents of state and federal courts, to all members of the main party executive committees (CDU/CSU, SPD, FDP) and chairmen of party working committees and standing committees in the Bundestag, to all full professors of public law teaching in German universities, to journalists from "high brow" newspapers and reporters of major broadcasting stations, and to a random sample of high civil servants and interest group leaders drawn from relevant national directories on civil servants and associations in West Germany. The associations involved were mainly labor, business, farm, and church groups. While questionnaires were

sent to the presidents of these organizations, a few of them were passed on to the group's legal counsel who in turn filled out the questionnaire; we have included them here. One hundred sixty-four completed questionnaires, representing thirty-four percent of the sample, were returned. The research instrument was drafted with the advice and assistance of Dr. Max Kaase of the Social Science Research Center at Mannheim University.

8. Respondents were asked to rank the importance of public and private institutions (federal cabinet, federal bureaucracy, federal bank, trade unions, Bundesrat, state governments, Catholic Church, the armed forces, party leaders in the Bundestag, etc.) on an eleven-point scale (0 to 10) ranging from "very important" to "no importance"). Table 16 was constructed from these data.

9. See Walter F. Murphy and Joseph Tanenhaus, "Public Opinion and the United States Supreme Court," in Joel B. Grossman and Joseph Tanenhaus (eds.), *Frontiers of Judicial Research* (New York: John Wiley, 1969), p. 275.

10. See Elisabeth Noelle and Erich Peter Neumann, *Jahrbuch der Oeffentlichen Meinung 1958-1964* (Allensbach and Bonn: Verlag für Demoskopie, 1965), p. 115.

11. Elisabeth Noelle and Erich Peter Neumann, *Jahrbuch der Oeffentlichen Meinung 1947-1955* (Allensbach am Bodensee: Verlag für Demoskopie, 1956), p. 24.

12. David Easton, *A Systems Analysis of Political Life* (New York: John Wiley 1965), p. 289.

13. Almond and Verba's cross-cultural study of civic cultures did show that Germans take considerably less pride in their governmental and political institutions than American, British, or even Mexican citizens. See Gabriel A. Almond and Sidney Verba, *The Civic Culture* (Princeton: Princeton University Press, 1963), p. 102. But the Almond-Verba data are at best a partial measure of support for the political system; furthermore, the data are old. More recent surveys point to general popular approval and satisfaction with democratic institutions in Germany, although the intensity of such feeling is not calibrated. In 1965, for example, the EMNID Press Service found that seventy-nine percent of Germans preferred democracy to any other type of political regime. See Arnold J. Heidenheimer, *The Governments of Germany*, 3rd edition (New York: Thomas Y. Crowell Company, 1971), p. 106. In 1967, the Allensbach Institute found that sixty-one percent of a random sample of West Germans preferred a system of democratic pluralism to one based on an elite composed of the "best men" in the country. Allensbach also found a large measure of support for the political regime generally, fifty percent expressing satisfaction with the development of the

Federal Republic since 1949, thirty-two percent expressing partial satisfaction, with only ten percent expressing dissatisfaction. See Elisabeth Noelle and Erich Peter Neumann, *Jahrbuch der Oeffentlichen Meinung 1965-1967* (Allensbach and Bonn: Verlag für Demoskopie, 1967), pp. 152 and 185.

14. These data, incidentally, are in need of qualification since only thirty-four percent or 164 of the respondents returned the completed questionnaire. It is possible that the data exaggerate support for the Court. Despite assurances of anonymity, the author discovered considerable reluctance on the part of the German public officials, especially judges, to disclose their views about the Court; they were particularly averse to reacting toward specific decisions. Hence, those with negative attitudes might disproportionately have declined to reply to the questionnaire. Yet it is worth mentioning that fourteen percent of respondents who for reasons of propriety chose not to fill out the questionnaire wrote letters instead, overwhelmingly in support of the Court.

15. For figures on the number of cases submitted to the Constitutional Court by various courts see Donald P. Kommers, *Frontiers,* op. cit., p. 113.

16. Confidential letters of August 30, 1968 and July 30, 1968.

17. Joel B. Grossman and Richard S. Wells, *Constitutional Law and Judicial Policy Making* (New York: John Wiley, Inc., 1972), p. 826.

18. BVerfGG, sec. 31 (2).

19. See Family Tax Case (First Senate), BVerfGE 6: 55 (1957) and Income Tax Act of July 26, 1957 (BGBl. I., p. 848).

21. Orphans Assistance Case, Decision of January 29, 1969 (First Senate), BVerfGE 25: 167, 181 (1969).

22. Children's Equal Protection Act of August 19, 1969 (BFBl. I., p. 1243).

23. See Apportionment Case, Decision of May 22, 1963 (Second Senate), BVerfGE 16: 130, 141 ff. (1963).

24. Sales Tax Case, Decision of December 20, 1966 (First Senate), BVerfGE 21: 12, 42 (1967).

25. Turnover Tax Act of May 29, 1967 (BGBl. I., p. 545).

26. Several examples of such cases are included in Wiltraut Rupp-v. Brünneck, "Admonitory Functions of Constitutional Courts—Germany: The Federal Constitutional Court," *American Journal of Comparative Law* 20: 395-399 (1972). Admonitory decisions have been severely criticized by German legal scholars. It is not the Court's function, they say, to proffer advice to the legislature or to encroach upon its turf by pressuring it into given lines of conduct. The Justices, however, view the admonitory decisions as a strategy of judicial-legislative cooperation. Justice Rupp v. Brünneck writes

that "advice to the legislature in the course of 'normal decision' . . . is a necessary element of sound judgment. . . . The Legislature or Executive, having failed in their first attempt to attain their object in accordance with the Constitution, are entitled to learn about the possible ways for a better—constitutional—solution." ibid., p. 401.

27. See Guardianship Case (First Senate), BVerfGE 10: 302 (1960) and Family Code Amendment Act of August 11, 1961 (BGB1. I. p. 1221).

28. See Party Subvention Case I, Decision of July 19, 1966 (Second Senate) BVerfGE 20: 56 (1967) and Political Parties Act of July 24, 1967 (BGB1. I., p. 773).

29. See Party Subvention Case II, Decision of December 3, 1968 (Second Senate), BVerfGE 24: 300 (1969) and Parties Amendment Act of July 22, 1969 (BGB1. I., p. 925).

30. For example, on February 26, 1965, Lower Saxony concluded an agreement with the Holy See on denominational schools. See Lower Saxony School Act of July 1, 1965, Gestz-und Verordnungsblatt (1965), p. 191.

31. See Schleswig-Holstein Election Case, Decision of April 5, 1952 (Second Senate), BVerfGE 1: 208 (1952). See also Elections Act of May 31, 1955, GVB1. (1955) p. 124.

32. University Governance Case, Decision of May 29, 1973 (First Senate), BVerfGE 35: 79 (1974).

33. *Relay from Bonn*, German Information Agency, New York, Vol. IV (No. 96), May 30, 1973, p. 4.

34. See, for example, the Constitutional Court's Chimney Sweep Case, Decision of April 30, 1952 (First Senate), BVerfGE 1: 264 (1952) and Refugee Case, Decision of May 7, 1953 (First Senate), BVerfGE 2: 266, 285 (1953). Compare with Federal Supreme Court Decision of June 10, 1952, BGHZ 6: 270 (1952).

35. See *Juristenzeitung* 11: 92 (1956).

36. See Decision of January 25, 1953, BGHZ 11 (1954): Appendix A, p. 33.

37. See Civil Servant Case, Decision of February 19, 1957 (First Senate), BVerfGE 6: 222 (1957). See also Gestapo Civil Servant Case, Decision of February 19, 1957 (First Senate), BVerfGE 6: 132 (1957).

38. Examples are Business Tax Case, Decision of January 24, 1962 (First Senate), BVerfGE 13 (1963): 318 and Personal Property Assessment Case, Decision of December 13, 1966 (First Senate), BVerfGE 21: 1 (1967). The interplay between the Federal Constitutional Court and the Federal Finance Court, and the impact of the former on tax policy, is discussed in Wilhelm Hartz, "Steuergerichte und Verfassung," *Sonderdruck aus die Auslegung der*

Steuergesetze in Wissenschaft und Praxis (Cologne-Marienburg: Verlag Dr. Otto Schmidt KG, 1965), pp. 106-118.

39. See Donald P. Kommers, "The Spiegel Affair: A Case Study in Judicial Politics," in Theodore L. Becker, *Political Trials* (Indianapolis: Bobbs-Merrill, 1971), pp. 14-15.

40. R. Taylor Cole, "The Political Impact of Constitutional Courts: A Critique," *Notre Dame Lawyer* 49 (June 1974): 1948.

41. Article 59, Clause 1, of the Basic Law of the Federal Republic of Germany (1949).

42. For instance, in the Commercial Treaty Case the Court gave an extremely restricted interpretation to the concept of "political treaty," limiting it to peace treaties, non-aggression pacts, disarmament agreements, general political alliances, and the like. Treaties are not political and therefore not subject to ratification, said the Court, "merely because they deal with public affairs, the good of the community, or affairs of state." See Decision of July 29, 1952 (Second Senate), BVerfGE 1: 372, 381 (1952). In the Petersberg Case the issue was whether the Allied High Commission was a "foreign state" within the meaning of the Basic Law's treaty provisions. See Decision of July 29, 1952 (Second Senate), BVerfGE 1: 351 (1952). For a related issue see also Decision of June 30, 1953 (Second Senate), BVerfGE 2: 347 (1953).

43. Decision of March 26, 1957 (Second Senate), BVerfGE 6: 309 (1957).

44. Decision of July 30, 1958 (Second Senate), BVerfGE 8: 104 (1959).

45. Still the Court's byword had been caution in cases calling into question the constitutionality of treaties. An example is the Court's treatment of the European Saar Statute of 1954 which provided for a referendum on the future of the Saar, formerly German territory placed under French control after the war. Under the statute, residents could choose to have the Saar internationalized or opt for its reunification with Germany. The SPD, fearing the permanent dismemberment of the Saar from Germany, claimed that the statute would violate the Constitution since the basic rights of Germans living in the Saar were at stake. The Court admitted that Saar residents might lose their rights as Germans, but did not wish to anticipate the outcome of the referendum or second guess the government relative to the wisdom of the Statute. Given the general political context of the agreement between France and Germany over the Saar, the Court felt that its only alternative was to sustain the statute.

46. Decision of July 30, 1952 (First Senate), BVerfGE 1: 396 (1952).

47. See *Rheinischer Merkur*, October 10, 1952.

48. Opinion of December 8, 1952 (Plenum), BVerfGE 2: 79 (1953).

49. Decision of March 7, 1953 (Second Senate), BVerfGE 2: 143 (1953).

50. See *Der Kampf um den Wehrbeitrag* (Munich: ISAR Verlag, 1953), II: 822-828.

51. See *Verhandlungen des Deutschen Bundestag*, 252. Sitzung, March 4, 1952, pp. 12099-12112.

52. Radio address by Hermann Höpker-Aschoff over the South German Radio Station, March 14, 1953 (mimeographed).

53. See *Stuttgarter Nachrichten*, December 19, 1952.

54. See Article 73 (1), as amended by the Federal Law of March 26, 1954 (BGB1. I., p. 45).

55. Statement of federal government spokesman Armin Grünewald, quoted in *Relay from Bonn*, IV/96, German Information Center, May 30, 1973, p. 3.

56. *Die Zeit*, June 15, 1973, p. 2.

57. Rottmann Exclusion Case I, Decision of May 29 (Second Senate), BVerfGE 35: 171 (1974).

58. See Hans Schueler, "Karlsruhe: die falsche Adresse," *Die Zeit*, June 8, 1973, p. 1.

59. Intra-German Basic Treaty Case I, Decision of June 4, 1973 (Second Senate) BVerfGE 35: 193 (1974).

60. Rottmann Exclusion Case II, Decision of June 16, 1973 (Second Senate), BVerfGE 35: 246 (1974).

61. *Der Spiegel*, June 25, 1973, p. 36.

62. Intra-German Basic Treaty Case II, Decision of June 18, 1973 (Second Senate) BVerfGE 35: 257 (1974).

63. Intra-German Basic Treaty Case III, Decision of June 19, 1973 (First Senate), BVerfGE 35: 280 (1974).

64. Hans Schueler, "Das Orakel der Zweiten Senats," *Die Zeit*, June 15, 1973, p. 2.

65. Intra-German Basic Treaty Case IV, Decision of July 31, 1973, (Second Senate), BVerfGE 36: 1 (1974).

66. Supplement to *The Bulletin*, Press and Information Office of the Government of the Federal Republic of Germany, January 29, 1974, p. 6.

8

CONCLUSION

We may now summarize some of the main points advanced in this study. First, judicial review, although not firmly anchored in Germany's constitutional tradition, has gained acceptance in the political system of the Federal Republic. Judicial review has worked in Germany because it has been used almost daily as an instrument in the process of settling constitutional disputes: It has been used by judicial institutions to raise and adjudicate questions of wide import under the Basic Law; by large numbers of Germans who have come increasingly to identify the Constitutional Court with the protection of their constitutional liberties; and by legislative minorities, political parties, and governmental organs as an alternative forum for the resolution of constitutional controversies which do not get settled satisfactorily elsewhere. Indeed, the German experience seems to show that judicial review, once regarded as a unique feature of American constitutionalism, can flourish in constitutional traditions substantially different from the American.

It is important to add, however, that cultural and political conditions in West Germany have constituted a favorable environment for effective judicial review. West Germany's political system has been sufficiently bipartisan, federal, and pluralistic to enable the Court to win support among centers of power and vital political forces in and outside government. The Court has not been engaged in a zero-sum game. Its losses have never been total; nor have its winnings. The Court has been able to trade off one source of support for another. Thus, in West Germany's middle-class society, sustained as it is by a thriving economy and stable system of checks and balances, judicial review has taken root in fertile soil.

Second, the Constitutional Court has achieved, apart from its acceptability by the larger political community, a remarkable measure of internal stability and autonomy. The Court's decision-making procedures have become regularized; its administrative operations and budget have been freed from the control of the Ministry of Justice; its internal organization has developed into a highly structured and efficient mechanism; its judicial output has remained steady, and the volume input of cases has been coursing along annually on a rather uniform upward curve. Relative equilibrium has been achieved in the workloads of the two senates while jurisdictional conflicts between them have been held to a minimum, mainly because the Court itself has won the right, subject to parliamentary approval, to amend the statute governing their jurisdiction. Finally, a fixed twelve-year term has become the rule for all Justices after years of experimentation with a dual system of tenure, and the Justices' long fight for the right to publish dissenting opinions has been won.

Third, political considerations have been an important factor in the recruitment of Federal Constitutional Court Justices. Although Parliament formally elects the Justices, their selection has been the product mainly of negotiation among party leaders in both state and federal governments. We have seen that the typical Justice has been a person recruited from a high-ranking position in the judiciary, in the civil service, or in the federal parliament's party hierarchy. If he has not had a background in partisan politics, he almost always has been a person with political views associated with one of the major parties or with close personal links to major party leaders. While the Justices have been almost evenly divided numerically between those associated in some way with the Christian Democratic Party and those associated in some way with the Social Democratic Party, they have been mainly middle-class and centrist in political orientation and fully committed to liberal democratic values. One consequence of these recruitment patterns is that, ideologically and politically, the Justices have on the whole not been far out of line with predominant feeling in the country or too far in front of—or behind—parliamentary opinion.

Fourth, the Constitutional Court has been the main source and articulator of constitutional doctrine in the Federal Republic. Moreover, the Justices have been aware of the significant role which they as individuals and the Court as a whole can play in the formulation of constitutional law and policy. But influence over policy development inside the Court has not been evenly distributed among the Justices. The Court's deliberative processes have been a severe test of each Justice's capacity to influence the judgment of his colleagues. At the same time, a Justice's individual capacity to influence the content of constitutional policy has been limited by certain norms of the Court as a whole, such as the pervading and continuing belief in the propriety of handing down single and anonymous institutional opinions. Still, as the recent dissenting behavior on the Second Senate has shown, the Justices have not been able successfully to conceal the inherently conflictual nature of constitutional policy-making.

Fifth, the Constitutional Court has played a number of important policy-making roles in the Federal Republic. Among the Court's manifest roles have been those of protector of individual rights, equalizer of socioeconomic opportunity, umpire of the federal system, and custodian of party democracy. Among the Court's less manifest, but equally important, roles have been those of ratifier of governmental policy and teacher of constitutional values. Here a brief comment about the Court's vigilance over the political system will suffice. While there is no logical reason for believing that the political liberty of a people is safer in the hands of a constitutional tribunal than in the hands of representative assemblies, the fact remains that the Constitutional Court has been more protective of minority political interests and more tolerant of dissident political groups than parliamentary bodies or other judicial tribunals. This has not meant that the Court has always chosen the most democratic alternative among possible solutions to a problem of political representation.

Here the Court's banning of the Socialist Reich's Party and the Communist Party may be cited. Doctrinally, the German Constitutional Court has created less space for maneuver by radical political dissenters and movements than has the U.S. Supreme Court. But then the Basic Law incorporates express language, absent in the U.S. Constitution, forbidding activity which endangers the liberal democratic political order.

Finally, the Court's political impact in West Germany has been substantial: The Court has been highly visible among and high in the esteem of various publics; it has experienced a notable degree of compliance with its decisions on the part of Parliament, the high federal courts, and federal and state governments; it has received considerable diffuse and specific support in the political community; and it has been able to cope with stressful situations that threatened to undermine its institutional independence. Specifically, the Constitutional Court has emerged from the controversies surrounding the European Defense Community Treaty and the Intra-German Basic Treaty, which we defined as stressful or near-crisis situations for the Court, with its authority intact and its institutional integrity preserved. The treaty cases also have shown that, while the Constitutional Court's impact on the formulation of major public policy goals has been marginal, it nevertheless has been a crucial element in the totality of intergrovernmental relationships out of which such policies emerge.

Whatever the circumstances of these relationships may have been at any one time, the Justices have steadfastly and at all times defended the Court as the ultimate guardian of constitutional democracy in the Federal Republic. They have not been wholly unsuccessful, as we have seen, in getting Germans to accept this way of looking at the Court. The Justices' identification of the Court with human dignity, liberal democracy, and the rule of law is, of course, good judicial strategy. It is plausible to think, although empirically difficult to show, that the Court's identification with these values has been a fundamental source of its power and influence in the political system. In reality, however, the Justices have been a shrewd and dexterous group of men and women. So far, as we have seen, they have exercised their authority with relative restraint and a fairly decent respect for the opinions of other governmental branches. Pragmatic as their counterparts on the U.S. Supreme Court, they have realized that a good constitutional ruling is often a combination of sound policy and bad law.

The placement of the Constitutional Court in West Germany's parliamentary democracy deserves one last comment. Politically, the Court represents a sharp break away from a constitutional tradition associated with the subordination of the judiciary to executive and parliamentary institutions. In this connection, some West Germans have reacted with unease to the handing down of judicial decrees in Karlsruhe at variance with policy decisions made in Bonn. Old-line jurists and law professors whose intellectual roots lie deep in the German tradition of legal positivism tend to view the Constitutional Court's mere existence as a violation of the principle of separation of powers, and they see the Justices as "high priests," ordained to disturb the unity of the state. They decry the "politicization of justice."

But the Court's scholarly critics also include those who deplore the "judicialization of politics." For them, judicial review is incompatible with democracy and contrary to the principle of parliamentary supremacy. Occasionally, too, practicing politicians have been known to lament what they perceive as the Court's inordinate influence over certain aspects of the political process. They have even come forth with proposals to limit the Court's power by changing its jurisdiction or altering judicial selection procedures. So far, these and other efforts to undermine the Court's institutional integrity have failed and, barring any shattering political upheaval in West Germany, they are likely to continue to fail.

A quarter of a century is not long in the light of a political or legal institution, but it is long enough to test an institution's durability and the probability of its continuity. The Federal Constitutional Court has survived this first test.

INDEX

ABOUT THE AUTHOR

Donald P. Kommers is Professor of Government and International Studies and Adjunct Professor of Law at the University of Notre Dame. He is also Director of Notre Dame's Center for Civil Rights. He received his B.A. from Catholic University of America and his M.A. and Ph.D. from the University of Wisconsin. During 1971-72 he was an Alexander von Humboldt Fellow on the law faculty of the University of Cologne in West Germany. His work on German politics and comparative constitutional law has been published both in the United States and in the Federal Republic of Germany. His most recent publication, co-authored with Arnold J. Heidenheimer, is *The Governments of Germany*, fourth edition (New York: Thomas Y. Crowell, 1975).